D1578696

'Knives, Tanks, and Missiles': Israel's Security Revolution

Eliot A. Cohen
Michael J. Eisenstadt
Andrew J. Bacevich

The Washington Institute for Near East Policy

A Washington Institute Monograph

© 1998 by the Washington Institute for Near East Policy

Published in 1998 in the United States of America by the Washington Institute for Near East Policy, 1828 L Street N.W. Suite 1050, Washington, DC 20036

Library of Congress Cataloging-in-Publication Data
Cohen, Eliot A.
    'Knives, tanks, and missiles' : Israel's security revolution / Eliot A. Cohen, Michael J. Eisenstadt, Andrew J. Bacevich.
    p.   cm.
    ISBN 0-944029-72-8 (pbk.)
    1. Israel —Defenses. 2. National Security —Israel. 3. Israel —Tseva haganah le-Yisra'el. I. Eisenstadt, Michael. II. Bacevich, A. J. III. Title
UA853.I8C623 1998   98-10302
355'.03305694 —dc21   CIP

Cover design by Debra Naylor, Naylor Design Inc. Photo © Photodisc 1998.

A Note About the Title

The title of this study—'Knives, Tanks, and Missiles': Israel's Security Revolution—derives from an oft-repeated metaphor used by former Foreign Minister Shimon Peres to describe the threat Israel faces following the end of the Cold War. According to Peres, Israel had traditionally prepared to deal with the threat posed by "the tank"—that is, the conventional military forces possessed by its neighbors. This had caused Israel to "think in an old-fashioned way" that prevented it from facing "the new danger" that came from terrorism ("the knife") and weapons of mass destruction ("the missile").[1] This paper examines Israel's efforts to come to terms with the new threat environment captured by the Peres metaphor, as well as its efforts to grapple with broader changes in the political, military-technical, and socioeconomic spheres.

---

[1] Shimon Peres interview quoted in *Mideast Mirror*, April 6, 1993, p. 2; and Shimon Peres interview aired on the *Charlie Rose Show*, May 18, 1994.

The Authors

Eliot A. Cohen is professor of strategic studies at the Paul H. Nitze School of Advanced International Studies (SAIS) of the Johns Hopkins University. He received his B.A. and Ph.D. degrees from Harvard University, where he was an assistant professor of government from 1982 to 1985. Between 1985 and 1990 he taught in the strategy department at the Naval War College. Following a brief period of service on the policy planning staff of the Office of the Secretary of Defense, he was appointed to the chair in strategic studies at SAIS. From 1991 to 1993, he directed and edited the *Gulf War Air Power Survey*, the U.S. Air Force's six-volume official study of the 1991 war with Iraq. He is the author (with John Gooch) of *Military Misfortunes: The Anatomy of Failure in War* (Free Press, 1991) and of two other books and numerous articles.

Michael J. Eisenstadt is a senior fellow at The Washington Institute for Near East Policy. He has an M.A. in Arab Studies from Georgetown University, and his publications include *Iranian Military Power: Capabilities and Intentions*; *Supporting Peace: America's Role in an Israel-Syria Peace Agreement* (with Carl Ford and Andrew Bacevich); and *Like a Phoenix from the Ashes? The Future of Iraqi Military Power*. In 1992 he took a leave of absence from The Institute to work on the U.S. Air Force's *Gulf War Air Power Survey*. In that capacity, he contributed a chapter on Iraqi strategy and plans prior to the Gulf War. Before coming to The Institute, he worked as a military analyst with the U.S. Army. He is also a reserve officer in the U.S. Army and served in Turkey and Iraq as part of Operation Provide Comfort.

Andrew J. Bacevich is executive director of the Johns Hopkins Foreign Policy Institute at SAIS. A graduate of the U.S. Military Academy, he received his Ph.D. from Princeton University. Prior to beginning his academic career, Dr. Bacevich served for twenty-three years as an officer in the U.S. Army, to include tours in Vietnam, Germany, and the Persian Gulf. He is the author of two books: *The Pentomic Era: The U.S. Army Between Korea and Vietnam* and *Diplomat in Khaki: Major General Frank Ross McCoy and American Foreign Policy, 1898–1949*. Dr. Bacevich is also the coauthor of *American Military Policy in Small Wars: The Case of El Salvador* and *Supporting Peace: America's Role in an Israel-Syria Peace Agreement*.

• • •

Contents

Acknowledgments

Many Israeli and American officials, journalists, and experts shared their views with us—often under condition of anonymity, which we have preserved—and we are grateful to them. Efraim Inbar of the BESA Center for Strategic Studies at Bar Ilan University gave us valuable substantive and administrative support during our research visit to Israel in the spring of 1996, which considerably eased our task there. He and his colleague, Stuart Cohen, shared their scholarly insights with us. Shimon Naveh and his associates, and in particular Zvi Lanir and Dov Tamari, arranged for us a series of meetings in Israel that provided indispensable insights into the IDF. Ze'ev Schiff, dean of Israeli defense correspondents, gave us the benefit of his encyclopedic knowledge of Israeli security matters. Robert Satloff of The Washington Institute for Near East Policy has supported this effort since its inception, lending particularly valuable logistical support during its early phases. Tehilla Kalisky and Lawrence Kaplan helped us assemble and organize a variety of sources, providing invaluable research assistance. Adam Garfinkle of the *National Interest* suggested the title. Stuart Frisch, Karen Dunn, Eytan Fisch, Elyse Aronson, Jonathan Lincoln, John Wilner, and Monica Neal of The Washington Institute for Near East Policy provided invaluable assistance in editing and preparing the monograph for publication.

We received comments on earlier drafts from a number of individuals, including James Carney, Stuart Cohen, Efraim Inbar, Marvin Feuer, Thomas Keaney, Azriel Lorber, Andrew Marshall, Kenneth Pollack, Uri Reychav, Stephen Rosen, Thomas Welch, Ehud Ya'ari, Yedidiah Ya'ari and others, including serving officers in the IDF whose identities we have kept anonymous. Their views contributed greatly to this book. We stress, however, that we take exclusive responsibility for what follows.

Eliot A. Cohen
Michael J. Eisenstadt
Andrew J. Bacevich

Preface

While the day's headlines focus on the stalemate in the Arab–Israeli peace process, the necessity of deterring and—potentially—fighting war remains the supreme challenge for Israel's leaders. Indeed, history provides few examples of a country taking risks for peace with some of its neighbors while remaining under threat of attack from others. Security and peace may go hand in hand, but ensuring one while attaining the other is no easy feat.

Complicating this effort is the remarkable pace of technological change that has created what experts term a "revolution in military affairs." As the new century approaches, the very concept of war and conflict is undergoing fundamental change. Weapons are "smarter" and more lethal than ever before, terrorism can now pose a strategic threat and missiles can now bring an enemy thousands of miles away to a nation's borders. Readying soldiers, sailors, and airmen, mostly reserves, to fight an "old fashioned" conventional war—while preparing for these new challenges—is a herculean task.

To understand the answers Israeli military planners and strategic thinkers have given to these critical questions—so as to glean appropriate lessons for the U.S. armed forces—the Pentagon's Office of Net Assessment commissioned a team of respected scholars to undertake this special study. Working under the joint banner of The Washington Institute and the Foreign Policy Institute at Johns Hopkins University's Paul H. Nitze School of Advanced International Studies, the trio of Eliot Cohen, Michael Eisenstadt, and Andrew Bacevich undertook extensive research and traveled together to Israel for intensive discussions with active and retired Israeli officers and officials.

Their findings, presented here, constitute a comprehensive assessment of the changing face of Israel's security challenges and the varied responses the Israeli government has devised to meet them. We concur with the Pentagon in believing there is much for Americans to learn from the Israeli experience, but we also publish this study out of a conviction that increased knowledge of Israeli security dilemmas can assist the United States in advancing the cause of peace.

Mike Stein   Barbi Weinberg
President   Chairman

Executive Summary

Born a small, beleaguered state, outnumbered and surrounded by enemies committed to its destruction, Israel early in its history formulated a distinctive set of principles for its basic defense policy. To outside observers, Israel's approach became emblematic of, indeed, in some respects indistinguishable from its national character. Throughout the quarter-century immediately following independence, the national security concept derived from those principles served Israel well. Beginning with the shock of the 1973 war and continuing through the next two decades, however, events tested that concept severely and raised doubts about its durability. Prodded by these events, Israeli leaders sought to update, amend, and reinterpret the principles underlying essential national security policies. They did so always with an eye toward preserving the basic policy framework, thereby lending an essential continuity to Israel's approach to defense.

Now much of that seems likely to change. Technological, strategic, economic, and social forces are combining to render Israel's traditional approach to national security obsolete. As a result, in the decade to come, Israel faces the prospect of deep-seated and irrevocable change that will transform its national security policy and its armed forces. Altogether, these developments augur a veritable revolution in Israel's security affairs that will manifest itself in dramatic changes in the organization, role, and capabilities of the Israel Defense Forces (IDF) and in the relationship between the IDF and Israeli society.

This revolution in security affairs is likely to affect Israel's armed forces in the following ways:

• **The abandonment of universal military service.** Israel is unlikely to shift to an all-volunteer force or to jettison entirely its reliance on seasoned reservists. Over time, however, the IDF is likely to adopt a hybrid system, retaining the principle of near universal service, but establishing in practice multiple distinctive tracks: for the average soldier, a period of basic training followed by Swiss-style reserve duty; for volunteers (perhaps encouraged by financial incentives), a longer period of active service; for career-oriented professionals (whose numbers can be expected to rise), renewable, long-service contracts.

• **A reduction in force structure.** More than most militaries, the IDF has wrestled with the tension between quality and quantity. In the future, Israel will trade quantity to preserve quality, as the cost of first-line helicopters, tanks, and sophisticated artillery systems make a mass army unaffordable. Moreover, as the Israeli security perimeter shifts outward, toward Iran and beyond, the IDF will acquire increasingly costly systems that can be effective at considerable distances from the Levant.

- **A rebalanced force.** The IDF's long romance with the tank, although hardly over, is giving way to a far more complex military, including an ever-growing helicopter force and a more sophisticated artillery arm. The role of Israeli armor will diminish, particularly as attack and transport helicopters take over more of the maneuver role once dominated by the tank. Although the Israeli Air Force (IAF) will still support the ground forces, it will play an increasingly independent role, hunting surface-to-surface missiles or striking nonconventional weapons-related facilities in neighboring states and beyond. The navy will retain much of its independence, though it will assume a more prominent role as a strategic strike force. A different kind of rebalancing may occur if Israel shifts responsibility for day-to-day security to professional units designed for that purpose. Israeli efforts to suppress the *intifada* with conventionally organized units, both active duty and reserve, damaged morale and disrupted training without yielding success. In the end, specialized units such as Border Guards assumed a greater responsibility for this work, a trend likely to recur in future "current security" contingencies.

- **An "Americanized" officer corps.** Recognizing that its officer corps requires significant overhaul, the IDF has begun to imitate some—not all— features of the American approach to officer development and compensation. Existing programs for educating more senior officers are clearly inadequate. Already under consideration are proposals to convert the command and staff school to a two-year course, and perhaps to create a military academy that would confer academic degrees.

- **A revised strategic doctrine.** Rarely in the past have Israeli planners considered the political impact of military actions on Israel's relations with its neighbors, save in terms of deterrence. Since 1991, however, the Arab–Israel negotiations have constrained Israel's use of force. Henceforth, all conflicts will be "wars after peace," conducted with an understanding that permanent postwar settlements (and not mere armistices) may be a real possibility. How will Israeli strategic doctrine change as a result? Three possibilities stand out:

  1. *An emphasis on defensive and counteroffensive operations in lieu of offensive ones.* While never disavowing the preemptive option, Israel will face ever-greater political obstacles to its use. Aside from prospective attack with weapons of mass destruction, a scenario in which Israel will launch large-scale operations without some precipitating use of violence against it is difficult to imagine.

  2. *The pursuit of regional partners.* Acceptance of Israel as a legitimate player in the region leads other countries to see new opportunities in an alliance with the region's most advanced military power. Israel will capitalize on those opportunities by aggressively seeking tacit or overt alliances with nearby states and working in cooperation with foreign partners.

3. *Military operations directed at destroying enemy forces rather than seizing terrain.* In past wars, territorial gains offered Israel the prospect of a barrier or buffer against attack, useful as a diplomatic bargaining chip and as a means of enhancing border security. As long as the Soviets willingly replaced lost Arab hardware, the mere destruction of enemy forces promised little comparable payoff. Today, a crippled enemy can no longer turn to Moscow for reconstitution. Furthermore, occupied land is likely to include a hostile populace that greets occupiers with bombs and booby traps. Ground, once taken, becomes difficult to control yet difficult to return.

The most painful changes brought on by the revolution in security affairs, however, may well have to do with civil–military relations. The concern, voiced privately by some active and retired IDF officers, that a growing sense of "alienation" divides the army and society in Israel is overstated. Israeli civil–military relations are not headed toward estrangement and outright antagonism. Nonetheless, the unusually intimate relationship that has prevailed since independence along with the extraordinary deference accorded the army are a thing of the past.

Israeli military history has turned a corner. The revolution in security affairs inaugurates a new post-heroic age in which Israeli warriors are likely to find moral clarity and epic undertakings to be in equally scarce supply. Henceforth, the IDF will find itself obliged to perform tasks possessing neither the glory, say, of the June 1967 War nor the heroic resonance of the Entebbe rescue. Internal security, counterterrorism, counterinsurgency: such will be the dirty work that increasingly defines the lot of the Israeli soldier. For a proud and mighty army, the rewards that derive from that modified role will be mixed at best.

Israel's pattern of civil–military relations has allowed for an extraordinary degree of permeation of the society by the military and vice versa, including a very high level of participation in politics by general officers immediately upon their retirement from active duty. That practice, and certain institutional arrangements—for example, the weakness of the civilian Ministry of Defense bureaucracy and the absence of a national security council—may serve Israel poorly in the years to come. Future Israeli civil–military relations are likely to resemble those of other advanced democracies: complicated, contentious, and inextricably linked to a larger domestic and international political context. At the same time, the adjustments will produce a civil-military relationship congruent with the social and political realities of Israel.

Israel's revolution in security affairs will perpetuate its status as the dominant conventional power in the Middle East. Drawing on a more literate and technically sophisticated populace, and equipped with military hardware comparable, at its best, to that fielded by the United States, the IDF will decisively overmatch the armies and air forces of its neighbors.

The Israeli revolution in security affairs will alleviate, albeit slowly, the three-way tension between manpower, military requirements, and society. A new model IDF, with a larger professional component, will adapt to demographic and cultural changes in Israeli society that have made the old militia system untenable. That new model IDF will look, at first glance, rather more like the U.S. armed forces—high-tech, combined-arms forces, perhaps developing an ethos that places it at some remove from much of Israeli society. Yet this process of "Americanization" will have distinct limits. Indeed, the pressures leading the IDF to incorporate aspects of American military practice will themselves generate resistance aimed explicitly at preserving the IDF's distinctive identity. Thus, the tactical and technological responses that Israel devises to its security problems will, in the final analysis, retain a unique Israeli flavor.

The Israeli revolution in security affairs will widen the breach of Israel's diplomatic isolation. Israeli strategists have long dreamed of being *bündnisfähig*—an attractive potential coalition partner for regional or great powers. Such hopes—whether to serve as a *place d'armes* for British or American forces in the Middle East, to construct a grand coalition of minorities in the region, or to build a grander coalition yet of non-Arab states on its periphery—have never completely borne fruit. Now, the combination of Israel's military sophistication and a more relaxed political atmosphere makes Israel an increasingly plausible military ally.

Despite such beneficial effects, the Israeli revolution in security affairs is likely to leave other problems unresolved. Israel's sensitivity to casualties, for example, will mitigate Israel's dominance in the conventional realm. In the 1940s and 1950s Israelis accepted tens of losses in routine security operations, and hundreds (even thousands) killed in "wars of no choice." Yet, the traumas of 1973 and 1982, along with general societal changes, are fostering a heightened aversion to high-risk military actions in peacetime and brinkmanship during crises. These developments so reduce the tolerance for casualties that even successful military enterprises become politically unaffordable. As a result, the revolution in security affairs will make it even more difficult in the future to generate public support for "wars of choice"—such as the 1982 war in Lebanon. Furthermore, the prospect mass civilian casualties caused by nonconventional weapons will make it increasingly difficult for Israel to go to war for any purpose other than self-defense or survival, and it will make Israel psychologically vulnerable to Arab strategies that exploit Israeli casualty sensitivity.

In addition, the revolution in security affairs will not remove or even greatly reduce Israel's vulnerability to terror or insurgency or to attack by nonconventional (chemical, biological, or nuclear) weapons. Indeed, to the extent that Israel's conventional dominance grows, potential opponents will rely ever more on these instruments of violence that Israel finds difficult to counter. Through just such means, one can argue, the Palestinians have succeeded in achieving much of their political agenda—recognition of the Palestine Liberation Organization (PLO) and an autonomous political entity comprising Palestinians living in the West Bank and Gaza, pointing toward eventual creation of an independent state. Technology is not likely to give Israel a substantial edge in waging low intensity conflict if the true objective is not military victory as such but mobilizing a civilian population on behalf of a cause and influencing world opinion.

Transformations of the kind discussed here also give rise to their own complications. One may identify at least three in Israel's case. First, given Israel's new diplomatic standing in the region, its expanding web of regional relationships, and changing popular attitudes with regard to war, Israeli governments will find their military options far more restricted than in the past. Concerns about world opinion, relations with the United States, and the stability of neighboring Arab states will diminish the utility of Israeli military power. Fighting terrorism and perhaps engaging in limited wars against its remaining enemies without harming ongoing negotiations or endangering existing peace treaties will challenge political leaders and military commanders. During the Cold War, Israel often chafed under United Nations or U.S. pressure that would prevent it from achieving decisive battlefield victories. In the future, an adversary facing conventional defeat might unleash a biological or chemical attack against Israeli population centers, a prospect that dramatically increases the risks inherent in allowing IDF field commanders a free hand.

A second new problem relates to Israel's relationship with the United States. Simply put, Israel's strategic dependence on its patron will grow in coming years. Developing an effective defense against missiles and nonconventional weapons will require a high level of technological cooperation. Likewise, with some of the most dangerous threats facing Israel coming from comparatively distant countries, the importance of intelligence cooperation with the United States will increase. Finally, although the principle of self-reliance may remain theoretically intact, Israel is likely in a future war to require some form of direct U.S. assistance, continuing the precedent established in 1991 when U.S. Patriot batteries defended Israel against Iraqi missile attacks.

Yet even as Israeli dependence on the United States increases, Washington's commitment to Israel will come under increasing pressure. To be sure, mutual interests in curbing religious extremism, terrorism, and the proliferation of nonconventional weapons should provide an adequate basis for sustaining the strategic partnership. Having said that, the end of the Cold War has already severed one common bond. The demographic stagnation of the American Jewish community and corresponding growth in the Arab–American and Muslim communities within the United States undermines another. Relations with the American Jewish community have also come under strain over debates in Israel about "who is a Jew?" Differences between Washington and Jerusalem over the peace process or the sale of Israeli military technology to countries such as China could induce the United States to curtail strategic cooperation. These factors, combined with the fact that Israel's share of the foreign aid budget looks increasingly at odds with that country's growing economy and the supposed outbreak of peace, cast some doubt on Israel's prospects of sustaining accustomed levels of U.S. support.

A final problem will emerge as a byproduct of Israel's gradual abandonment of its nation in arms concept. The IDF is already backing away from its longstanding role as "school of the nation." Indeed, the army reached a milestone when, as occurred recently, its Nahal (*noar halutzi lohem*—"fighting pioneer youth") units began training young Israelis to become urban entrepreneurs rather than hardy farmers on border *kibbutzim*. At a time when the Jewish state faces growing internal fissures, the demise of the IDF's role as a unifying and assimilating force in a country of immigrants may well leave a void at the very center of Israeli society. In that sense, the effects of Israel's revolution in security affairs will extend well beyond Israeli security.

The Israeli revolution in security affairs will not be a panacea for the Jewish state. Once complete—a process that might take a decade or more—Israeli conventional military power will appear to its neighbors more potent than ever before. The IDF will dominate neighboring armies and acquire the capability to deliver damaging blows to more distant ones. For a nation that was born in war and that has lived, ever since, in its shadow, the prospect of surmounting such threats is no small accomplishment. Hard experience has taught the Israelis, however, the limits as well as the utility of military power, and the ways in which superiority in one form of conflict can merely goad an opponent to develop others. Israel's security will continue, as in the past, to require large sums of money and a spirit of dedication from soldier and civilian alike. But more than ever it will require a willingness on the part of Israeli politicians and the leaders of the IDF to change.

Chapter 1

Introduction

During the last several years American defense analysts, both within and outside the government and the military, have debated the likelihood of an imminent "revolution in military affairs" (RMA)—a transformation of warfare resulting, in at least one view, from the application of information technologies to weapons and the organizations that control them. Although much disagreement exists about how precisely one might define this RMA, and although some would discount its existence altogether, most senior military leaders would nonetheless say that some such transformation is under way, and that it may have already occurred.

The RMA was first a Soviet and then an American concept. Although isolated groups of defense analysts and officers in other countries have discussed it, they have not engaged in a broader debate comparable to that under way in the United States and, in some measure, in post-Soviet Russia. And yet if an RMA is indeed in progress, it has profound implications for the security of many countries, particularly technologically sophisticated ones. This study looks at one such state: Israel. More specifically, we intend to ask four questions:

- To what extent, if at all, do the Israel Defense Forces (IDF) and Israeli military thinkers believe in the existence of an RMA?
- To the degree that they do believe an RMA is under way, do they characterize it differently than do American analysts?
- What are the likely consequences of Israeli views for Israeli defense policy in coming years?
- What implications do Israeli views have for American thinking and what consequences might flow for U.S. policy from these views?

Although this study began as an attempt to delineate the Israeli view of the RMA, it quickly became apparent that few Israeli military experts accept that term—at least not in the way Americans do. Insofar as they are familiar with it they regard it as either excessively optimistic about the potential of technology in war, or as irrelevant for the challenges confronting the IDF. Yet, at the same time we found a consensus, barely articulated and indeed still in the process of formation, that Israel faces a broader transformation: one that the authors (not the

Israelis) term a *revolution in security affairs*. The Israeli defense establishment is in the midst of a transformation in several dimensions, and although individual aspects of that transformation receive sustained attention, it has yet to receive an integrated treatment. To prepare such an overall assessment of the Israeli "RSA," as we call it, became our objective. This "revolution in security affairs" reflects four forces:

- alteration of Israel's strategic position owing to the defeat of Iraq, the collapse of the Soviet Union, and the initiation of the Madrid peace process in 1991;
- technological developments in Israel and among its potential enemies;
- growth in the size and wealth of the Israeli economy; and
- changes in the composition and values of Israeli society.

As a result of these developments, Israel stands today on the verge of a dramatic change—revolution is a fair term—in how it copes with the problems of national defense that have played a central role in its history since 1948. An able and serious military leadership finds itself wrestling with problems caused by phenomena (a glut of conscripts and the challenges created by the tortuously evolving Middle East peace process, for example) that would have been inconceivable to most Israeli generals when they entered military service a quarter century ago. Their views and decisions will, of course, affect the security of their own country; they merit as well, however, the attention of Americans concerned not only with the Middle East, but with the future of U.S. defense policy as well.

This study thus addresses several audiences: students of Israeli defense policy and Middle East security issues, and Americans interested in the RMA debate. It follows in the footsteps of previous studies of the IDF and its doctrine that have appeared in recent decades, which, valuable though they are, require substantial modification in light of the events of the late 1980s and 1990s.[1]

---

[1]   Some of the major studies are Michael Handel, *Israel's Political–Military Doctrine* (Cambridge: Harvard University Center for International Affairs, 1973); Edward Luttwak and Dan Horowitz, *The Israeli Army* (New York: Harper & Row, 1975); Yoav Ben-Horin and Barry Posen, *Israel's Strategic Doctrine* (Santa Monica, Calif.: Rand, 1981); Hirsh Goodman and W. Seth Carus, *The Future Battlefield and the Arab–Israeli Conflict* (New Brunswick: Transaction, 1990); Michael Handel, "The Evolution of Israeli Strategy," in Williamson Murray, MacGregor Knox, and Alvin Bernstein, eds., *The Making of Strategy* (Cambridge: Cambridge University Press, 1994), pp. 534–578.

THE REVOLUTION IN MILITARY AFFAIRS: A PRIMER[2]

The notion that the world has entered a period of revolutionary change in the conduct of war has several origins. Beginning in the 1980s American analysts discovered, translated, and pondered the meaning of Soviet writings on the future of warfare. These works, which included studies written by the most senior leaders of the Soviet military, suggested that a new era of warfare was dawning in which conventional weapons would have the military effectiveness of tactical nuclear weapons.[3] Soviet writers spoke in terms of "reconnaissance-strike" or, later on, "reconnaissance-destruction" complexes, which would allow the near annihilation of large armored formations at depths of hundreds of kilometers in periods as short as thirty to forty-five minutes.

Awareness of the Soviet notion of a "military-technical revolution" did not immediately translate into an acceptance of it. Rather, the subject remained confined to a few defense specialists until the Persian Gulf War of 1991, which seemed to some Americans to validate the notion of an RMA. The lopsided battles in the deserts of Kuwait and southern Iraq and the seemingly effortless domination of Iraqi skies by coalition air forces indicated to many that warfare had indeed changed. In particular, the contrast between U.S. expectations of a bloody fight, and the reality of Iraqi collapse, struck many observers as an indication of fundamental change.

A third source of thinking about the RMA came from a single individual, William Owens, a nuclear submariner who rose to become a powerful vice chairman of the U.S. Joint Chiefs of Staff in 1994. In that capacity, he helped to create institutions designed to maximize the power of the central military

---

[2] This section is excerpted from Eliot A. Cohen, "American Views of the Revolution in Military Affairs," in Ze'ev Bonen and Eliot Cohen, *Advanced Technology and Future Warfare*, Security and Policy Studies No. 28, (Ramat Gan, Israel: BESA Center, Bar-Ilan University, 1996), pp. 3–18. See as well Eliot A. Cohen, "A Revolution in Warfare," Foreign Affairs (March/April 1996), pp. 37–54.

[3] One of the earliest American assessments of the Soviet view was Notra Trulock, Kerry L. Hines, and Anne D. Herr, "Soviet Military Thought in Transition: Implications for the Long-Term Military Competition" (Pacific Sierra Research Corporation, May 1988). A recent Russian view was Vladimir I. Slipchenko, "A Russian Analysis of Warfare Leading to the Sixth Generation," *Field Artillery* (October 1993), pp. 38–41. N.V. Ogarkov published two short books in 1982 and 1985: see, in particular, *History Teaches Vigilance* (Moscow: Voyenizdat, 1985). A short summary of Soviet thinking can also be found in M. A. Gareev and M. V. Frunze, *Military Theorist* (Moscow: Voyenizdat, 1985; Washington, D.C.: Pergamon-Brassey's, 1988), a work that deals with both contemporary and historical issues.

leadership at the expense of the services. The Joint Requirements Oversight Council (JROC), which he chaired, and which is composed of the vice chiefs of staff of all the services plus other military and civilian officials, had more than bureaucratic consequences. Its purpose, as envisaged by Owens, was to bring about an operational, and not merely an organizational, revolution, based on the integration of three sets of technologies: long-range precision strike, communications, and sensors. This "system of systems" would, in Owens's view, allow the United States, at will, to dominate segments of the earth's surface defined in 200-by-200-mile boxes.[4] More precisely, within such boxes the U.S. military could locate, track, and destroy enemy forces with virtual impunity.

From these three sources, a variety of views of the RMA have developed in the United States. Each may be defined in terms of answers to four broad questions:

- Is there a revolution under way?
- What is the fundamental dynamic of warfare that the RMA will change?
- Looking inward, what is the chief policy challenge to American defense planners in coming years, in light of the above?
- Looking outward, what is the chief threat that the U.S. armed forces face?

What follows, then, are "ideal-type" positions on the RMA, corresponding not so much to a single individual's views (although in some cases they do just that) but to clusters of opinion. They represent four perspectives, some well developed, others barely articulated, that cover a range from firm faith in the RMA to no less than a firm dismissal of it.

OWENS'S DISCIPLES: 'THE SYSTEM OF SYSTEMS'

The first group, Admiral Owens's disciples, has no doubts that an RMA has begun. It consists above all in the application of information technologies to warfare. In this view, the change under way represents not merely *a* revolution in warfare, but *the* revolution in warfare, a change that dwarfs all others, with the possible exception of the introduction of nuclear weapons half a century ago. Moreover, this revolution is one that only the United States can master.

The United States has accumulated phenomenal technological capacities for long-range precision strike, communications, and sensing, but it has yet to network them and thereby take full advantage of their power. In the view of

---

[4]   See William A. Owens, "The Emerging System of Systems," *Proceedings* of the U.S. Naval Institute (May 1995), pp. 36–39.

Owens and his followers, the challenge is not so much to create new technologies, but rather to exploit to their fullest those already fielded or on the verge of coming into service. Indeed, one of the greatest obstacles to the creation of the system of systems—a completely integrated web of military forces that can look, shoot, and communicate—is the U.S. military's ignorance of the full range of the systems at its disposal. Owens himself often showed senior military audiences a list (see Table 1) of some of the leading systems in each category and observed caustically that no one present, himself included, could explain each of the acronyms, let alone how all of the technologies operate. Owens's use of a table of this kind was more than a mere rhetorical device. In his view, his audiences' failure to master it captured the main problem of military professionalism on the verge of a new century.

Table 1. Owens's List of U.S. Military Technology

Precision Strike[5]	Communications	Sensors
SFW	GCCS	AWACS
JSOW	MILSTAR	RIVET JOINT
TLAM (BLK III)	JSIPS	EP-3E
ATACMS/BAT	DISN	JSTARS
SLAM	JUDI	HASA
CALCM	C4I FTW	SBIR
HAVE NAP	TADIL J	TIER 2 (+)
AGM-130	TRAP	TIER 3 (-)
HARM	TACSAT	TARPS/ATARS
AIR HAWK	JWICS	MTI
SADARM	MIDS	REMBAS
HELLFIRE II	SONET	MAGIC LANTERN
TLAM (BLK IV)	LINK 16	ISAR

Underpinning the system of systems is the belief that until now most military activity has consisted of wasteful motion and effort. Infantrymen fired thousands of bullets that missed for every one that hit an enemy soldier; bombers dropped similar quantities of bombs for every one that landed on a factory, bridge, or tank. Logisticians accumulated vast quantities of supplies that armies never

---

5   Ibid., table slightly modified.

needed, aircraft patrolled air space that the enemy never violated, and lieutenants leading patrols crept through areas that the enemy did not occupy. According to Owens, much of what von Clausewitz described as "friction" and even more so, "the fog of war" resulted not from the innate characteristics and tendencies of war itself, but rather from the deficiencies of information gathering, assessment, and management—deficiencies that technology, intelligently managed, can now remedy. To be sure, the emotions engendered by war will always have a distorting effect on commanders' perceptions of the battlefield, but these can be vastly reduced. To believe otherwise is to resemble a primitive man who refuses to believe in the possibility of anything but blurry vision because he cannot conceive of the existence of eyeglasses.

The chief challenge to the U.S. armed forces, therefore, consists of an architectural problem: building the system of systems. The overarching idea is simple—making sure that targeting information acquired by any system can be passed, in a timely fashion, to another system that can then fire effectively. In practice, however, the implementation of the system of systems will require an extraordinary effort to standardize protocols and provide seamless procedures that, for example, would allow an Army helicopter firing a long-range missile to hit a mobile radar located by an Air Force unmanned aerial vehicle, or a Navy warship launching a tactical cruise or ballistic missile to strike a moving column of armor detected by satellite moments before.

To enable these technical changes to take root would require profound organizational and even psychological transformations. In a system of systems there exists no room for service-specific solutions to military problems. Ultimately, it would be desirable (if, in all likelihood, impractical) to merge the services into one joint military organization. Beyond this, however, the Owens vision would seem to require an officer corps of both greater technical sophistication and greater operational flexibility than any yet known in the United States. It is no accident that Owens, himself emerged from among the ranks of nuclear submariners, a group notable for high levels of tactical skill (admittedly, of a specialized type) and advanced technical knowledge.

The system of systems advocates have not identified any particular country as a future opponent of the United States. Indeed, given their technology-centered view of warfare, they do not need to. The current technologies, properly meshed, will allow the United States to achieve "dominant battlefield knowledge" over any 200-by-200-mile square of the earth's surface. The United States still outspends the next largest military power in the world by a factor of five or more, and it has, moreover, an unparalleled capital stock in the form of satellites, aircraft carriers, and the like. For that reason the United States alone can build the system of systems and thus dominate any future conventional competitor.

The real threat, therefore, is not so much external as internal—the resistance of the services to the development of truly joint organizations and modes of warfare, and the refusal of the officer corps to accept the challenge of a new era of warfare. Indeed, Owens himself was in many respects thwarted by the bureaucracies he attempted to subdue, and he retired after only a single two-year term as vice chairman of the Joint Chiefs of Staff, when he might reasonably have been expected to serve for longer. The system of systems revolution, however, does not rest exclusively on the vision of one man. It is, to some extent, implicit in the reforms of the last 20 years, and above all in the Goldwater–Nichols Department of Defense Reorganization Act of 1986, which increased the power of the unified commands and the Joint Staff at the expense of the services. Owens himself may have left the bureaucratic battlefield, but the impediments to achieving his vision have diminished and will continue to do so.

THE UNCERTAIN REVOLUTIONARIES

For a somewhat larger group of defense analysts, the promise of drastic change in the conduct of war is clear, but its course is not. If a revolution in warfare is under way, it has yet to progress beyond its early stages. The Gulf War and minor eruptions of force since then—for example, Operation Deliberate Force, the U.S.-led bombing campaign in Bosnia in 1995—offer hints or samples of what might lie ahead. The maturation of the RMA lies in the future, its final shape and likely consequences shrouded in uncertainty.

In this view, the current (or, more accurately, emerging) revolution is but one in a series of dramatic changes in the conduct of war. Others include the advent of armored operations in the interwar period or, in the nineteenth century, the use of the railroad and telegraph in conjunction with the rifle to make possible the effective use of the mass armies that dominated Europe from the 1860s through World War I. Such revolutions have a number of features in common. A single country usually leads in their implementation, although an initial pioneer may stumble by the wayside (as the British did, for example, in forfeiting their lead in armored warfare during the 1920s). Civilian technologies often (though not always) drive radical military change, as the example of the railroad, the telegraph, and later the internal combustion engine suggest. The human means for taking advantage of technology are often more important than the tools of warfare themselves.

This latter point addresses the question "what drives warfare?" by pointing to the synthesis of technology, operational concept, and organization to achieve a quantum improvement in military effectiveness. As has often been noted, the Germans did not defeat the French and British in 1940 because they had uniformly superior tanks or greater numbers of them, but rather because they had developed both an organization (the Panzer division) and an operational concept (armored penetration) that allowed them to exploit the new technology. Thus, like Owens's disciples, the uncertain revolutionaries rely less on technology *per se* than on technology as exploited by human ingenuity. But where Owens's disciples define the challenge of transforming warfare as a straightforward architectural problem, the uncertain revolutionaries see a more complex picture with many more intangible elements and a far less certain outcome.

The Germans succeeded in developing armored warfare for a number of reasons, including a military tradition of mission-oriented tactics *(auftragstaktik)* that fit well with the new weapons of war. They operated as well in favorable financial and strategic circumstances: well funded if small, the interwar German army could pick and choose its officers and men and could afford to equip and train them well, within the bounds of the Versailles treaty limitations. The German military had no competing demands on its attention and energies, unlike the British, for example, who were preoccupied with imperial policing at the expense, oftentimes, of attention to planning for ground war against a major opponent.[6] Even so, the Germans had by no means solved all of the problems of modern mechanized warfare by 1940. Nor were they able to retain their lead indefinitely. Rather, they had a passing advantage and exploited it. In time, others developed equal competence at many of the techniques Germany had pioneered.

For the uncertain revolutionaries, therefore, the chief challenge to the U.S. armed forces lies in fostering experimentation and innovation.[7] Inclined to mistrust the certainty of Admiral Owens, and having a greater belief in the persistence of friction and the fog of war, they do not believe in any one system of systems or any other neat crystallization of the RMA. They expect the armed forces to develop a variety of weapon systems, organizations, and operational concepts. Some of these initiatives may fail, but they do not fear such missteps. Rather, they worry chiefly about the increasing reluctance of the U.S. military to tolerate radical experimentation. They note, for example, that during the interwar period, which was particularly fruitful for the development of naval aviation, the Department of the Navy was willing to invest large sums of money on such

---

[6]   Where no such distractions existed—in the case of air defense, for instance—the British did much better in the interwar period.

[7]   See Stephen P. Rosen, *Winning the Next War: Innovation and the Modern Military* (Ithaca, N.Y.: Cornell University Press, 1991).

abortive concepts as the use of dirigibles to transport and launch aircraft and did not penalize the men who pioneered them. Today, however, when the defense acquisition system has grown ever more cautious and ponderous, and when many within the U.S. armed forces tend to think that they already have the answers to tomorrow's operational problems, innovation has become ever more difficult.

The uncertain revolutionaries applaud a diverse array of programs under way and seek to nurture and protect them—the Navy's arsenal ship, the Marine Corps' Sea Dragon, the Army's digitization of the battlefield initiative, and the Air Force's first steps toward the sustained exploitation of unmanned aerial vehicles. In their view, it will not be enough, however, merely to fund a few prototypes or field a new squadron or two. It may be necessary to build half a dozen types of arsenal ship before hitting on the optimal design, even as it took more than 15 years of experimentation with operational aircraft carriers before U.S. naval architects developed the Essex-class design that won the carrier war in the Pacific. It will be necessary to cultivate new types of officers whose career paths and backgrounds will differ from those of today—UAV operators, for example, attempting to make their way in a service dominated by fighter pilots.

Where Owens's disciples see tremendous opportunities blocked only by bureaucratic self-interest and obstinacy, the "uncertain revolutionaries" have more sobering concerns. They note that most of the technologies driving the RMA arise from the civilian sector, and hence will be available to possible opponents of the United States. Moreover, even more narrowly military technologies such as stealth are increasingly available in an international arms market that lacks the structure and controls of the Cold War period. At a deeper level yet, the uncertain revolutionaries worry about the distractions caused by the operations tempo of U.S. forces deployed around the world, which reduces the resources, time, and attention that the services can focus on the longer term development of conventional military forces.

The uncertain revolutionaries believe that the United States may, and probably will, face a "peer competitor" in the next two or three decades. By peer competitor they mean a country that can field forces capable of inflicting serious damage on the U.S. military or denying it the ability to operate in a theater of war. A peer competitor need not equal the United States in economic size or military sophistication—Japan possessed less than 15 percent of the economic resources of the United States in 1941, after all. Rather, a peer competitor must meet only certain thresholds of physical and economic size and military sophistication and have the motivation to see in the United States a potential opponent. Even if such competition does not lead to overt warfare with the

United States (as, indeed, the Cold War did not), the results could still adversely affect American foreign policy and national interests.

The most likely peer competitor, and one publicly acknowledged with increasing frequency, is China. In the early years of the next century, China's economy may match the American economy in order of magnitude, if not absolute size. Chinese interests clash with those of the United States in a number of areas (including Taiwan and the South China Sea) and China has a long and sophisticated military tradition. That China's military today is, by and large, bloated and obsolete offers small comfort in this view. By exploiting civilian technology, investing large sums of money in defense, and concentrating on military capabilities that serve its strategic interests (rather than merely mirroring the forces of the United States) China might, before very long, pose a serious military challenge to the United States. And the danger, in the view of the uncertain revolutionaries, is that the U.S. armed forces, preoccupied by peacekeeping and perpetual overseas deployments, complacent about their technological edge, and confined by a "zero-defects" procurement and force development system, may find themselves some day overmatched by an opponent whom they viewed with disdain only a decade or two before.

THE GULF WAR VETERANS

Both of the foregoing are minority views. The bulk of the officer corps, in its heart, is more likely to have the outlook of what one might call "the Gulf War veteran." The veteran too believes in revolutionary change in the conduct of war, but would argue that the decisive revolution has already come to pass. In fact, it occurred in the 1980s or even slightly earlier, though it was fully revealed only in the American war with Iraq in 1991. This revolution rests on the thorough exploitation of modern military technology by highly trained soldiers; indeed, for the Gulf War veteran, the American training revolution of the 1970s embodies the essence of the RMA. The creation of sophisticated training areas such as the National Training Center at Fort Irwin, California, or instrumented ranges such as those at Nellis Air Force Base, coupled with careful recruitment and retention policies have, in this view, created armed forces that are in a different class than those of most countries. Whereas in the past, hardy peasants using second-rate equipment could put up a stiff fight against a developed country's force, that is no longer the case. The combination of increasingly sophisticated hardware, ever more realistic training, and personnel policies that attract, cultivate, and retain highly intelligent and well-educated soldiers, has combined to produce revolutionary advances in capability. The seemingly effortless triumph of the coalition over the Iraqis, in a victory whose cheapness surprised even many of the soldiers who helped achieve it, demonstrated that warfare had in fact undergone a revolution.

For the Gulf War veteran, technology is certainly important, but no more so than quality training. Acutely conscious of the difference between the all-volunteer force of today and the conscript force of yesterday, the veteran attributes the edge between American and other armed forces to a military way of life quite different from that of the days of the draft. Whereas in the past American soldiers would spend much of their time peeling potatoes or painting rocks, engaging in only episodic and stylized training, today they spend most of their time soldiering. Only militaries that can draw on a technologically advanced population, and that can afford to give soldiers constant and realistic (and hence expensive) training, can fully exploit the possibilities of contemporary weapons.

The internal challenge for the Gulf War veteran is essentially a budgetary one. The U.S. defense budget has shrunk roughly 40 percent from its peak during the Cold War, as the government has gone from spending some 5.5 percent of gross domestic product on defense to some 3.4 percent, with projections heading downward from there. The U.S. armed forces have shrunk in size by a bit less than a third, however, and the operational tempo of deployed forces remains high. Because American defense leaders understand the imperative of maintaining quality, they will not skimp on pay or training. Because forces are continually in action overseas, they cannot decrease readiness. As a result, procurement of new hardware has absorbed the steepest cuts—of more than 50 percent—to $43 billion or less annually. Gulf War veterans may agree with these priorities, but they nonetheless want to sustain the continuous, incremental force modernization familiar since the beginning of the 1980s. For the veteran, the central problem of the future is one of balance: sustaining those attributes of the U.S. military that have made it so successful thus far, while continuing to improve it. The veteran's greatest anxiety, in this regard, is a return to the conditions of the late 1970s, when conditions in the military deteriorated because of substandard recruits, slack discipline, and the lack of a clear operational focus.

The Gulf War veteran tends to believe that, given continued investments in pay, training, and operations and maintenance, the United States will maintain an overwhelming conventional superiority over any potential opponents. In fact, the veteran believes, this superiority may have paradoxical consequences. Rather than attempt to compete on terms favorable to the United States—namely, high-technology conventional warfare—potential opponents will resort to measures at either end of the spectrum of conflict. They will either resort to terrorism and unconventional means of fighting to evade American conventional superiority—information warfare, for example—or, instead, use chemical, biological, or nuclear weapons of mass destruction to neutralize it. In the worst of both worlds they might combine both. Against such strategic challenges the United States is far more poorly positioned to react than it was when faced with the action of a Saddam Hussein invading Kuwait. But conventional superiority still retains, in this view, enormous value. As difficult as the new threats might prove, they represent lesser difficulties (for the moment at any rate) than would a world safe for conventional warfare. If the United States can make conventional military operations against it virtually unthinkable—and, by and large, the Gulf War veteran thinks this is within reach—the United States will have achieved a very great deal.

THE SKEPTICS

The final school of American thought regarding the RMA regards the entire notion with suspicion and even derision. In this view the whole notion of revolutionary change in warfare is misplaced and even dangerous. An odd coalition of military historians and experienced soldiers join in opposing the very instance of discontinuous change in warfare. The historian notes that virtually every case of revolutionary transformation detected in the past turns out to have taken place far more gradually, and over a longer period of time, than at first appears to have been the case. The transformation of warfare in the Napoleonic period had its roots in the simplified tactics of French drill masters thirty years earlier; the German blitz of 1940 emerged as a byproduct of infiltration tactics developed during World War I; and the same goes for many so-called revolutionary technologies today, such as precision-guided munitions, which first appeared in crude form toward the end of World War II.

The antipathy of some orthodox soldiers to the idea of revolutionary change stems from a visceral disagreement with the idea that technology, rather than human nature, dominates the battlefield. Unlike the Gulf War veteran, the skeptic believes that the war with Iraq represented an anomaly—a unique circumstance created by an unusually stupid opponent who presented the U.S. military with an ideal array of targets. Had the Iraqis fought with somewhat greater determination and cunning (had they been as tough and as clever as the North Vietnamese, for instance) they might have administered a severe battering to the coalition, even if they would have succumbed in the end. The military skeptic views with grave doubt Owens's belief that technology can substantially eliminate the fog and friction of war. For the skeptic, these phenomena are inherent in the very nature of conflict and cannot be removed from war until combat ceases to be an activity directed by, and on behalf of, human beings.

Herein resides the military skeptic's theory of war: the human element dominates. Not necessarily hostile to technology, the skeptic views with mistrust the claims of technologists and those who put their faith in technology. The skeptic wants the best weapons, of course, but worries far more about having the right soldiers (especially women as combat soldiers) in battle. For the skeptic, the cultivation of the warrior spirit is more than a matter of designing the right training ranges and simulation facilities: it is the heart of the military profession.

Like the Gulf War veteran, the skeptic sees the forthcoming challenge to U.S. defense policy as one of balance: keeping a substantial force structure and being wary of substituting high technology for soldiers while maintaining its quality and sustaining modernization. The skeptic has a further concern, however. Where the Gulf War veteran believes that the right mix of monetary and educational incentives for would-be recruits, along with generous pay and tough, realistic training for those who serve, will sustain the qualitative edge of American soldiers, the skeptic views such confidence with alarm. Rather, the skeptic fears the intrusion of the values of contemporary American society—which are viewed as hedonistic, overly egalitarian in relations between men and women, and much too tolerant of lax standards of personal conduct—into the U.S. military.

Paradoxically, perhaps, like Admiral Owens and his disciples, the military skeptic sees the chief enemy as coming from within. Doubting the possibility of human foresight, the skeptic is unwilling to predict what kind of strategic threat the United States will face in the next century. Rather, the skeptic tends to believe in the value of a generalized preparedness for a variety of forms of conflict, and to view with suspicion the idea of focusing on a single, dominant threat. The skeptic's true enemies, therefore, are the arrogance of the Gulf War veteran and the excessive cleverness of both the Owens group and the uncertain revolutionaries.[8] Arrogance and excessive cleverness are the perennial temptations of militarily successful nations, and he is skeptical enough about the United States to believe that it might well fall into a similar trap.

WHY STUDY ISRAEL?

If an RMA is indeed under way, and not merely the culmination of a single country's military development, such a phenomenon should be reflected in other states. Other countries, after all, have access to the same civilian technologies that drive the RMA in the United States. Indeed, some analysts fear the erosion of the U.S. military edge through the commercialization and diffusion of such

---

[8]   For a good example, see Warren Caldwell, "Promises, Promises," *Proceedings of the U.S. Naval Institute* (January 1996), pp. 54–57.

technologies as space-based imaging and precision navigation. Israel offers an interesting test case for the RMA hypothesis because it has the means, motives, and sophistication to pursue its own transformation of war.

For all of these groups—Admiral Owens and his adherents, the uncertain revolutionaries, the Gulf War veterans, and the skeptics—Israel offers a particularly interesting case. One of the world's most sophisticated militaries, the IDF takes its responsibilities with deadly seriousness because it, unlike many of its counterparts, must stand ready on a moment's notice for a variety of forms of combat, from border skirmishing with guerrillas to all-out conventional war, from terrorist attacks on city buses to strikes by chemical-tipped ballistic missiles. The IDF has acquired in half a century a fund of hard-won experience in warfare: its views demand attention. At the same time, Israel's difference in scale and military culture from the United States provides a very different perspective on the future of warfare.

The RMA debate is laden with American assumptions about technology, strategy, and operations, and about military organizations and the societies from which they spring. American defense analysts debate the RMA from the vantage point of a country that spends some four or five times as much on defense—even after the Cold War—as any other country. The very notion of Admiral Owens's system of systems rests on a defense budget of enormous size, overlaid on defense capital accumulated through decades of military acquisition. The institutional problems posed by the existence of three traditionally independent service departments and four services (one of them, the Marine Corps, on a scale vastly larger than that of any comparable naval infantry force) preoccupy American strategists, who also take for granted a global command-and-control structure and the opportunities and problems to which it gives rise. U.S. forces operate from a continental base that, even in an age of intercontinental ballistic missiles and terrorist truck bombs, has been relatively safe from attack. They are, particularly in the post–Cold War period, invariably expeditionary in nature, and play a dominant role in any coalition in which they take part.

A NOTE ON SOURCES

The student of the IDF soon becomes aware of a number of obstacles to the study of Israel's armed forces. First and foremost is Israeli secrecy, a necessity in a country at constant risk of war but that now reflects deeply ingrained habit as well. Israeli officers below the rank of brigadier general usually appear in the press or in professional publications identified only by their first name, or even their first initial. Only recently was the name of the head of Israel's civilian foreign intelligence service, the Mossad, publicly acknowledged. Israel still does not publish official data on order of battle or many of the basic manpower statistics that are routinely available in less embattled states. It is difficult to discover the table of organization and equipment for a standard armored brigade, for example—and even when obtained, the prevalence of special organizations and variation in unit structures make such information unreliable. With some few exceptions (the elite 7th armored brigade, for example, or the *Golani*, *Givati*, and 35th paratroop brigades) unit designations are classified. Divisions are frequently described in the press by their commander's name. Information about most aircraft accidents is classified, and Israelis were horrified recently when a British journal published order of battle data about the Israeli Air Force, most of which would be fairly readily available to a student of the U.S. Air Force.[9] Israeli journalists have traditionally submitted to censorship, though of a relatively light kind. More than in most countries, a journalist has been liable to think twice before revealing information that could jeopardize national security, if only because the journalist's own fate, and that of friends and relatives, may be at stake. And, it must be said, the Israelis have made and continue to make frequent and successful use of deception to mislead potential adversaries about their real military capabilities.

A second set of problems stems from a dearth of scholarly source materials. Israeli military archives are not open, except on an infrequent and exceptional basis, to researchers, though access has improved in recent years. Although the IDF has efficient military history units, their work has remained, for the most part, classified. Secondary works on the IDF are relatively few and now dated. Furthermore, because Israel is an informal country, much of what is important in Israeli military doctrine and thinking is not written down or widely distributed.

In more recent years, however, the situation for students of the IDF has improved. The general opening of the Israeli defense debate in the wake of the October 1973 War and the controversial Lebanon conflict of 1982 have produced more public inquiry about defense matters, and far more critical journalistic coverage than in the past. Israeli journalists have become adept at evading censorship by citing stories that have appeared in the foreign press—and, in some cases, leaking stories to foreign correspondents so they can then publish them domestically. A large and growing memoir literature sheds light on Israeli military culture, and the foreign trade press (including journals such as *Aviation Week and Space Technology* or *International Defense Review*) devote much

---

[9]   See Douglas Davis, "A 'Must-Read' about Israel's Military Machine," *Jerusalem Post,* August 9, 1996, p. 9; Josh Kalman, "Report on Air Force Stuns Israelis," *Washington Times,* July 31, 1996, p. 15.

attention to Israel. In recent years several think tanks and scholars have begun to write knowledgeably about the IDF, its troubles, and its successes. Government sources have also opened up, to include, most recently, the creation of a surprisingly extensive home page for the IDF on the World Wide Web, complete with extensive fact sheets and historical material. We have supplemented all of these sources with intensive interviews with a number of Israeli officials and journalists, most of whom have requested anonymity.

OUTLINE OF THE WORK

Chapter 2, "Israel's National Security Doctrine: Continuity and Change," describes the fundamental features of the Israeli military establishment today. These include first, the core Israeli national security doctrine established in the early years of the state, which exercises a profound effect on Israeli military thought to the present day; and second, a description of the evolution of Israeli force structure, to include special warfare, conventional, and strategic forces, as well as Israel's defense industry. Chapter 3, "Israeli Military Culture: Conservative Innovation," moves beyond the skeleton and sinew of the Israeli military establishment described in the preceding chapter to the spirit that animates it. The chapter analyzes those forces favoring innovation and change, on the one hand, and those retarding it, on the other. Its title suggests the paradoxical pattern that we have found in Israeli military practice: relentless and aggressive improvement and change on the margins, resting on a bedrock of relatively unchanging institutions and fundamental outlooks. Chapter 4, "The Israeli Revolution in Security Affairs," begins by examining the IDF as a whole as it evolved in response to the changed military environment of the post-1973 period. In particular, it describes what Israeli military experts have referred to as "the saturated battlefield," which guided much of Israeli force structure and operational thinking in the late 1970s and 1980s. It then surveys Israeli views of the Gulf War, which reveal much about Israeli views of an RMA more broadly. The chapter then describes the technological, strategic, economic, and social changes that are setting the stage for a broad-based change in the Israeli approach to warfare and the institutions that comprise the larger security establishment. It concludes by speculating about the contours of the Israeli defense establishment of the future. The final chapter, "Implications," explores the likely consequences of these changes for Israel and the United States.

Chapter 2

Israel's National Security Doctrine: Continuity and Change

Born a small, beleaguered state outnumbered and surrounded by enemies committed to its destruction, Israel formulated a distinctive set of principles for its basic defense policy early in its history.[1] The national security concept derived from those principles ably met Israel's needs in the quarter-century immediately following independence, and in the eyes of many, it came to be seen as emblematic of the Israeli national character.

Beginning with the shock of the October 1973 War and continuing through the next two decades, events severely tested Israel's security doctrine and raised doubts in some quarters about its durability. Prodded by these events, Israel's leaders sought to update, amend, and reinterpret the basic principles underlying its national security policies. But they did so always with an eye toward preserving the basic policy framework, thereby lending an essential continuity to

---

[1] In addition to the studies of Israel's national security concept and strategy cited in the previous chapter, see Dan Horowitz, "The Israeli Concept of National Security and the Prospects of Peace in the Middle East," in Gabriel Scheffer, *Dynamics of a Conflict: A Reexamination of the Arab–Israeli Conflict* (Atlantic Highlands, N.J.: Humanities Press, 1975), pp. 235–275; Maj. Gen. Israel Tal, "Israel's Defense Doctrine: Background and Dynamics," *Military Review* (March 1978), pp. 22–37; Efraim Inbar, "Israeli Strategic Thinking After 1973," *Journal of Strategic Studies* (March 1983), pp. 36–59; Maj. Gen. Israel Tal, "The Offensive and the Defensive in Israel's Campaigns," *Jerusalem Quarterly* (Summer 1989), pp. 41–47; Ariel Levite, *Offense and Defense in Israeli Military Doctrine* (Tel Aviv: Tel Aviv University, Jaffee Center for Strategic Studies, 1989); Efraim Inbar and Shmuel Sandler, "Israel's Deterrence Strategy Revisited," *Security Studies* (Winter 1993–94), pp. 330–358; Efraim Inbar, "Contours of Israel's New Strategic Thinking," *Political Science Quarterly* (Spring 1996), pp. 41–64; Avner Yaniv, ed., *National Security and Democracy in Israel* (Boulder, Colo.: Westview, 1993). There is, of course, also a very rich Hebrew literature, including most recently Israel Tal, *National Security: The Few Against the Many* (Tel Aviv: Dvir, 1996) but also older works such as Yigal Allon, *Curtain of Sand: Israel and the Arabs Between War and Peace* (Tel Aviv: Hakibbutz Hameuchad, 1981).

Israel's approach to defense, even as evidence accumulated that the principles supporting the concept no longer sufficed.[2]

ISRAEL'S NATIONAL SECURITY CONCEPT

Strategic Defense, Operational Offense

"The IDF's doctrine at the strategic level is defensive, while its tactics are offensive. Given the country's lack of territorial depth, the IDF must take initiative when deemed necessary and, if attacked, to quickly transfer the battleground to the enemy's land."[3] For nearly half a century, the Israel Defense Force (IDF), believing the hostility of its Arab neighbors to be virtually immutable, has clung to a combination of preemptive, preventive, and retaliatory action—a combination that, it hoped, would develop Israel's deterrent capacity and eventually convince its Arab opponents of the impossibility of a military resolution of the Arab–Israeli conflict.

Israel lacks natural strategic depth.[4] In its pre-1967 borders, Israel was only 14 km wide at its narrow waist, making it vulnerable to attempts to cut the country in half. Moreover, its long coastline and frontiers—relative to its total land area—make its borders difficult to secure. And because some two-thirds of the country's population live along the narrow coastal strip between Tel Aviv and Haifa, cross-border raids or invasion can put much of its civilian population at immediate risk.[5] Israel could not, according to the framers of the doctrine, afford to adopt a defensive approach because it could not trade space for time. The Israeli military planners decided early on that war must take place on enemy terrain, and that Israeli ground forces must carry it there, thereby creating a kind

---

[2]   Tal, *National Security*, p. 218.

[3]   This is a quote from the Israeli Ministry of Foreign Affairs' website dealing with the Israel Defense Forces. "The State: Israel Defense Forces (IDF)," www.israel-mfa.gov.il/facts/state/fstate11.html, December 10, 1996.

[4]   For an extensive discussion of strategic depth in the Israeli context see *Strategic Depth in Modern War*, Elazar Papers no. 2 (Tel Aviv: Tel Aviv University, Elazar Memorial Association, 1979).

[5]   Steven J. Rosen, *Military Geography and the Military Balance in the Arab–Israeli Conflict,* Jerusalem Papers on Peace Problems no. 21 (Jerusalem: Hebrew University, The Leonard Davis Institute for International Relations, 1977). For a particularly trenchant discussion of the issue of strategic depth in the Israeli context, see Aharon Yariv, "Strategic Depth—an Israeli View," *Ma'arachot* (October 1979), pp. 21–25 (Hebrew).

of artificial strategic depth. To be sure, after the 1967 war, and even after the 1973 war, some senior Israeli planners moderated their enthusiasm for the offense.[6] Even as offensive-minded a leader as Chief of Staff Rafael Eitan declared that "when an army is well prepared and ready for the coming attack, it is much easier to annihilate the enemy when on the defensive."[7] Nonetheless, for the most part, the IDF has viewed a defensive on the ground as but a brief phase—unavoidable or desirable depending on circumstances, but a short interlude nonetheless—before passing to the attack.

Israel will, therefore, whenever feasible, move the war quickly to enemy territory by deep, flanking movements through gaps in the enemy's dispositions or—if no other options exist—by breakthrough battles. The option taken depends on topography, the nature of enemy deployments, and the personal style of the commanders involved. For instance, in the 1967 war, Israeli forces in the Sinai employed a combination of approaches, flanking Egyptian positions to encircle the enemy where possible while attacking Egyptian positions where necessary (Abu Ageila, most notably). On the Golan, narrow frontages meant the IDF could not avoid bloody battles involving frontal attacks on Syrian forces. During the 1973 war, counterattacking Israeli forces in the Sinai struck the seam between two Egyptian armies, penetrated it and outflanked Egyptian forces, encircling the Egyptian Third Army. In the Golan, again, terrain and the density of enemy deployments forced the Israelis to drive Syrian forces back through a series of costly frontal counterattacks.

Short Wars for Limited Ends

From the outset, Israel has sought to win its wars quickly.[8] War between Israel and its Arab neighbors threatened the stability of the region, raised the specter of U.S.–Soviet confrontation, and endangered Western access to Middle Eastern oil. As a result, Israeli leaders expected the major powers to use diplomatic pressure or the threat of military intervention to stop a war before Israel could achieve its war aims, or worse, after the Arab states had achieved some of theirs. This reinforced the Israeli predisposition for short-war strategies. So too did the sensitivity to casualties in a society in which every dead soldier's picture appears bordered in black in the newspapers, because (it was hoped) quick and decisive

---

[6]   Inbar, "Israeli Strategic Thinking," pp. 36–59.

[7]   Ibid., p. 39

[8]   A useful preliminary discussion may be found in Stuart A. Cohen and Efraim Inbar, "A Taxonomy of Israel's Use of Military Force," *Comparative Strategy* (1991), pp. 121–138.

offensive action would keep losses low.[9] A rapid battlefield decision, moreover, would allow Israel to avoid having to fight Arab expeditionary forces from countries like Iraq, or to react to Soviet intervention on behalf of its enemies.[10] Furthermore, lacking a massive military–industrial base, Israel would have to fight its wars from existing stocks of munitions and supplies; a short-war strategy would allow it to end a conflict without having to petition a foreign patron for emergency resupply and thereby risk forfeiting its strategic or operational freedom of action. Finally, some military planners believed that short wars reduced the possibility that a conflict would escalate to involve the bombardment of civilian population centers.[11]

Despite their quest for the swift and crushing blow, however, Israeli military leaders have not thought it likely that any given clash of arms would produce decisive political results. In 1991, Yitzhak Rabin, then the former chief of staff and defense minister, said, "Israel cannot formulate a security policy involving the imposition of preferred peace arrangements following upon the defeat or conquest of Arab countries. This is not a pleasant situation—but it is a given!"[12]

Israel could neither occupy the capital cities of its enemies (though it might menace or raid them), nor prevent hostile powers from rearming those enemies after each war. Rather, Israel aimed to achieve its principal goal—acceptance by its Arab neighbors—through the cumulative effect of limited but clear-cut battlefield victories that might eventually convince its adversaries of the futility of efforts to eliminate it. In wartime, Israel sought to destroy enemy forces and seize territory for use as a bargaining chip in postwar negotiations, and as a means of achieving more secure borders that would enable it to absorb an enemy surprise attack without risking its survival. This would also, Israeli planners

---

[9]   Moshe Netiv, "IDF Manpower and Israeli Society," *Jerusalem Quarterly* (Summer 1984), pp. 142–144.

[10]   Tal, "The Offensive and the Defensive in Israel's Campaigns," p. 43. See also Uri Bar Joseph and J. P. Hannah, "Intervention Threats in Short Arab–Israeli Wars," *Journal of Strategic Studies* (1988), pp. 437–467.

[11]   Yitzhak Rabin, "After the Gulf War: Israeli Defense and Its Security Policy," speech of June 10, 1991, reprinted in BESA Center, *Yitzhak Rabin and Israeli National Security* (Ramat Gan, Israel: Bar Ilan University, 1996), pp. 7–8. Rabin describes a meeting with then–Prime Minister David Ben Gurion in 1955 in which the latter responded furiously to army officers who dismissed the impact of a few bombs landing in civilian areas. "'You weren't in the Blitz on London. I was! I do not want the Israeli home front exposed, in any degree, to that which the British home front endured.' He never explained why." The truth is that Ben Gurion had doubts concerning the resilience of Israeli morale.

[12]   Ibid., p. 3.

hoped, enable it to create a more stable postwar status quo. After 1967, based on the new, and more favorable geographic positions held by the IDF, more than one Israeli expressed a cautious appreciation for the value of the defensive; however, the overwhelming preference remained for the attack.[13]

A Nation in Arms

Shortly after independence, Israel created a military built around the core of a standing army consisting of conscripts and career soldiers, and a much larger reserve force that was well-trained, experienced, and available on short notice. Through this system of near total mobilization of the country's available population, Israel was able to achieve rough numerical parity with its enemies.[14] Modeled in part on Swiss practices and in part on its own experience of operating a large underground militia in the pre-state period, the IDF created an army in which, in the words of a former chief of staff, Israelis are, in effect, "soldiers on eleven months' annual leave." Traditionally, men as well as women have performed two to three years' active duty in the army, which thus has constituted a rite of passage to adulthood and full membership in society. Reserve service (*miluim*) has, for decades, been a constant feature in the life of Israeli men through their forties and fifties. They have, by and large, willingly accepted this burden, which has taken them from work and family for a month or more each year. Reserve units, commanded at the brigade and division levels by active duty colonels and generals, constitute the bulk of the military's ground order of battle. Israel's reserve units include some of the most skilled and experienced units in the IDF. Many crews have served together for years (both on active duty and in the reserves) and have substantial combat experience.

Not all branches of the IDF, however, depend equally on reservists. Although the army largely comprises reserve formations, the intelligence corps, air force, and navy consist largely of active units. Intelligence provides the early warning the army's reserve units need to mobilize and deploy under the protection of the standing ground forces and the air force, which must hold the line until they arrive.

---

[13] This is particularly true at the tactical level. One reserve officer interviewed for this project noted that he could barely remember any training in his officers' candidate school for defensive operations. For an early case for the defense made by one of the founders of the IDF, Yigal Allon, see *The Making of Israel's Army* (New York: Universe Books, 1970), pp. 99–100. See also Levite, *Offense and Defense,* pp. 25–62.

[14] Horowitz, "The Israeli Concept of National Security and the Prospects of Peace in the Middle East," p. 241.

Israel's reliance on reserves puts a premium on strategic early warning to permit the mobilization of forces before the outbreak of war, a predicament that, on more than one occasion, has placed before Israeli leaders an unenviable choice: Mobilize the reserves and be safe, but strain the economy and the army's citizen-soldiers, or continue normal deployments and run the risk of surprise attack. Both courses have been taken at various times.[15] The 1973 war illustrated the costs of failure to mobilize in time.[16] It demonstrated, moreover, that even with early warning, political considerations could prevent Israel from taking the steps dictated by Israel's national security doctrine (such as preemptive air attack) required to achieve a rapid victory or at least to forestall extensive losses.[17] After the 1973 war, to hedge against the possibility of surprise, the IDF dramatically increased the size of its standing forces and took steps to reduce the time required to mobilize its reserves. Call-up procedures were streamlined and vehicles and equipment were put into carefully controlled dry storage.[18] As a result, call-up times were reduced even from the standards of 1973.

The nation in arms concept has even extended to assigning reservists to serve as senior commanders in wartime—a fact of considerable importance from the points of view of civil–military relations and the high command. Reserve generals helped direct operations in both Sinai and the Golan Heights in 1973, serving as divisional commanders and, in one case (Lt. Gen. Chaim Bar Lev, a retired chief of staff of the IDF) effectively substituting for the southern front commander. In peacetime it has not been uncommon for reserve colonels and generals to return to active duty for extended periods of time. At the same time, the Israelis have traditionally retired generals from active duty at young ages. During the 1950s and 1960s, for example, a new chief of the general staff was typically a man in his late thirties, and a career of more than twenty years was unusual.[19] This has changed since the 1970s, however: Recent chiefs of staff have begun their tenure in their late forties or early fifties. Similarly, the reliance on reserve generals has diminished somewhat over time.

---

[15]   One lesser known case is the 1960 "Rotem" mobilization of the IDF. See Uri Bar Joseph, "Rotem: The Forgotten Crisis on the Road to the 1967 War," *Journal of Contemporary History* (July 1996), pp. 547–565.

[16]   See, *inter alia,* Eliot A. Cohen and John Gooch, *Military Misfortunes: The Anatomy of Failure in War* (New York: Free Press, 1990), pp. 95–132.

[17]   Maj. Gen. Ehud Barak, "On Intelligence," *IDF Journal* (Winter 1987), pp. 11–15.

[18]   Aharon Ben-David, "Controlled Humidity Storage," *IDF Journal* (Summer 1986), pp. 19–20.

[19]   Reuven Gal, *A Portrait of the Israeli Soldier* (Westport, Conn.: Greenwood, 1986), p. 172.

The militia system traditionally served not merely as a means of national defense, but as a tool for the assimilation and acculturation of Israel's large immigrant *(olim)* populations. The IDF, which won various educational prizes for its work, taught immigrants Hebrew, gave many of them basic skills, and provided a common rite of passage for young people entering society. Although this role remains intact in some ways, it clearly has diminished in importance in recent years, as the IDF has sought to devote its attention mainly to training and security.[20]

Tank and Fighter-Bomber: The Land–Air Team

The basic role and hierarchy of the various arms of the IDF have not changed substantially since the late 1950s. Because enemy ground forces posed the primary threat to Israel's existence, the IDF's own ground forces were seen as the key to victory on the battlefield and thus to the survival of the state. For this reason, the IDF is structured primarily around its ground forces, although the air force shares with it the bulk of the military budget.[21] The ground forces dominate the IDF's general staff, always providing the chief of staff (the only lieutenant general on active duty), the other two services having merely an "officer commanding" who is subordinate in rank. The IDF general staff is also far more powerful than the Ministry of Defense, which is composed largely of civilians.[22]

Within the ground forces, priority after 1956 went to the armored corps and, to a lesser extent, various special operations units and the IDF's active paratroop and infantry brigades.[23] The 1973 war, however, convinced the IDF that it had to strengthen its infantry, combat engineer, and artillery capabilities to enable the tank to operate effectively on the modern battlefield.[24] Still, the tank, with its

---

[20]   See Stuart A. Cohen, "Small States and Their Armies: Restructuring the Militia Framework of the Israel Defense Force," *Journal of Strategic Studies* (December 1995), pp. 78–93.

[21]   Reliable up-to-date figures concerning how the IDF allocates its budget among the various branches of its armed forces are not available. Figures from the 1970s are available, however, and show that during that decade the IDF spent between 40 percent to 60 percent of its budget on the ground forces, 25 percent to 55 percent on the air force, and 3 percent to 5 percent on the navy.

[22]   See Yehuda Ben Meir, *Civil–Military Relations in Israel* (New York: Columbia University Press, 1995).

[23]   Tal, "Offensive and Defensive," p. 45.

[24]   Maj. Gen. Moshe Bar-Kochba, "The Place of the Tank on the Future Battlefield," *Ma'arachot* (July 1982), pp. 60–61 (Hebrew).

combination of firepower, protection, and mobility, continues to hold pride of place in the ground forces.

At the same time, the IDF has come to rely on domination of the air to cover its mobilization and to make possible the offensive thrusts that its operational style requires. Thus, a powerful air force, designed first to neutralize enemy air and air defense forces and then to interdict and destroy enemy forces on the ground, has been an essential feature of the Israeli military. The air force is the most flexible branch of the armed forces and can deliver blows against distant targets with little advance notice. As for the Israeli Navy, it has traditionally come a distant third in obtaining a share of the defense budget and in terms of the quantity (though not quality) of its manpower.

Quality versus Quantity

The founders of Israel's national security doctrine recognized the tremendous disparity between Israel and its Arab neighbors in terms of size, population, political influence, and economic resources. For that reason, they sought advantage over their potential enemies by pursuing qualitative superiority— measured in terms of superior motivation, initiative, tactical proficiency, improvisational skills, and technology. As retiree Maj. Gen. Israel Tal has written, "Israel has to turn to all of its national resources in wartime, and to rely on the quality of its society in all areas: moral, social, scientific–technological, as well as on professional military virtuosity. The qualitative difference between Israel and the Arabs must be one not of degree but of kind."[25] In terms of materiel, this emphasis on the qualitative factor found expression in Israel's maintenance, since 1967, of a technological edge over its enemies in terms of its equipment, and the achievement of high equipment readiness rates, high sortie rates for its combat aircraft, and the rapid repair of battle-damaged equipment. The qualitative edge was seen as well in the ability to concentrate superior force at the point of decision, despite overall inferiority in numbers, and a capacity for fast-paced wars of decision requiring great striking power.[26]

'Red Lines' and Punishment: Israeli Deterrence Theory

Israel has at various times identified "red lines" whose violation could lead to war. This list of *casus belli* has included major arms buildups that threaten the military balance (1956); the deployment of non-Jordanian forces in the West Bank (1950s); the concentration of large forces along its borders (1967); the imposition of a naval blockade (1967); the entry of Syrian or Iraqi forces into

---

[25]   Tal, *National Security,* p. 70.

[26]   Tal, "Offensive and Defensive," p. 44.

Jordan (1970); the deployment of Syrian surface-to-air missiles into Lebanon or the movement of Syrian forces toward Israel's border (1976); and the acquisition by a hostile state of the capability to produce nuclear weapons (1981). In nearly every case, violation of a red line, even without overt hostile action directed at Israel, has brought a swift and violent response—Israel's passivity in the face of Iraq's missile attacks in 1991 being a notable exception.

Israeli military thinkers have believed that only immediate and severe responses to even minor threats could prevent Arab miscalculations of Israel's military capacity or its political will. Israel has hoped that sharp and swift responses to small provocations would ward off larger conflicts. At least one Arab–Israeli war—in 1967—arose from miscalculation by the Arabs; by indicating its willingness to fight, Israel has hoped to avoid any recurrence of this experience. Israel has also sought to strengthen its deterrent posture—and, no less important, domestic morale—by projecting an image of invincibility. It has therefore put a premium on daring covert operations and commando raids far from its borders, and, in war, the swift and complete destruction of enemy forces. Over time these policies have become central to the self-perception of the Israeli public. The acute discomfort felt even by dovish Israelis over the state's failure to react militarily to Iraqi missile attacks during the 1991 Persian Gulf War—a decision that made overwhelming political sense—shows how deeply these principles have settled into the Israeli psyche. Israeli strategists have also sought to ward off low-level violence that, over time, could undermine the will and sap the economic strength of a population that yearns for a normal life.

Israel has traditionally sought decisive victory through the destruction of enemy forces and seizure of enemy territory. In the case of Syria, however, geographic and military realities since 1967 (the density of Syrian defenses facing the Golan and the proximity of Damascus to the front) made seizing additional territory a costly option that risked provoking superpower intervention. Accordingly, Israel has in recent years threatened to destabilize the regime in Damascus in the event of a Syrian-initiated war.[27]

---

[27]   See the interview with Defense Minister Yitzhak Mordechai in which he warned that Israel would inflict "a hard blow on Syria, whose regime would probably be at risk" if Syria used chemical weapons against Israel: Arieh O'Sullivan, "Mordechai Warns Asad against Chemical Attack," *Jerusalem Post,* November 18, 1996, p. 1. Regime targeting first emerged as an instrument of Israeli deterrence during the 1969–1970 War of Attrition with Egypt, when Israel resorted to commando operations and deep penetration raids by its air force against targets designed to humiliate and undermine the Cairo government.

Finally, concerns over resource asymmetries between Israel and the Arabs spurred Israel to develop nuclear weapons as an ultimate deterrent. Israel has probably possessed nuclear weapons since before the 1967 war, and it has adopted a policy of studied ambiguity regarding its nuclear potential (though much of this ambiguity has vanished in recent years).[28] It has, however, avoided formally integrating nuclear weapons into its war-fighting doctrine, which relies exclusively on conventional means to deter or defeat conventional attack.[29] Israel has, nonetheless, threatened massive (presumably nuclear) retaliation for Arab use of nonconventional weapons.[30]

Self-Reliance

The Jewish experience of vulnerability and powerlessness during two thousand years of exile and persecution, and the action-oriented character of modern political Zionism, have imbued Israel and its people with a strongly held ethos of self-reliance.[31] Essential to this is the belief that Israelis alone should determine their own future and that they should not rely on others when it comes to their security.[32] This has had a far-reaching impact on Israel's defense posture. It was the main driving force behind Israel's development of an indigenous arms industry (to limit its vulnerability to embargoes or supply disruptions), and its

---

[28]   Avner Cohen, "Cairo, Dimona and the June 1967 War," *Middle East Journal* (Spring 1996), pp. 208–210.

[29]   Saadia Amiel, "Deterrence by Conventional Forces," *Survival* (March/April 1978), pp. 58–62; Oz Chen, "Reflections on Israeli Deterrence," *Jerusalem Quarterly* (Summer 1982), pp. 26–40.

[30]   For instance, then–Defense Minister Yitzhak Rabin explained in a July 1988 interview that "one of our fears is that the Arab world and its leaders might be deluded to believe that the lack of international reaction to the use of missiles and gases (during the Iran–Iraq War) gives them some kind of legitimization to use them. They know they should not be deluded to believe that, because it is a whole different ball game when it comes to us. If they are, God forbid, they should know we will hit them back 100 times harder." Israel Radio, July 21, 1988, in FBIS-NEA, July 21, 1988, pp. 28–29.

[31]   This attitude is well expressed by David Ben Gurion's famous dictum that Israel's fate would be determined "not by what the nations of the world think, but by what the Jews do." Michael Brecher, *The Foreign Policy System of Israel: Setting, Images, Process* (New Haven, Conn.: Yale University Press, 1972), p. 231.

[32]   This dictum has been violated only twice. In 1956, Israel requested that France dispatch combat aircraft to Israel to protect its airspace during the Anglo–French–Israeli attack on Egypt. And during the 1991 Gulf War, U.S. and Dutch Patriot SAM crews were dispatched to Israel to defend against Iraqi missile attacks.

insistence that only Israelis should be responsible for the defense of their country—even while seeking the support of a great power. It was also a key factor driving Israel's nuclear weapons program.

The Search for a Great Power Patron

Despite this insistence on self-reliance, Israel has also consistently sought out a great power patron as part of its efforts to offset Arab military might and Soviet political and military support for its enemies. At independence, Israel hoped to become a member of the British Commonwealth. In the early 1950s, Israel tried to engage the United States, and then Britain and France, as allies. These efforts led to the successful conclusion of an alliance with France from 1956 through 1967, based on their common opposition to radical Arab nationalism. During this time, France became Israel's main source of arms and provided crucial assistance to the latter's nuclear program. After the 1967 war, France—in a dramatic policy reversal—imposed an arms embargo on Israel, thereby giving impetus to the nascent Israel–U.S. relationship. Relations between the two countries grew stronger as the United States became Israel's main source of arms after the 1967 war. Since the 1973 war, the Israel–U.S "special relationship" has remained a fixed feature of the strategic landscape of the region.

U.S. support for Israel (in the form of diplomatic support, arms and technology transfers, arms purchases, and economic and military aid) has become a key component of Israel's national security equation and a critical element of its deterrence. Between 1949 and 1996, the United States provided some $71 billion in aid to Israel; since 1979, the amount has varied between $2 billion and $5 billion a year.[33] No less important has been the intelligence cooperation between the two countries—dating to the 1950s—and the strategic cooperation between Israel and the United States conducted on a routine basis since the early 1980s. Nonetheless, some Israelis still worry that dependence on the United States could constrain Israel's freedom of action in certain situations and would leave it isolated and vulnerable if the United States were to abandon it, as France previously did.[34]

---

[33]   Clyde Mark, "Israel: U.S. Foreign Assistance," Congressional Research Service Issue Brief, May 20, 1996.

[34]   Moreover, some Israelis believe that Israel's dependence on the United States is corrosive to the Jewish state's sense of self-reliance and autonomy, see Tal, *National Security,* p. 226ff. For more, see Shai Feldman, *The Future of U.S.–Israel Strategic Cooperation* (Washington, D.C.: The Washington Institute for Near East Policy, 1996), pp. 7–15.

ANATOMY OF ISRAEL'S FORCE STRUCTURE

Israel's doctrine, with only a few modifications, has lasted for almost a half century. If that doctrine has survived more or less intact, however, the forces tasked to implement it have undergone dramatic changes in size, sophistication, and their relative importance to Israel's defense. What follows is a discussion of the four main components of Israel's force structure: special, conventional, and strategic forces, and the defense industries.

Special Forces

Special forces play a unique role in the IDF. Dating back to pre-state days, when the elite Palmach (strike companies) trained a generation of leaders, Israel's special forces have exercised a disproportionate influence on the entire armed forces. For instance, many senior generals and one chief of staff, Ehud Barak, have served in *Sayeret Matkal*—the IDF's premier commando unit—or other special operations units.[35] Moreover, Israel's special forces have played a unique role in molding the image of the IDF abroad and at home. The dashing commando raid or the daring hostage rescue have done as much to define Israel's military reputation as have the IDF's achievments on the conventional battlefield.[36] Finally, to a degree that may be unusual in other militaries, Israel's special forces units often operate in conjunction with conventional forces, resulting in a unique Israeli "integrated operational style" that was first pioneered by its special forces in the late 1960s but that has been successfully used since then by the rest of the armed forces.

Israel's special forces trace their origin to Unit 101, founded in August 1953 to carry out reprisal raids against Arab states harboring Palestinian infiltrators and guerrillas, after the IDF's regular infantry units bungled a series of retaliatory actions. Although Unit 101 never numbered more than 45 men, it carried out several dozen missions prior to its merger with the newly formed 890th paratroop

---

[35]   For instance, Chief of Staff Lt. Gen. Amnon Shahak and his former deputy, Maj. Gen. Matan Vilna'i, both served in the 35th paratroop brigade. Likewise, former Mossad Chief Maj. Gen. Danny Yatom, Director of Military Intelligence Moshe Ya'alon, Chief of the General Staff Planning Branch Maj. Gen. Shaul Mofaz, and OC Central Command Maj. Gen. Uzi Dayan, all served in *Sayeret Matkal. Shin Bet* Chief Maj. Gen. Ami Ayalon is a former naval commando.

[36]   Parts of this section are based on Michael Eisenstadt, "Israel's Approach to Special Operations," *Special Warfare* (January 1994), pp. 22–29.

battalion in January 1954. Unit 101 not only became a small, elite unit that achieved impressive results in raids; it set standards for the entire armed forces. Unit 101's informal atmosphere, unique *esprit de corps*, and standards of combat leadership ("follow me") became norms for the IDF and part of the combat lore on which generations of IDF officers and enlistees have been raised. Unit 101's successors have perpetuated the original group's spirit in the IDF.

As a result of this early experience, the IDF has created various special units (*sayarot*, or reconnaissance units) in accordance with its operational requirements.[37] The existence of several units fulfilling similar roles is seen as a way to promote healthy competition and thereby raise combat standards in the armed forces overall. In the late 1950s the IDF created three regional reconnaissance units—*Sayeret Egoz* in the northern command, *Sayeret Haruv* in the central command, and *Sayeret Shaked* in the southern command—to undertake border security and cross-border actions in their respective areas of operation.[38] At the same time, the IDF also created *Sayeret Matkal*, which remains the IDF's premier special operations unit, and which was responsible for such spectacular coups as the assassination of senior PLO leaders in Beirut and Tunis in April 1973 and April 1988, and the rescue of hostages in Entebbe in July 1976.[39] Through the 1960s the regional units were particularly busy countering infiltrators and engaging in cross-border operations, particularly in the Gaza strip, southeastern Israel (the Arava), and the West Bank. The IDF disbanded *Egoz* and *Haruv* after the 1973 war, however, when it decided that it could no longer retain so many specialized counter-insurgency units at the expense of its regular infantry.

Furthermore, the reconnaissance companies of the IDF's three elite active infantry brigades (*Sayeret Golani*, *Sayeret Tzanchanim*, and *Sayeret Givati*) and the *Kommando Yami* (the naval special warfare unit) also conduct special operations.[40] Moreover, the IDF possesses a number of smaller, highly

---

[37]   The IDF refers to these units as reconnaissance units, even though they may fulfill a range of other special missions, such as raids, hostage rescues, intelligence gathering, and prisoner or equipment snatches.

[38]   For an account of *Sayeret Shaked,* see Uri Milstein and Dov Doron, *Sayeret Shaked* (Tel Aviv: Miskal, 1994) (Hebrew).

[39]   For more on Sayeret Matkal, see Moshe Zander, "The Chosen," *Ma'ariv Weekend Supplement*, May 27, 1994, pp. 54–71 (Hebrew).

[40]   The Israel Border Guard, a military style gendarmerie under the Interior Ministry, also has a special counterterrorist unit, *Yamam* (*yechida neged michablim*) which competes with various military units for recognition and a greater role in the counterterrorist effort. Established in May 1974, the unit has operated in Israel, the West

specialized units (some of which remain secret) for specific types of missions. For instance, after the outbreak of the *intifada* (the Palestinian uprising), in December 1988 the IDF created undercover squads *(mista'arvim)* who disguised themselves as local residents. Similar units had existed as early as World War II, when the Palmach formed units of Arabic- and (in British service) German-speaking soldiers. The modern *mista'arvim*—who operated in the West Bank and Gaza—were responsible for identifying and apprehending leaders of the Palestinian uprising. One unit, code-named "Samson" *(Shimshon)*, operated in Gaza, while another, code-named "Cherry" *(Duvdevan)*, operated (and continues to operate) in the West Bank.[41] In 1995 the Israelis resurrected *Sayeret Egoz* in the North as a counter to the guerrillas of Hizballah in Lebanon.[42] All of these units work closely with Israel's intelligence services in the areas concerned. And within the ground and naval forces, Israel's special forces act as centers of excellence that attract the best soldiers (they are, of course, volunteer units) and provide them with intensified training and extensive operational experience, creating a skilled and experienced leadership cadre.

Special forces have a particularly important role in dealing with day-to-day security challenges as well as in preparing for large-scale conventional warfare. These units have taken the lead (backed by IDF's four active infantry brigades: *Golani*, 35th Paratroop, *Givati*, and *Nahal*) in Israel's protracted conflict with terrorist and guerrilla organizations. The IDF launches special operations designed to disrupt enemy preparations, kill enemy personnel, destroy military equipment and facilities, and force the enemy to allocate additional resources to self-defense and security. Moreover, these operations may generate pressure on host states to constrain the terrorists or guerrillas, and thus may have a deterrent effect.[43]

Bank and Gaza, and South Lebanon. In its first high-profile operation, it rescued a busload of Israelis held by Palestinian guerillas near Dimona in March 1988. Topaz Carmi, "We Proved Our Worth," *Bamahane,* September 22, 1988, p. 9 (Hebrew).

[41] For more on one of these units, see Sima Kadmon, "Voices of Duvdevan," *Ma'ariv Weekend Supplement,* July 5, 1991, pp. 6–10 (Hebrew). A very good overall account is Stuart A. Cohen, "Mista'arvim—IDF 'Masqueraders': The Military Unit and the Public Debate," (Ramat Gan: Bar Ilan University, BESA Center, 1993).

[42] Amir Rappoport, "The IDF's Secret Weapon against Hizballah," *Yedi'ot Ahronot,* December 5, 1996, pp. B2–3. Chen Kotz, "Hard Nuts to Crack," *Ma'ariv Weekend Supplement,* December 6, 1996, pp. 44–46, 48, 50, 83 (Both Hebrew).

[43] Maj. Gen. Ehud Barak, "Facing Terrorism," *IDF Journal* (May 1985), pp. 82–83. For more on Israel's approach to reprisals and counterterrorist operations, see Barry Blechman, "The Consequences of Israeli Reprisals: An Assessment" (Ph.D. Dissertation,

Although these units have often excelled in undertaking special operations in peacetime, in wartime they have (like similar units in other armies) often been employed as high-quality infantry—an area in which the IDF has had persistent shortages. Lightly armed and trained for different tasks, however, they have not always performed well in this role[44] and have often suffered the heavy casualties typically incurred by infantry in wartime, impairing their ability effectively to undertake special operations afterwards.[45] Indeed, the founder of *Sayeret Matkal,*

Georgetown University, 1971); Daniel Kurtzer, "Palestine Guerilla and Israeli Counterinsurgency Warfare: The Radicalization of the Palestine Arab Community to Violence, 1949–1970" (Ph.D. Dissertation, Columbia University, 1976); Jonathan Shimshoni, *Israeli Conventional Deterrence: Border Warfare from 1953–1970* (Ithaca, N.Y.: Cornell University Press, 1988); and Ariel Merari, Meir Amit, Yitzhak Rabin, and Ehud Barak, "Perspectives on Terror," *IDF Journal* (Fall 1986), pp. 30–36.

[44] Lt. Col. Beni M., "Special Forces," *Ma'arachot* (January 1985), pp. 3–14 (Hebrew). According to the author,

> the IDF has had all the problems in developing special forces as most armies since WWII. The IDF continues to learn the hard way—through experience. The expression of this is the process that began with the merging of Unit 101 with the paratroops—emphasizing special operations at the expense of conventional infantry combat. It is sufficient to see what happened to the IDF's infantry as a result of this approach, in order to understand where the emphasis should be. The paratroopers, which operated reasonably well in reprisal operations, failed in conventional infantry operations in 1956, 1967, and 1973. . . . [On the other hand] it appears that the IDF's infantry units—the paratroopers and Golani— that fought so well in 1982 on the conventional battlefield, surely have their priorities straight when they train for battle in Beirut, before preparing for raids on Beirut. By this, we will preserve our ability to conduct special operations, because neglect, and the incorrect approach take many hard years to correct. (See p. 8).

This phenomenon of elite light infantry being pressed into regular infantry duty for which they are not suited is quite common. See Eliot A. Cohen, *Commandos and Politicians: Elite Military Units in Modern Democracies* (Cambridge, Mass.: Harvard University Center for International Affairs, 1978).

[45] During both the 1973 and 1982 wars, the Golani brigade suffered heavy losses, including in its reconnaissance unit. Out of a total of perhaps some 2,500 soldiers in the brigade, it lost in 1973 about 130 dead and 310 wounded, including the brigade's deputy commander, two battalion commanders, and the commander of *Sayeret Golani*. In 1982, it lost 46 dead, including the commander of *Sayeret Golani,* and 10 other *Sayeret* personnel. See Avi Bettelheim, *Golani: The Fighting Family* (Golani Brigade Command,

Avraham Arnon, said "a *Sayeret Matkal* fighter is much too valuable for the chaos of war."[46] Some of the most promising commanders in the IDF have been killed in operations with these units, robbing the IDF of many of its rising stars.

Because of the politically sensitive nature of special operations, planning is often conducted at the general staff level. The most senior and experienced personnel in the IDF (including the chief of staff, director of military intelligence, chief of the general staff operations branch, and the chief paratroop–infantry officer) are involved in all facets of the operation. As a result, during peacetime these operations tend to preoccupy the general staff and divert them from preparations for war.

Israel's special units cannot, however, deal with all aspects of current security without the help of regular line infantry and other units. Indeed, the Israelis would waste valuable resources by committing special units to routine border security duties in the South Lebanon security zone or police duties in the West Bank and Gaza. On the other hand, the regular line units involved in such duties must interrupt their training schedule to do so. Aside from the undercover units and the Border Guard (*Mishmar Hagvul*), the IDF has resisted creating formations exclusively dedicated to *intifada* duty. Instead, the IDF has tried to spread the burden of policing the occupied territories by regularly rotating active and reserve units through Gaza and the West Bank. The possibility of a renewed *intifada* ensures that this will remain a problem for the indefinite future. Similarly, the IDF regularly rotates infantry, armor, and artillery units through its so-called "security zone" in South Lebanon. In light of the growing effectiveness of the Hizballah, the IDF recently initiated, a counter-guerrilla course for these units.[47]

During the late 1980s, the IDF began shying away from using special units in Lebanon when the mission could be accomplished by attack helicopters and fixed wing aircraft with less risk.[48] This shift from relying largely on special forces to the air force in conducting the war against terror in Lebanon, stemmed from a desire to limit casualties, and the growing ability of the air force to hit terrorist

---

July 1980), p. 166; and idem., *Golani in Peace for Galilee* (Golani Brigade Command, October 1982), pp. 62–63 (both Hebrew).

[46] Muki Betser with Robert Rosenberg, *Secret Soldier: The True Life Story of Israel's Greatest Commando* (New York: Atlantic Monthly Press, 1996), p. 112.

[47] Arieh O'Sullivan, "IDF Sets Up Anti-Guerrilla Combat Training School," *Jerusalem Post: Internet Edition*, November 28, 1996.

[48] Steve Rodan, "Danger in the Deep," *Jerusalem Post International Edition*, December 28, 1996, p. 17.

and guerrilla targets in areas deemed too dangerous for special forces.[49] Increased reliance on the air force, moreover, has relieved some of the pressure on the IDF's special units and spread the routine security burden more equally throughout the IDF.

Conventional Forces

Ground Forces. From 1948 to 1956, the Israeli ground forces consisted primarily of leg and motorized infantry backed by modest amounts of armor. After the 1956 war, however, the IDF decided to build the ground forces around the tank, and the all-tank formation became the foundation of the army. To this day, the standard Israeli armored brigade, for example, has only a single organic, mechanized infantry company; this is a far smaller infantry complement than would be considered appropriate in most other militaries. Until the 1973 war, Israeli doctrine called for tanks to spearhead the IDF's armored thrusts, with regular infantry serving as a follow-and-support force to consolidate their gains. Because the air force had proven so effective in 1967 in destroying enemy ground forces after defeating Arab air forces, artillery received short shrift, and was used primarily as a means to neutralize enemy infantry.[50]

The 1973 war exposed major shortcomings in the ground forces, beginning with Israeli armor. Subsequent to the war, the IDF improved tank firepower and survivability with the development of an improved antitank round (the *chetz*); the addition of reactive armor; and the fitting of automatic smoke projectors, machine guns, and a turret-mounted 60 mm mortar. More broadly, however, the IDF recognized the need to move toward a more balanced combined arms force,

---

[49]   Thus, in a 1988 interview, the chief of current operations in the IAF stated that there is no doubt that the air force is a relatively easy solution compared to the other means at the disposal of the IDF. However, the principal reason that it is chosen to conduct missions in Lebanon is the fact of its unusual effectiveness. It is possible for aircraft to go anywhere the terrorists are located. . . . A decisive additional factor in the employment of aircraft is its ability to bear the price for sustained periods of time. The price the IDF pays when it uses the air force against the terrorists is a price it can afford to pay for many years. Minimizing losses is a fundamental objective of the IDF since its founding. This is a supreme, hallowed, value . . . (and) the danger to air force aircraft in the course of operations in Lebanon amounts to only a few percent. And if we continue with suitable tactics, it will remain thus.

See Dror Marom, "The Air Force: The Most Capable and Precise Means in the War Against the Terrorists," *Bita'on Heyl HaAvir* (January 1988), pp. 10–11 (Hebrew).

[50]   Luttwak and Horowitz, *The Israeli Army*, pp. 148–153, 186–192.

if the tank were to retain its dominance on the battlefield. Specifically, the IDF boosted the quality and quantity of its infantry. It enhanced infantry protection and mobility with the purchase of large numbers of M-113 armored personnel carriers, which were then further upgraded with smoke projectors, machine guns, and add-on armor. The 1973 war also demonstrated that the Israeli Air Force (IAF) might not always be available to support the ground battle, obliging ground combat units to rely instead on field artillery for fire support. Therefore, artillery was modernized with the procurement of new target-acquisition means and automated fire control systems, numbers were increased, and mobility and survivability improved by the acquisition of more self-propelled M-109 guns. Finally, the combat engineer corps received higher priority, and the IDF developed new mine- and obstacle-clearing means. In addition, the IDF recognized the tremendous potential represented by the attack helicopter, with its great flexibility and responsiveness. It therefore acquired the AH-1 Cobra in 1975 and the MD-500 Defender in 1980.

The 1982 Lebanon war confirmed many of the lessons of 1973, though it also demonstrated that the ground forces had still not created a true combined arms doctrine for the ground forces. As a result, the IDF set up the Ground Corps Command in 1983, responsible for creating a balanced combined arms force structure and doctrine.[51]

Following the war, the IDF continued its efforts to improve the firepower, protection, and mobility of the tank with the development of the *Magach* 7 (a much upgraded M-60) and the Merkava II and III. The 1982 war also made clear that the IDF still lacked infantry in sufficient numbers, leading it to create (actually, to reestablish) a fourth active infantry brigade (*Givati*) in June 1983. To compensate for the vulnerability of the M-113 on the modern battlefield, the IDF experimented with improvised infantry fighting vehicles based on the Centurion (*Nagmashot*) and the T-55 tank (*Achzarit*). The IDF also has worked to improve the antitank armament of its infantry, introducing the B-300 and Mapats infantry antitank weapons, and, more recently, a family of fire-and-forget top-attack antitank weapons: Small Spike, Spike, and Long Spike.[52] The IDF's artillery branch improved the accuracy and responsiveness of its fires with new position location and automated fire control systems and with target-locating radars. Finally, the engineer corps acquired additional mine- and obstacle-clearing

---

[51] Jeff Abramowitz, "The Evolution of the Ground Corps Command," *IDF Journal* (Summer 1986), pp. 8–14.

[52] *Jane's Defence Weekly*, July 2, 1997, p. 16.

equipment and a new engineer assault vehicle based on the Centurion tank chassis—the Puma—as well as armored protection kits for its bulldozers.

The Israeli Air Force. During and immediately after the 1948–1949 war, the IDF had a "balanced" air force consisting of small numbers of fighters, light bombers, and heavy bombers. The IAF soon realized, however, that it lacked the resources to maintain a balanced force. Nor did a country that depended on a short-war strategy need to maintain a fleet of heavy bombers useful primarily in campaigns of attrition.

The origins of the modern IAF can be traced to the decision in 1953 to create an air force based on the multirole combat aircraft par excellence: the fighter-bomber. Air force doctrine crystallized during the 1950s and 1960s and has since then remain largely unchanged. It has stressed two roles: attaining air superiority through offensive counter-air operations (suppression of enemy air defenses, raids on enemy airfields, and air-to-air combat) to enable the ground forces to mobilize and fight without interference by enemy air forces, and participating in the land battle by flying battlefield and deep interdiction missions.

During the 1956 war, Prime Minister David Ben Gurion, who lacked confidence in the capabilities of the IAF, prevented it from being used to its full potential. As a result, it was not until the 1967 war that the IAF was able to prove itself.[53] The 1973 war, however, raised questions in some quarters about the efficacy of IAF doctrine and more broadly, about the ability of manned aircraft to operate in the teeth of modern air defenses. During the war, the IAF was forced to provide urgent support to the embattled ground forces before it had suppressed enemy air defenses and achieved air superiority. It paid a heavy price for doing so. The IAF concluded from its experience during the war that although the manned aircraft retained its efficacy, the IAF needed to overhaul its approach to suppressing enemy air defenses. Overconfident in 1973 of its ability to smash Egyptian and Syrian air defenses with a combination of antiradiation missiles and well-placed bombs, the IDF soon shifted to more sophisticated methods to neutralize or destroy enemy air defenses,[54] including decoy and deception drones, ground- and air-launched antiradiation missiles, air-delivered precision munitions, and long-range artillery fires—paving the way for the dramatic

---

[53]   Luttwak and Horowitz, *The Israeli Army*, pp. 119–126. *Jane's Defence Weekly,* July 2, 1997, p. 16.

[54]   On IAF attitudes between the War of Attrition and the October 1973 War, see, *inter alia*, Ze'ev Schiff, *October Earthquake*, trans. Louis Williams (Tel Aviv: University Publishing Projects, 1974), pp. 258–261.

successes against Syrian surface-to-air (SAM) missile batteries in Lebanon in 1982.[55]

Following 1973, the IAF took steps to improve coordination between air and ground forces and to enhance the distribution of target intelligence.[56] In addition, Israeli industry developed world-class electronic warfare systems (including a variety of self-protection systems, jammers, and the Samson and Delilah deception drones) to enhance the survivability of Israeli combat aircraft, and a range of weapons such as the Python 4 air-to-air missile; electro-optically and laser-guided air-to-ground weapons such as the Pyramid, Opher, Griffin, Guillotine, and Popeye; and a new guided container weapon—the Modular Stand-Off Vehicle (MSOV)—that will be capable of delivering munitions at ranges of 100 km or more.

Although the development of the IAF since the early 1950s has been marked by more continuity than change, two new, potentially revolutionary, weapons entered the IAF during this time. The introduction of attack helicopters in the mid-1970s provided the IAF with a potent new means to participate in the land battle and provide true close support to ground forces—something the IAF had rarely done in the past.[57] In addition, the integration of attack UAVs into the IAF starting in the late 1980s—for air defense suppression, anti-armor, and missile defense roles—could result in further changes in the IAF's force structure.

The Israeli Navy. The navy exists primarily to protect Israel's long and vulnerable coastline against surface attack and, to the degree possible, to protect her sea lines of communications. Amphibious assault has never been a great threat, but given the concentration of Israel's population, industry, and military facilities on the coast, ship-to-shore attack is. No less important, the navy offers the IDF another offensive option against the Egyptian and Syrian coastlines, consistent with the larger doctrinal preference for operationally offensive solutions to a strategically defensive problem. And in recent years, the Israeli

---

[55]   Maj. Gen. Binyamin Peled, "The Air Force in the Yom Kippur War," in Louis Williams, ed., *Military Aspects of the Israeli–Arab Conflict* (Tel Aviv: University Publishing Projects, 1975), pp. 238–245; Colonel Y. and Major Y., "The Aircraft and Ground Combat: End of the Road or Turning Point?" *Ma'arachot* (November 1978), pp. 43–46 (Hebrew); Lt. Col. Uri Dromi, "Where is the Air Force?" *Ma'arachot* (October 1983), pp. 72–76 (Hebrew).

[56]   Lt. Col. Yehuda Weinraub, "The Israel Air Force and the Air-Land Battle," *IDF Journal* (Summer 1986), pp. 22–30.

[57]   Brig. Gen. Nehemia Dagan, "Integrating Attack Helicopters into Defense Doctrine," *IDF Journal* (Summer 1987), pp. 23–26; Weinraub, "The Israel Air Force and the Air-Land Battle," *IDF Journal* (Summer 1986), pp. 26–27.

Naval Force (INF) has acquired an additional mission: to launch attack helicopters and cruise missile strikes against distant enemy shores.

During the War of Independence, the Israeli Navy achieved some notable but minor combat successes using commando tactics learned from Italian and other special operations veterans of World War II. Through the 1950s, the INF possessed a small balanced fleet built around relatively traditional combatants such as destroyers and submarines. Following the 1956 war, however, the INF concluded that its small fleet, which enjoyed neither qualitative nor quantitative advantages over the vessels deployed by its adversaries, were ill-suited for securing Israel's coastline. As a result, the INF decided to shift to a fleet based on small missile boats. Budget problems, however, prevented the INF from implementing this plan until the 1960s.[58] The sinking of the destroyer *Eilat* by an Egyptian missile in 1967 quickened the desire of Israeli naval officers to move to a navy based on smaller and more agile craft.

In late 1967, the INF acquired its first missile boats. By the time of the 1973 war, the INF had transformed itself into a modern force built around a relatively large number of such craft. During that war, the INF sank twelve Arab missile boats, without any INF losses, thereby validating the small missile boat concept.[59]

Since then, the INF has begun to shift to somewhat larger ships—such as the Sa'ar V corvette—with technological capabilities second to none in their class. It is also acquiring three modern Dolphin-class submarines from Germany. The INF apparently believes that only larger, more heavily armed boats have the ability to accommodate the necessary mix of offensive and defensive weapons particularly while conducting operations far from Israeli shores.[60] Finally, it should be noted that the Israeli Navy has conducted limited amphibious operations, including commando operations and an amphibious assult in Lebanon in 1982. Indeed, the reestablished *Givati* brigade had as one of its first missions the development of expertise in amphibious warfare. Yet, Israel's amphibious craft are aging and it appears that the IDF's leaders have doubts about the viability of similar ventures in the future.

---

[58]   Commodore Eli Rahav, "Missile Boat Warfare," *IDF Journal* (Fall 1986), p. 38.

[59]   For a succinct explanation of the INF's small boat philosophy, see Commodore Eli Rahav, "To the Health of the Small Boats," *Ma'arachot* (July–August 1985), pp. 19–25 (Hebrew). For details of the evolution of the missile boat program, see: Commodore Eli, "The Gabriel Boats: Building the Force that Brought Victory at Sea in the Yom Kippur War," *Ma'arachot* (December 1984), pp. 31–40 (Hebrew).

[60]   Abraham Rabinovich, "Deep-Sea Visionary," *Jerusalem Post International Edition*, August 20, 1994, p. 14.

Strategic Forces

The IDF has operated its forces primarily against the militaries of the states immediately surrounding it, and, for most of its history, has postured itself for a conventional, all-arms struggle. But it has also developed strategic forces, including an arsenal of nuclear weapons, associated delivery means (cruise and ballistic missiles and strike aircraft), and missile defense systems.

Israel's nuclear arsenal was originally created to counter the existential threat posed by the large ground forces of its neighbors. The initial decision to investigate a nuclear option was taken in 1948, shortly after the founding of the state. Following the politically disastrous 1956 Sinai campaign, Israel signed a contract with France for a nuclear reactor, built near Dimona, and completed in 1962. Israel is believed to have produced its first nuclear weapon by the time of the 1967 war.[61] Since then, it has amassed a substantial nuclear stockpile. Credible estimates place Israel's nuclear arsenal at sixty to one hundred weapons, including "enhanced radiation" weapons. This inventory in all likelihood includes missile warheads (mounted on Jericho I/II MRBMs—medium-range ballistic missiles), aerial bombs, artillery rounds, and mines.[62] If true, this suggests Israel may possess nuclear weapons for tactical as well as strategic use.

Events in recent years have partially raised the veil of secrecy surrounding Israel's nuclear deterrent. The leaking of details concerning Israel's nuclear program to the foreign press by a disgruntled nuclear technician in October 1986, frequent references to Israel's nuclear capabilities by Arab diplomats involved in peace negotiations, and the attention focused on Israel's program prior to the Nuclear Non-Proliferation Treaty review and extension conference in May 1995, have all served to diminish the ambiguity surrounding Israel's nuclear capabilities.

This has resulted in a more open—albeit still cautious—treatment of this subject in Israel. The most important recent statement in this regard was made by the then director general of Israel's Ministry of Defense, David Ivri, in a 1995 interview in which he claimed that Israel required a strategic deterrent force

---

[61]   Leonard S. Spector, *Nuclear Ambitions: The Spread of Nuclear Weapons 1989–1990* (Boulder, Colo.: Westview, 1990), pp. 151–155; Shlomo Aronson with Oded Brosh, *The Politics and Strategy of Nuclear Weapons in the Middle East* (Albany: State University of New York Press, 1992), pp. 50–52; Cohen, *Commandos and Politicians,* pp. 208–210.

[62]   Spector, *Nuclear Ambitions,* pp. 149–174; Seymour Hersh, *The Samson Option: Israel's Nuclear Arsenal and American Foreign Policy* (New York: Random House, 1991), pp. 199–200, 215–217, 276.

based on a "second strike capability."[63] Although he did not elaborate, Ivri alluded to the U.S. Cold War doctrine of mutual assured destruction by nuclear means as a model for Israel, thereby implicitly acknowledging Israel's own nuclear capabilities. Although Ivri's intentions in raising this issue publicly are unclear, he may have been motivated by a desire to enhance Israel's deterrent capability vis-à-vis adversaries who might soon be armed with nuclear weapons.

Nonetheless, day-to-day deterrence and defense planning are based on the conventional balance of forces; accordingly, nuclear weapons have never been integrated into Israel's war-fighting doctrine. On only two occasions is Israel believed to have placed its nuclear forces on alert: during the 1973 war—when the existence of the state seemed imperiled—and during the 1991 Gulf War—when an Iraqi chemical attack seemed possible.[64]

At the same time, since the mid-1970s Israel has tried to stem the proliferation of nonconventional weapons in the region via demarches to potential suppliers of production technology, covert operations to prevent the transfer of these technologies, and occasionally the assassination of key personalities involved in these programs. These efforts have delayed, but not prevented, the proliferation of chemical and biological weapons in the region. Israel has, moreover, proven willing to risk retaliation and censure by taking preventive military action to stem nuclear proliferation. Its attack on Iraq's Osiraq reactor in June 1981 is a model in this regard. Potential proliferators, however, are more likely to disperse and hide nuclear facilities in the future, making a successful repeat of the Osiraq raid unlikely.

The creeping proliferation of nonconventional weapons in the Middle East during the 1970s and 1980s and the erosion of norms against their use during the Iran–Iraq War (in which both sides made extensive use of chemical weapons and missiles) had a profound effect on Israel. The Israelis began to see their nuclear force not just as a hedge against conventional defeat (a prospect that seemed increasingly remote), but as a deterrent to a growing nonconventional threat. Following the emergence of Iraq as a major regional power in the 1980s, Israel came to see the need to augment its long-range strike capability.

The 1991 Gulf War reinforced these tendencies. Iraq's bombardment of Israeli cities with modified Scud missiles, and Israel's decision not to retaliate lest it fracture the Gulf War coalition, raised questions about the efficacy of its

---

[63] Aluf Ben, *Ha'aretz*, December 27, 1995, p. A3, in FBIS-NES, December 29, 1995, p. 34.

[64] Hersh, *The Samson Option*, pp. 225–236, 318.

deterrent.[65] The Gulf War, moreover, provided Israel a possible glimpse of wars to come, in which civilians might be subject to direct attack. These considerations spurred Israel to enhance its civil defenses, improve defensive measures against the missiles that are considered the primary delivery means for nonconventional weapons, develop new means to strike at missile launch sites and nonconventional weapons facilities in the outer-ring states, and enhance its long-range strike capability

In November 1991, Israel established a separate Home Front Command to oversee civil defense preparations and operations. Building on an existing civil defense organization, the Home Front Command refined the nationwide air-raid siren alert notification system, modified building codes to require the creation of shelters in all existing and new buildings to offer protection against chemical attacks, replaced substandard protective masks distributed to civilians during the 1991 war with more effective masks, and took measures to better coordinate civilian emergency services in wartime.[66] At a deeper level, the creation of the Home Front Command represented an acknowledgment that the old strategic concept, which placed overwhelming emphasis on security through deterrence and operational offense, no longer sufficed.

The Gulf War also lent greater urgency to Israeli efforts begun in the mid-1980s to develop anti-missile defenses. Although in retrospect the Israelis viewed U.S.-made Patriot missile batteries as ineffective against Iraqi Scud missiles, they pressed on with the development of active missile defenses. These efforts involve at least three elements: the Arrow missile system, a UAV-based boost-phase intercept (BPI) system, and the Tactical High-Energy Laser (THEL) system. The Arrow will reportedly be deployed in two or three batteries with four launchers and fifty missiles each. Early warning will be provided by U.S. satellites and battle management by an advanced command-and-control system of Israeli design, while the missiles will be guided to their targets by a locally produced fire-control radar.[67] Little is known about the UAV-based BPI system, although Israel is believed to be working on a high-altitude, long-endurance UAV design mounting an extended-range version of the Python 4 air-to-air missile, code-

---

[65]   For the debate about the 1991 Persian Gulf War and Israeli deterrence, see Ze'ev Schiff in *Mideast Mirror,* October 8, 1991, pp. 9–10; and Shai Feldman, "Israeli Deterrence and the Gulf War," in Joseph Alpher, ed., *War in the Gulf: Implications for Israel* (Boulder, Colo.: Westview, 1992), pp. 184–208.

[66]   Interview with Home Front Commander Maj. Gen. Ze'ev Livne in *Bamahane,* June 3, 1992, pp. 11, in JPRS-NEA, July 15, 1992, pp. 14–15.

[67]   *Compass News,* October 28, 1996.

named "Moab."[68] The THEL, which is being jointly developed by the United States and Israel, is a mobile laser system that will provide protection against rockets and cruise missiles. Each fire unit will carry fuel for sixty kills and the system will have a probability of kill approaching 100 percent at 5 km, with a maximum effective range of 10 km The system has been undergoing developmental testing in the United States and is expected to undergo operational testing and evaluation in Israel from early 1999.[69]

The decision to develop the Arrow spurred a major policy debate in Israel. The defensive nature of the system and its high cost (estimates range from the official $1.6 billion to critics' $6 billion) have prompted many observers in the press, the IAF, and industry to question the wisdom of sinking so much money into this one project. These critics contend that the Arrow can be rendered useless by various countermeasures, and that enhancing Israel's preemptive strike capability (i.e., the air force) and its second-strike capability (i.e., long-range aircraft and perhaps a new family of inexpensive surface-to-surface missiles) would provide a more effective deterrent.[70] Furthermore, they argue, money spent enhancing the capabilities of the air force will yield benefits in other areas, as aircraft are multipurpose platforms, although the Arrow is a single-purpose system. Development of the Arrow has gone forward despite these objections (in part because U.S. support for the program takes most of the burden off the Israeli defense budget), and it is expected to have a limited initial operational capability by 1999.

Israel has also intensified efforts to enhance its long-range reconnaissance capabilities. Israel is reportedly working on a high-altitude long-endurance reconnaissance UAV[71] and in April 1995 put its first military reconnaissance

---

[68] Aluf Ben, "Over the Enemy's Head," *Ha'aretz*, December 24, 1992, p. B3, in JPRS-NEA, February 3, 1993, pp. 13–14; *International Defence Review*, July 1996, p. 5; *International Defence Review,* August 1997, p. 5.

[69] Mark Hewish, "Israel and U.S. Forces Warm to High-Energy Laser Weapon," *International Defense Review* (February 1997), p. 5.

[70] Journalist and former fighter pilot Reuven Pedatzur has been the most vocal public critic of the Arrow. For a sampling of his opinions, see Reuven Pedatzur, "Investing in Deterrence," *Ha'aretz*, April 3, 1989, p. 11, in FBIS-NES, April 4, 1989, pp. 25–26; idem., "The Israeli ATBM: The Errant Arrow," *Breakthroughs* (Spring 1994), pp. 17–22; idem., "A New Threat to the Arrow," *Ha'aretz*, October 15, 1995, p. B1, in FBIS-NES, October 16, 1995.

[71] In a 1995 interview, then–IAF commander Maj. Gen. Herzl Bodinger declared that "this (high-altitude long-endurance) UAV will be developed and it will be acquired and

satellite—the Ofeq 3—into orbit, some seven years after launching its first experimental satellite. These satellites will help Israel to follow developments in countries far from its borders and provide target intelligence for the growing number of long-range strike systems in its inventory.

To deal with the over-the-horizon threat, some IDF planners have reportedly advocated that Israel not rely exclusively on its air force and navy, but that it also build large numbers of inexpensive conventional surface-to-surface missiles ("1,000 little missiles") capable of hitting distant enemy population centers. This would enable Israel to deter enemy missile strikes on its own cities without putting its pilots at risk, violating the airspace of neighboring countries, or being left without a retaliatory option in the event that the air force is neutralized. It is not clear whether Israel is actively pursing this option at this time.[72]

DEFENSE INDUSTRY

The origins of Israel's domestic arms industry can be traced to the small clandestine arms manufacturing workshops of the pre-state *yishuv* (Jewish settlement) and the arms research and development (R&D) and production organizations created by the IDF and the Ministry of Defense in the early 1950s.[73] By the late 1950s, for a new and underdeveloped country, Israel already had a small but impressive arms production and upgrade capability. Yet, Israel became a major arms producer only after France imposed an arms embargo following the June 1967 War, cutting the IDF off from its main arms source.

As a result of this traumatic experience, Israel sought to achieve near total self-sufficiency in arms production. It did so by encouraging the expansion of its military industries and their involvement in the production of everything from

---

integrated into the air force." Sharone Parnes, "Israeli Air Force Eyes More Missions for Unmanned Aircraft," *Defense News*, July 3–9, 1995, p. 8.

[72]   A key proponent of this approach is Maj. Gen. Israel Tal, a former deputy chief of staff and deputy minister of defense. See Aluf Ben, *Ha'aretz*, January 22, 1993, p. B3, in JPRS-NEA, February 25, 1993, pp. 15–16; Aluf Ben, *Ha'aretz*, November 26, 1996, p. B2, in *Mideast Mirror*, November 26, 1996, pp. 4–7.

[73]   The latter include Israel Military Industries, a producer of light arms and ammunition; the Ministry of Defense's research and development (R&D) organization, which later became Rafael; the Bedek aircraft maintenance plant, which later became Israel Aircraft Industries (IAI); and Tadiran, a producer of military electronics. "Israel's Defense Industry: Evolution and Prospects," in U.S. Congress, Office of Technology Assessment, *Global Arms Trade* (Washington, D.C.: U.S. Government Printing Office, 1991), pp. 85, 93–94.

ammunition to major weapons systems. Key systems produced as a result of this initiative were the Reshef class missile boat in 1973, the Kfir fighter in 1974, and the Merkava tank in 1979. The drive for self-reliance, however, was not the only reason for Israel building up its defense industrial base. Rather, the effort was part and parcel of Israel's across-the-board effort to increase its qualitative edge over its enemies.

Table 2. The IDF at a Glance, 1996[74]

Special operations forces	Perhaps 1,500 men; *Sayeret Matkal, Sayeret Tzanchanim/Golani/Givati, Sayeret Egoz*, naval commandos, and several classified units
Conventional forces	175,000 standing, 425,000 reserves, 600,000 on mobilization.
Ground forces	135,000 standing, 365,000 reserve, 500,000 on mobilization; 12 armored divisions, 13 infantry brigades; 3,850 tanks (incl. 1,000 Merkava, 1,400 M-60s, 1,000 Centurions); 8,000 APCs (incl. 5,900 M-113s, and perhaps 100–200 *Nagmashot* and *Achzarit*); 1,300 artillery pieces (incl. 550 M-109 SP guns, 9 MLRS launchers).
Air force	32,500 standing, 54,000 reserve, 86,500 on mobilization; 450 combat aircraft (incl. 60 F-15 [with 25 F-15I on order], 205 F-16, 100 F-4E, and 40 AH-64, 40 AH-1, and 35 MD-500 attack helos).
Navy	9,000 standing, 10,000 reserve, 19,000 on mobilization; 30 major surface combatants (incl. 3 Sa'ar V corvettes, 3 submarines, 24 Sa'ar 1-4.5 Fast Attack Craft, 40 fast patrol boats).
Strategic forces	60-100 nuclear weapons, three Jericho I/II missile squadrons; Arrow anti-missile system (under development).

Israel's military industries produce equipment tailored to the precise operational requirements of the IDF and the threat it faces. Moreover, because of

---

[74] Sources: Shlomo Gazit, ed., *The Middle East Military Balance: 1993–1994* (Boulder, Colo.: Westview, 1994), pp. 315–332; International Institute for Strategic Studies, *The Military Balance: 1996–1997* (London: Oxford University Press, 1996), pp. 134–136.

the close working ties between the military industries and the IDF (many companies are run by former military officers), the needs and preferences of operators are more likely to be factored into the design of weapons than in other countries. Indeed, while performing their annual reserve duty, defense industry technicians may well find themselves relying on systems they designed and developed. For these reasons, many Israeli military planners favor home grown equipment over items produced overseas. The fact that many weapons are developed in Israel or "in house" (in the case of Rafael, the defense ministry's weapons development authority) also facilitates efforts to achieve technological surprise, since the capabilities of weapons produced in the United States—or elsewhere—may be familiar to Israel's enemies. It should be noted, however, that some leading Israeli policymakers, most notably Yitzhak Rabin, rejected this approach, favoring the purchase of foreign (above all, U.S.) systems whenever they were cheaper or superior to Israeli products.

Table 3. Israel's Defense Industry: Representative Products

Decade	Product
1940s	Hand grenades, submachine guns, mortars, armored cars
1950s	Uzi submachine gun
1960s	Fouga Magister jet trainer (licensed production); Gabriel antiship missile, Jericho intermediate-range ballistic missile
1970s	Unmanned aerial vehicles, Galil assault rifle, Reshef missile boat, Kfir fighter, Merkava tank, Barak surface-to- air missile
1980s	Harpy attack drone, Lavi fighter (canceled), Popeye air-to-ground missile
1990s	Python 4 air-to-air missile, Arrow anti-missile missile, Ofeq reconnaissance satellite, high-altitude, long-endurance UAVs

The limited size of the domestic market has long compelled Israeli arms producers to export their wares to remain economically viable. In addition, production for export permits economies of scale that result in lower unit costs for the IDF. Consequently, Israeli governments past and present have as a rule supported foreign military sales and helped industry market its products abroad. Thus, production for the IDF is in effect subsidized, to some extent, by foreign military sales,[75] which have averaged between $1.6 billion and $1.9 billion annually since 1980.[76]

By the early 1980s, Israel's military–industrial sector counted more than 150 entities employing nearly 70,000 people; this amounted to more than 4 percent of the total work force and 20 percent of the industrial labor force.[77] It produced an impressive array of items, including major weapons systems for the ground, air, and naval forces, an extremely diverse range of equipment and subsystems, and munitions of all types.[78] There was also, however, a growing realization in Israel that thanks to government bailouts and subsidies, the defense industrial sector had become bloated; that it was characterized by waste, inefficiency, and duplication; and that a small country like Israel could no longer afford this state of affairs. The IDF also sometimes resented Ministry of Defense pressure to use limited procurement funds to "buy Israeli" when less expensive versions of a system were available from the United States or elsewhere.[79]

---

[75]   This is not true for all defense items produced in Israel. Some, whose existence is kept secret, are barred from export, to enable the IDF to achieve technological surprise in wartime.

[76]   *International Defence Review*, July 1991, p. 766; *Armed Forces Journal International* (January 1992), p. 30; *Jane's Defence Weekly*, November 19, 1994, p. 23. These published figures probably understate the total volume of defense exports. Israel often prefers not to identify its foreign arms trade partners, to avoid embarrassing clients sensitive about their ties to Israel, or to avoid political problems with the United States over arms sales to controversial countries such as China.

[77]   These included privately owned companies, publicly owned corporations, the MoD's Rafael, and large state-owned enterprises such as IAI and TAAS. Rafael, the MoD's own military research and development authority, has traditionally occupied a key position in the Israeli military–industrial complex, for it is responsible for translating the military requirements of IDF field units into development projects, which are then pursued at Rafael, or submitted to the military industries for competitive bidding. For more on Rafael, see "Company Portrait: Rafael," *Military Technology*, June 1991, pp. 50–56. In addition, many defense firms possess an independent research and development capability and develop concepts and produce systems for the IDF or export on their own initiative. One example of this kind of venture is Soltam's Slammer self-propelled gun.

[78]   Imri Tov, "Government Policy Towards the Defense Industries," in Moshe Arens et al., *Israel's Defense Industries* (Ramat Gan: Bar Ilan University, BESA Center for Strategic Studies, 1995), p. 51.

[79]   The most notable instance of this was the Lavi fighter. The IDF preferred the U.S. F-16 for its future fighter, whereas the Ministry of Defense supported the Lavi (which would have cost twice as much) to boost the country's defense industrial sector. See

A turning-point in the development of Israel's military–industrial sector came in the mid-1980s when government efforts to rein-in runaway inflation through a series of economic reforms led to deep cuts in domestic procurement and overall defense spending. At about the same time, debt and liquidity crises in many developing-world countries (in the early 1980s) and the end of the Cold War (in the late 1980s), coupled with the disappearance of the Iranian and South African markets for Israeli arms, led to a downturn in foreign demand for Israeli systems. The subsequent cancellation of the Lavi fighter aircraft project in 1987 under U.S. pressure was a major blow not only to IAI (Israel Aircraft Industries) but to the entire defense industrial sector. Israeli domestic purchase of hardware for its new American F-16 fighters offered only partial compensation for these blows. These developments forced a painful restructuring of Israel's defense sector.

Israel's defense industries were forced to undertake massive layoffs,[80] to look for new markets for their products (mainly in Eastern Europe, after the fall of communism, and in East Asia), to form joint ventures to preserve their share of a shrinking market (for instance, IAI and Tadiran merged their UAV operations to create a new company, Mazlat), and to increase production for the civilian sector. Israel's extensive experience in upgrading older systems, including tanks and aircraft, provided a base for work in these areas. In addition, Israeli firms increasingly sought joint ventures with foreign—particularly American—firms to penetrate the United States and other large markets that might otherwise be closed to them.

The result of this restructuring has been a smaller, leaner military–industrial sector consisting of more than 200 firms employing some 40,000 people. (Some duplication still exists; for example, at least seven firms in Israel produce night vision equipment.[81]) The focus now is less on the production of major systems or platforms (although at least three major efforts—the Merkava IV, the Arrow, and the Ofeq satellite—are underway) and instead on systems that act as force

---

Chief of Staff Lt. Gen. Dan Shomron in *Le Figaro*, October 28, 1988, pp. 150–151, in FBIS-NES, November 3, 1988, p. 31.

[80]   For instance, IAI cut its labor force from 20,000 in 1987 to 13,000 today. TAAS likewise cut its labor force from 14,600 in 1985 to 5,000 today. And Soltam cut its labor force from 2,400 workers in 1987 to 315 today. Arens et al., *Israel's Defense Industries*, p. 25; Office of Technology Assessment, *Global Arms Trade*, pp. 96, 98; SIBAT (Foreign Defense Assistance and Export Organization of the Ministry of Defense), *Defense Sales Directory*, 1995–1996 (Tel Aviv: Israel Ministry of Defense, 1995), pp. 449–450, 462–463.

[81]   SIBAT, *Defense Sales Directory, 1995–1996*, pp. 440–466.

multipliers (such as night vision, command-and-control, and electronic warfare systems and precision munitions) and efforts to modernize and upgrade older platforms (such as the M-60/Magach 7 tank, the F-4/Phantom 2000 fighter, and the CH-53/Puffin 2000 helicopter programs).[82]

Israel's military–industrial base remains an important asset, though Israel's leadership has yet to define its place in a revised national security concept. Such issues as the degree of permissible foreign ownership of Israeli defense companies remain to be resolved. In the meantime, Israel's defense industry will continue to rely heavily on foreign sales, particularly to the United States, Eastern Europe, and China. This solution, of course, poses political problems and, in some cases, the potential for Israeli technology coming back, in unfriendly hands, to threaten the Jewish state.

The IDF of 1998 looks outwardly to be far different than the rag tag army that won Israel's struggle for independence half a century ago. Vastly stronger in all respects, it boasts not only soldiers trained to a very high level, but excellent equipment, much of it of indigenous manufacture. It has come a very long way from an army that had to count every rifle bullet, and whose best piece of homegrown equipment was an inaccurate, but very noisy, homemade mortar. Yet the Israeli military's continuity with its predecessors is also very strong, not only in the lineage of its units, but in its manpower system, its doctrine, and its concept of organization.

In Israel today, popular support for the traditional Israeli national security concept remains. In many respects, the precepts embodied in that concept—the nation in arms, self-reliance, qualitative superiority, pre-emption, and the emphasis on offensive action to achieve rapid decision—still describe the framework within which public discussion of national security occurs. But the overall concept itself, as well as its constituent parts, have come under critical scrutiny in recent years. Despite a concerted effort by the Israeli defense establishment to adapt and reinterpret traditional practices to fit new conditions, evidence accumulates—manifested most notably in the ongoing transformation of Israel's force structure and in a public debate about the place of the IDF in Israeli society—suggesting that the concept itself may soon require drastic revision. Should this prove to be the case, the IDF may be entering an era of profound change, at least as disconcerting as the turbulent years after the 1973 war, and more likely to resemble the formative period of the early 1950s. Such an era of change will place a premium on the IDF's capacity for innovation.

---

[82]   See OTA, Global Arms Trade, pp. 83–103; Arens et al., *Israel's Defense Industries.*

Chapter 3

Israel's Military Culture: Conservative Innovation

All militaries, British military historian Michael Howard once said, get it wrong to some degree before a war starts. What matters, he went on to say, "is their capacity to get it right quickly when the moment arrives."[1] Such a calculation, he conceded, might represent too great a concession to English disdain for *a priori* theorizing or (a non-Englishman might add) the comfortable margin of security possessed by an insular power. Certainly, the ability to improvise in the chaos of battle matters a great deal; but to embattled states with enemies on their frontiers, if not their very doorsteps, much hinges on the ability to anticipate change during peacetime. All armies have different styles of innovation: This chapter examines that of Israel.

A RECORD OF INNOVATION

At virtually every level of war (except, perhaps, the highest: that of strategy) the IDF has demonstrated throughout its history a proclivity for the dashing, the unusual, or the creative solution to military problems. It is indeed the popular image of Israeli military innovation that accounts for much of the respect (and occasionally envy) with which foreign commentators view it. Israeli military culture is pre-sumed by most observers to reflect levels of military proficiency and adaptability similar to that of Germany in its heyday. And yet, as we shall see below, this highly creative and innovative military is, in some fundamental ways, extremely conservative. In this respect, as well as some others, the IDF is not quite as *sui generis* as it would sometimes like to believe.

Although Israelis began to win such accolades early on—Basil Liddell Hart was an admirer already in the years following Israeli independence in 1948, and the American military expert S. L. A. Marshall in the aftermath of the 1956 Sinai campaign—the high point of such creativity is generally considered to have been the June 1967 War. Following preemptive air strikes that smashed the air forces

---

[1]   Michael Howard, "Military Science in an Age of Peace," *Journal of the Royal United Services Institute for Defence Services* (March 1974), p. 264.

of four Arab states (Egypt, Syria, Jordan, and, to a lesser extent, Iraq), Israeli ground forces seized the Sinai peninsula, the hills of the West Bank, and the Golan Heights, some 27,000 square miles in all. Here, it seemed to outside observers, was a military achievement comparable to that of the German blitz through France and the Low Countries in six weeks during the spring and early summer of 1940. Indeed, for Israelis themselves, the 1967 victory came to typify the model of war as it should be fought—short, on enemy territory, and begun with a preemptive attack. The myth of 1967, grounded though it was in reality, explains much of Israeli military culture since then. It crystallized some features of Israeli military doctrine and culture that linger to the present day, and fixed the reputation of the IDF as a brilliant military force.

The June 1967 War remains the archetypal victory of a small, dogged, and clever military against larger but clumsier opponents. It established the ideal toward which the IDF would aspire for the next generation, albeit never with complete success. That reputation has since been burnished in a variety of smaller operations, both within larger conflicts and in the intervals between them. In the first category fall such episodes as the audacious dash across the Suez Canal in the October 1973 War, while in the latter category are a variety of daring commando raids, such as the snatch of an advanced Russian radar from the Egyptian side of the Suez Canal in 1969 or the Entebbe hostage rescue operation of 1976.

The high tolerance for tactical risk revealed in such operations has been matched by no less adroit cleverness in set-piece operations. These include the assault at Abu Ageila on the Egyptian front in 1967 and the successful suppression of Syrian air defenses in the Bekaa Valley in 1982.[2] Even the *intifada*, clearly the most frustrating of Israel's many wars, revealed a pattern of rapid Israeli countermeasures to the tactics adopted by a rag-tag but determined group of Palestinian insurgents.[3]

In addition to operational and tactical innovation, since the days of pre-1948 underground military workshops, the Israelis have cultivated a military industry

---

[2]   On the Abu Ageila operation, see George W. Gawrych, *Key to Sinai: The Battles for Abu Ageila in the 1956 and 1967 Arab–Israeli Wars* (Fort Leavenworth, Kansas: Combat Studies Institute, 1990).

[3]   For an overall account, see Ze'ev Schiff and Ehud Ya'ari, *Intifada*, Ina Friedman, trans. (New York: Simon and Schuster, 1990). Also of value are Reuven Gal, ed. *The Seventh War: The Influence of the Intifada on Israeli Society* (Tel Aviv: Hakibbutz Hameuchad, 1990) (Hebrew); Efraim Inbar, "Israel's Small War: The Military Response to the Intifada," *Armed Forces and Society* (1991), pp. 29–50; and Stuart Cohen, "How did the Intifada Affect the IDF," *Conflict Quarterly* (1994), pp. 7–22.

capable of technological innovation as well. Modern innovations include unmanned aerial vehicles (UAVs), reactive armor on tanks, specialized long-range precision munitions, and indigenous missile systems such as the Barak ship defense anti-missile missile, the Gabriel anti-ship missile, and the Python air-to-air missile.

From an organizational point of view as well, the IDF has been willing to change. In the course of two generations of officers it went from an army based on brigades (in the 1950s), to one oriented on the task-organized division *(ugda misimati)* in the 1960s, to standing divisions in the 1970s, to a corps-level organization *(gayis)* in the 1980s. New special operations organizations have come into existence, been abolished, and reappeared; and although the central command system has remained essentially the same since its inception, new organizations (particularly a command for Israel's ground forces and its rear) have come into being.

Thus, on all levels—operational, tactical, technical, and organizational—the IDF has won a reputation for creativity and innovation, and it has established those qualities as central to its theory of war.[4] What explains the Israeli record?

THE SOURCE AND NATURE OF ISRAELI INNOVATION

Ein Breira: Necessity as the Mother of Invention

The simplest explanation for Israeli military innovation can be summed up in these two words, *ein breira*, meaning "no choice"—a phrase often used by Israeli leaders to explain their success. Born in the face of a threat to its very existence, and continuing to develop in the face of the avowed intention of its enemies to eliminate it from the map, the IDF has had every motivation in the world to develop clever solutions to its problems. Stark necessity, in other words, explains Israeli innovation.

One must immediately qualify this judgment in two ways, however. First, although the existential threat to Israel explains the *motivation* to innovate, it does not explain Israel's success; many countries, after all, have failed where

---

[4]   See (then-Col.) Yitzhak Ben-Israel, "Where did Clausewitz Err? Clausewitz and the Principles of War in Light of Modern Technology," *Ma'arachot* (February–March 1988), pp. 16–26 (Hebrew). Ben-Israel argues that Clausewitz systematically underrates the importance of cunning, intelligence, surprise, and technological innovation; he proposes adding to the "principles of war" the "principle of anticipation," with regard to time, place, and psychological preparedness, and he cites Israel's successes against Syrian air defenses in 1982 in this regard.

Israel has triumphed. Second, the existential threat to Israel, although hardly absent even today, diminished greatly in the late 1970s for a variety of reasons, including the eventual withdrawal of Egypt from confrontation with the Jewish state, and the demonstration that Israel had the diplomatic and economic support of the United States in the event of war. And yet, to an impressive extent, Israeli innovation flourishes to the present day.

The Israeli military style has developed, to a remarkable degree, in isolation from that of the United States and other leading countries. Barbara Tuchman, in a particularly perceptive summary of interviews with Israeli generals immediately after the Six-Day War, noted that "one theme they notably and unanimously maintain is refusal to acknowledge any debt to foreign methods or doctrines and insistence on their independent development. There are no foreign experts or advisers in the IDF."[5] One Israeli lieutenant colonel returned from his year at the U.S. Army's Command and General Staff College with the sure assessment that, "In the narrow domain of commanding military formations, of course, I had no need to broaden my resources of information and experience."[6] Despite ever increasing attention to U.S. military developments and technology (noticeable, for example, in long articles dealing with the United States in *Ma'arachot,* the Israeli general staff journal), the IDF retains a strong sense of the superiority, or at least the appropriateness, of its own methods.[7] Thus, for example, one of Israel's leading military psychologists is sharply critical of American officer recruitment practices, observing severely, that "the American concept of command cannot be based on the 'Follow Me' model that we know."[8] (One must note that few graduates of the U.S. Army Infantry School at Fort Benning, Georgia, whose motto is "Follow Me," would agree with this assertion, though it accurately reflects an Israeli sense of exceptionalism in this area.)

---

[5]   Barbara Tuchman, "Israel's Swift Sword," in her book of essays, *Practicing History* (New York: Ballantine, 1982), p. 178. This essay was originally published in *Atlantic Monthly,* September 1967.

[6]   Avigdor Kahalani, *A Warrior's Way* (New York: Shapolsky, 1994), p. 267.

[7]   For an example of the kind of careful treatment of U.S. developments, see Beni Michaelson, "The U.S. Army into the 21st Century," *Ma'arachot* (February 1995), pp. 10–16 (Hebrew). Michaelson is a reserve colonel and a senior officer in the IDF's military history office.

[8]   Reuven Gal, "For a Review of the Current Model of the Israeli Officer," *Ma'arachot* (February 1996), p. 19 (Hebrew). Gal was chief psychologist of the IDF. It should be noted that Gal goes on to find deficiencies in the IDF's officer recruitment system, as noted below.

Although early in Israeli history a distinct British influence pervaded the IDF, and although Israeli officers frequently attend American courses, the fundamental features of the Israeli military system remain indigenous. This stems from a variety of reasons. The prewar Israeli para-state developed its own military forces, particularly the elite Palmach *(plugot machatz*—strike companies), which self-consciously adopted a different military culture than that of the British authorities.[9] This style was then perpetuated after independence through the influence of such figures as Moshe Dayan and Yitzhak Rabin, as well as non-*palmachniks* such as Ariel Sharon, who first made his mark as a commander of Unit 101 in the early 1950s. Even after the development of close relations with the United States, the Israelis have been careful not to share too much of their tactics and technology with their superpower patron, fearing leaks to their Arab enemies. This explains Israeli reluctance to participate in the U.S. Air Force's Red Flag exercises at Nellis Air Force Base in Nevada, or initial Israeli reticence in sharing lessons from the 1982 Lebanon war.[10]

Despite Israel's slender physical and modest demographic dimensions, and its insular military culture, its armed forces have contained contradictory currents: Ex-British officers and *Palmachniks* and even some veterans of the Red Army, paratroopers and tankers, hyper-aggressive commanders and more cautious ones.[11] This diversity has produced a rich mix of tactical styles. Because no single solution to Israel's operational challenges has emerged, the Israeli military has continued to experiment and play with a variety of solutions to its problems. At the technical level, isolation very early (including a variety of unilateral and multilateral arms embargoes) led to the development of an indigenous arms industry dedicated to production for the IDF.

All militaries may be understood by the traumas that mark them. For the Israelis, there are many, including the bloody War of Independence, but at the

---

[9] For sharply contrasting views, see Meir Pa'il, *The Emergence of Zahal (IDF)* (Tel Aviv: Zmora, Bitan, Modan, 1979) and Yoav Gelber, *The Kernel of a Regular Hebrew Army* (Jerusalem: Yad Yitzhak Ben Zvi, 1986) (both Hebrew). The distinctive approach of the Palmach is captured in several books by its commander, Yigal Allon, including *The Making of Israel's Army* (New York: Universe Books, 1970), which incorporates documents as well as Allon's own views, and his *A Curtain of Sand* (Tel Aviv: Hakibbutz Hameuchad, 1959; expanded edition 1968) (Hebrew).

[10] Interview, Israeli general officer.

[11] Consider, for example, the debate over the creation of the Bar Lev Line following the War of Attrition, the product of sharp disagreements regarding fundamental operational doctrine in the IDF. See Yaacov Bar-Siman-Tov, "The Bar-Lev Line Revisited," *Journal of Strategic Studies* (June 1988), pp. 149–176.

purely technological level no trauma is more important than France's abandonment of Israel in 1967, with a resultant freeze on exports to Israel of advanced weapons, including fighter aircraft and missile boats. A similar, though lesser, shock occurred in 1969 when Great Britain suspended a sale of Chieftain tanks to the Israelis during the War of Attrition, an act that contributed to the development of the homegrown Merkava.[12] Even since the early 1970s, the United States has, from time to time, refused the transfer of advanced military technology to Israel, or has restricted the timing and scale of deliveries as a form of political pressure. Despite close ties with the United States, many Israelis still harbor a fear of abandonment by their superpower patron which will not, in any case, share all of its technological secrets with them. Moreover, the Israelis believe (with some reason) that they can best develop technologies that suit precisely their particular operational environment, and hence they see advantages in keeping a vigorous defense industry.

Important as technology may be, the IDF believes that its successes have rested on the skill, spirit and determination of its soldiers who, in its large wars (particularly 1948, 1967, and 1973) fought with desperate courage because they fought to protect their homes and families. Motivation to excel in peacetime too, in the duties of routine security or in training for war, rest on the spirit of *ein breira*. The result is a kind of motivation U.S. soldiers have not known since the Civil War. Israel has, until very recently, willingly accepted high casualty rates in training and on military operations. In 1953, in fact, Moshe Dayan reacted to a failed retaliatory raid by issuing an order that no officer was to suspend an attack unless his unit had taken more than 50 percent casualties on pain of relief for cause.[13] In several wars Israel paid a heavy price for objectives thought worth the price—the storming of Tel Fakhr by the *Golani* brigade on the Golan Heights in 1967, for example, or similar attempts by the same unit in 1973 to reclaim the Mt. Hermon observation posts seized by the Syrians. After Yitzhak Rabin compared the extremely low price in human life paid by the United States for its victory in the Gulf War with the much higher losses suffered by Israel in its wars,

---

[12]   The Israelis had, in fact provided the British with advice on the development of the Chieftain. See Peter Hellman, "Israel's Chariot of Fire," *Atlantic Monthly* 255 (March 1985), p. 81ff.

[13]   Edward Luttwak and Dan Horowitz, *The Israeli Army* (New York: Harper & Row, 1975), p. 108; Moshe Dayan, *Milestones*, (Jerusalem: Edanim, 1976), pp. 112–13 (Hebrew).

he remarked stoically: "Israel is forced to live with such differentials."[14] More recently, such willingness to accept casualties may be diminishing, as Israeli reactions to recent losses in training and operations in South Lebanon indicate.

The Israelis' preference for innovative solutions remains high, but, in the last resort, Israeli commanders fall back on the grit of their troops to carry the day. One of the outstanding platoon leaders in the IDF told an interviewer that it was far more important to develop discipline and the spiritual commitment of his privates than to develop their professional skills.[15] *Dvekut b'misima l'or hamatara* is a term that conveys more powerful emotional overtones in Hebrew than its English translation, "maintenance of the objective."[16] The IDF traditionally has relied less on technical inventions to secure victory than on the fighter's tactical proficiency and spirit of self-sacrifice, and this core belief sets one of a number of limits on the importance assigned to technological change.[17]

One might include in the philosophy of *ein breira* the psychological consequences of operating on a continuous war-footing. The casual visitor to Israel is immediately struck by the ubiquitous presence of armed soldiers in Israel's cities and towns; a trip to the IDF in the field (which may be no more than half an hour away from the heart of a major city) conveys the sense of an operational environment. Israeli soldiers are almost never found without weapons and live ammunition, and rarely a week goes by without skirmishes on Israel's frontiers. The constant possibility of terrorist attack from within or infiltration from without, combined with a vivid sense of the perennial possibility of large-scale conventional war, makes the IDF very much a field army. Constant

---

[14]   Yitzhak Rabin, "After the Gulf War: Israeli Defense and its Security Policy," in BESA Center for Strategic Studies, Bar Ilan University, *Yitzhak Rabin and Israeli National Security* (Ramat Gan, Israel: Bar Ilan University, 1996), p. 7.

[15]   Eren Alcavi, "They Will Stand by Virtue of Values, by Virtue of Understanding, and by Virtue of a Sense of Responsibility, and They Will Strive to Improve." *Ma'arachot* (August 1994), p. 28 (Hebrew). Alcavi was killed in Lebanon shortly after giving this interview, which was one in a series commissioned by the IDF's school of leadership.

[16]   Yair Burla, *Dictionary of Military Terms* (Tel Aviv: Dvir, 1988), pp. 85, 366. *Dvekut* carries a connotation of almost religious passion, and *matara* is best translated as goal or target.

[17]   See David Ben Gurion's speech to a 1955 officer's course, "The Spirit of Self-Sacrifice in the IDF," *Unity and Destiny* (Tel Aviv: Ministry of Defense Publishing, 1971), pp. 217–218 (Hebrew). Ben Gurion used the word *akedah,* which is usually used to refer to the binding and near sacrifice of Isaac by Abraham—an experience traditionally interpreted as a supremely voluntary act by both grief-stricken father and doomed son.

operational activity reinforces the pragmatism, flexibility, and penchant for simplicity that are hallmarks of the IDF, and dissolves many of the artificialities of garrison life and peacetime training that affect other armies. For higher-level commanders as well, the pressure of necessity acts as a solvent on some of the normal parochialism of military bureaucracies. One American officer with long experience in Israel noted that an Israeli air base commander had casually told him that he would rather fly an AH-64 Apache attack helicopter in combat than an F-16. It is unlikely that a senior U.S. Air Force officer would make such an admission, or that he would (as this officer did) have the opportunity to act on his preference.[18]

One final and paradoxical element of *ein breira* has to do with the consequences of a string of failures that have elicited successful responses from a leadership that believed it had little margin for error. The abortive and costly retaliatory raids of the early 1950s led to the creation of Unit 101, and with it the reinvigoration of Israel's infantry. The high price exacted by Egyptian and Syrian surface-to-air missiles and anti-aircraft artillery in 1973 led to the carefully orchestrated suppression of enemy air defenses in the Bekaa Valley in 1982. The searing losses brought about by Egyptian antitank teams, armed with rocket-propelled grenades and guided missiles, turned the IDF to combined arms tactics and the improved protection for tankers and infantry. The sinking of the *Eilat* in 1967 accelerated the Israeli Navy's turn to missile boats in following years, and the setbacks of the early days of the *intifada* resulted in the creation of generally successful undercover units. Although Israeli soldiers exhibit their share of vanity when dealing with the outside world, they have also had their experiences of complacency-shattering calamity. Col. Muki Betser, former deputy commander of the elite *Sayeret Matkal*, recalls the consequences of the disastrous raid on Karameh, Jordan, in early 1968, in which the IDF lost nearly thirty men killed (three of whose bodies were abandoned on the field of battle) and seventy wounded:

> In a single stroke, my perceptions of the IDF and its strength, and of my own invincibility, had changed forever. At Karameh I understood my own vulnerability, as well as the IDF's. Since then, before every battle, every operation, and every project I began, I have seen Karameh in my mind's eye, where I learned to learn. . . .[19]

---

[18]   Interview with a retired U.S. officer, March 12, 1997.

[19]   Moshe "Muki" Betser with Robert Rosenberg, *Secret Soldier: The True Life Story of Israel's Greatest Commando* (New York: Atlantic Monthly Press, 1996). Betser was the deputy commander at the daring 1976 Entebbe rescue operation. Former Deputy Chief of

'The Few Against The Many'

On Hanukkah, the Jewish holiday celebrating the long struggle of a Judaean rebellion against the Seleucid Greco-Syrians, Jews recite a prayer that thanks God, who "delivered the strong into the hands of the weak, the many into the hands of the few, the impure into the hands of the pure." This belief that modern Israelis too are "the few against the many," is deeply rooted in a broader Jewish self-concept, and indeed may be found in such Biblical stories as the struggle between Abraham and the five kings who kidnapped his nephew Lot, or Gideon and the Midianites, in which a force of three hundred routed a force of thousands. For Israeli military thinkers, the answer to their enemies' quantitative superiority is quality—a comprehensive quality that rests only partly on technology, and much more on fighting spirit, tactical skill, and social cohesion.[20]

The founding fathers of the IDF asserted that the few could beat the many by greater skill or cunning. "We have a unique military problem," Israel's first prime minister told the graduates of a platoon leader's course in November 1948.

> We are few and our enemies are many. In our recent war we stood seven or eight hundred thousand against thirty millions, and if war awaits us in the future—and no one can tell us that it does not—we must once again face this condition . . . And even if our numbers triple or quadruple—we will have to stand the few against the many, because there is no objective possibility that our numbers will equal those of our current and potential enemies in the future. And numbers, you know, are a powerful force in military matters, and generally decisive. How, then, have we stood until now, and how shall we stand in the future? On, and only on, our qualitative superiority, moral and intellectual. That is the great and

---

Staff Maj. Gen. Matan Vilnai made a similar point in a 1988 interview. Discussing a daring heliborne commando raid he led in 1968, he stated:

> Today, our special units have attained a degree of proficiency we did not have then—yet we have not conducted an operation like this one since. As a matter of fact, our capabilities today are much greater. The problem is—the audacity to take such a decision. . . . Today we see things differently. One must remember that in the intervening period we had the Yom Kippur War. The IDF of today is an army that has more than once failed, and it has learned to live with this. But this fact has its consequences. Today we know that we may fail. Back then, we didn't realize this.

Yosef Argamon, "Operation Shock," *Bamahane*, November 2, 1988, p. 49.

[20] The near-obsession of Israeli military thinkers with this subject is evident in a thoughtful collection of articles, Tzvi Ofer and Avi Kober, eds., *Quality and Quantity: Dilemmas in the Creation of Military Strength* (Tel Aviv: Ministry of Defense Publishing House, 1985) (Hebrew).

precious inheritance that Jewish history, Jewish education, Jewish suffering, and Jewish vision give us—the suffering of despised and persecuted generations, exiled and slaughtered, the education during thousands of years of constant dwelling in the tents of the Torah, and the primordial vision of prophets and sages.[21]

For David Ben Gurion, qualitative superiority was not a technical concept but a spiritual one. His successors have clung to this notion—hence the preoccupation of senior Israeli officers with the state of national morale and the willingness of young people to embrace, and not merely accept passively, the burdens of military service.

This concept of the few against the many runs like a thread through Israeli military thought down to the present day.[22] Moshe Dayan, in an article written several weeks before the June 1967 War, described the IDF's situation by comparing it to the Biblical story of David's combat with Goliath, in which the young shepherd rejected the heavy armor offered him by his king in favor of his own favored weapon—a sling.

> David did not forego arms for spirit, and did not rely on the Lord God of Hosts alone to do battle for him, but rather sought and found a way of fighting that gave him a military advantage over Goliath. But this approach to combat hinges on one thing: only he who 'has the spirit of God in him' can employ it. Only those who possess that spirit become daring, fearless fighters.

But, Dayan went on to say, "moral superiority must find military–technical expression if it is to carry any weight in battle."[23] Thus too, the Israeli pursuit of a lean, mobile, and agile fighting force and the admiration for the British military historian and theorist Basil Liddell Hart, who early on adopted the Israelis as his protégés.[24]

The emphasis on quality has always had some technological dimension. Even in the early 1950s, the IDF created a fledgling military research and development establishment to give it a technological edge over its opponents. Over time, the

---

[21]   Ben Gurion, *Unity and Destiny*, p. 43.

[22]   See, as examples, Allon, *Curtain of Sand*, pp. 35–51, a chapter entitled "The Few Against the Many," and most recently Israel Tal, *National Security: The Few Against the Many* (Tel Aviv: Dvir, 1996) (Hebrew).

[23]   Moshe Dayan, "The Fighter's Spirit," in Ruth Bondy, Ohad Zmora, Raphael Bashan, *Mission Survival* (New York: Sabra Books, 1968), p. 120.

[24]   For a reassessment of Liddell Hart's influence, however, see Tuviah Ben-Mosheh, "Liddell Hart and the IDF: A Reassessment," *Medinah, mimshal, v'yachasim beinleumiyim* 15 (1980), pp. 40–56.

weight assigned by Israel to technological superiority over potential opponents has grown in response to both opportunity and challenge. From the first the IDF sought to achieve technological superiority where possible, as evidenced, for example, by its investment in domestic missile development as early as the 1950s.[25] Over the last thirty years, technology has come to occupy an ever more important role in the IDF's self-understanding, although it did not and probably never will displace the IDF's emphasis on human quality. Still, a qualitative gap in the weapons of war, and not only the humans who handle it, is now part of the Israeli security concept—something quite different from the situation that existed until shortly before the 1967 war, when Israeli military hardware was not noticeably superior in kind to that of its Arab enemies. Even today, when some potential enemies (including Egypt and Saudi Arabia) have acquired U.S. weapons, the Israelis have a margin of superiority—in areas like software, munitions, and avionics—that creates a distinct technical edge over their enemies. The United States has pledged itself to maintain that technological margin of superiority, and the Israelis are determined to preserve it.

The rise of the air force as the cutting edge of the IDF, and the dominance within the ground forces, particularly during the 1970s and 1980s, of the armored corps, rested at least in part on a belief in technical quality as a way of counteracting the numerical superiority of Israel's enemies. More broadly, as Israel gained access to American arms, and as its military industry has developed, Israeli confidence that the IDF's weapons are not only handled more proficiently, but are more sophisticated than those of its opponents, rose in importance. Overall technical parity may have been tolerable if uncomfortable and undesirable for the Israel of 1967, but that is no longer the case today.

Two dimensions of "the few against the many" concept bear reflection. First, when carried to the strategic level, it embodied a deeply felt pessimism: None felt this more strongly than David Ben Gurion, Israel's Founding Father and still its most influential strategic thinker. The dark side of Ben Gurion's thought always set limits on what Israel could achieve by military action, precisely because the disparity between Israel's population and that of its opponents was so large that it could never hope to resolve the conflict militarily. Ben Gurion's strategic pessimism affected his disciples as well. Thus, Yitzhak Rabin, during his tenure as chief of the General Staff, concluded that all Israel's wars would be limited wars, because no Arab–Israeli conflict would be settled "the old-fashioned

---

[25]   See the interesting memoir by Munieh M. Mardor, *Rafael: In the Course of Research and Development for Israel's Security* (Tel Aviv: Ministry of Defense Publishing House, 1981; 5th ed., 1988).

way"—by seizing the enemy's capital and dictating peace terms.[26] To some extent, this reflected the dominating role of external powers (the United States and Soviet Union, and before them Great Britain) in the Middle East, but also the limits on Israel's resources. Thus, "the few against the many," while a source of military creativity, has also bounded Israel's military horizons, excluding, for example a shattering conventional *coup de main* that could resolve the Arab–Israeli conflict once and for all. Some Israeli military leaders have indeed asserted the need for "decisive force," in the event of war, but they have remained a minority.[27] Indeed, like most soldiers, senior members of the IDF have become increasingly aware of the intrinsic limits on the uses of military power—particularly after 1973.

The second point to bear in mind about "the few against the many" is that it is a myth in the proper sense.[28] Although true in certain respects, it also misrepresents Israel's strategy and its military reality. From the outset, Israeli military planners have thought it imperative to answer quantity with quantity insofar as they possibly could. At the highest level, this meant an obsession with increasing Jewish *aliyah* (immigration). But at the organizational level of war it has meant mobilizing the largest numbers possible of men, women, and machines. Indeed, in Israel's War of Independence in 1948 the fledgling state with a population of barely 600,000 was able to field larger armies than its Arab opponents. As Nadav Safran shrewdly put it, "The ghost of Voltaire might feel smug satisfaction that in this instance, too, God gave victory to the side with the 'biggest battalions.' But he would have to use intellectual legerdemain to explain how the side with the much smaller population was able to marshal the larger army."[29] Even at the time of the initial invasion, the two sides stood at rough

---

[26] Personal recollection, speech by Yitzhak Rabin c. 1980.

[27] See the article by the legendary armored leader, Maj. Gen. Moshe Bar-Kochba, "Strategic Decision on the Terms of the State of Israel," *Ma'arachot* (October–November 1989), pp. 7–13 (Hebrew). Bar-Kochba defines strategic decision as "breaking the will of the enemy and his national and military ability to resist, including control of vital areas in the depths of his country." Avi Kober, *Military Decision in the Arab–Israeli Wars 1948–1982* (Tel Aviv: Ministry of Defense Publishing House, 1995) (Hebrew). See Kober's article "A Paradigm in Crisis? Israel's Doctrine of Military Decision," *Israel Affairs* (Autumn 1995), pp. 188–211.

[28] That is, a "traditional story of ostensibly historical events that serves to unfold part of the world view of a people." *Webster's New Collegiate Dictionary* (Springfield: G. & C. Merriam, 1980), p. 755.

[29] Nadav Safran, *Israel: The Embattled Ally* (Cambridge, Mass.: Harvard University Press, 1978), pp. 49–50. For details, see Appendix B to this study.

parity, with some 30,000 troops on a side, although the Jews, as Safran notes, had been worn down by six months of battle against Palestinian guerrillas and still lacked much of the material advantages of the invaders. Following the truce of June 11, 1948, however, the Israelis nearly doubled their force, while the Arabs increased theirs by perhaps a third.[30] Moreover, a relatively large influx of hardware enabled the newborn IDF to meet its enemy on technologically comparable terms, as the Israelis acquired armored cars, tanks, artillery, and fighter and bomber aircraft from abroad.[31]

During the Six-Day War, the IDF attacked forces that were indeed superior in numbers. On the Sinai front, for example, some 70,000 Israelis and 750 tanks faced 100,000 Egyptians and 930 tanks; on the Jordanian and Syrian fronts, the ratios were comparable, though more favorable to the IDF on the former than the latter. The Arab armies operated under the disability of exposure to air attack and, in the case of the Egyptians and the Syrians, poor leadership that early on decided to withdraw toward their respective capitals. The Israelis lost most heavily to the smallest of their opponents, the Jordanians.[32] By exploiting interior lines of communication and superior organizational skills, Israel sought to gain numerical superiority, at least for brief periods of time. When disaster struck in 1973, and Israel found itself the victim of a surprise attack on two fronts, the postwar reaction was not merely to improve the armed forces in various ways, but to fully *double* the ground order of battle by increasing the active force and extending the scope of reserve service—a quantitative reaction, in other words, and not merely a qualitative one. As an Israeli military proverb says, "Quality is a wonderful thing, as long as you have a lot of it."

Thus, the Israelis have frequently tried to become "the many" rather than "the few" on the operational level, relative to their Arab enemies. Moreover, in many of the sources of military power—specifically, economic strength—Israel has long since surpassed its rivals in quantitative as well as qualitative terms. In the mid-1970s the Israeli gross national product was more than double that of Egypt, Syria, and Jordan combined; twenty years later it was roughly triple that of its three main neighbors combined.[33] Allowing for the uncertainty of all such

---

[30]   Safran, *Israel*, p. 57.

[31]   See Munieh Mardor, "Military Acquisition 1947–1948," in *Army on the Way to a State* (Tel Aviv: Ministry of Defense Publishing House, 1988), pp. 204–216 (Hebrew).

[32]   Data from Michael Clodfelter, *Warfare and Armed Conflicts: A Statistical Reference to Casualty and Other Figures, 1618–1991*, vol. II, *1900–1991* (Jefferson, N.C.: McFarland & Co., 1992), pp. 1041–1045.

[33]   World Bank, *World Development Report* (Washington, D.C.: World Bank, various years).

numbers, it nonetheless appears that Israeli economic growth has continued to outstrip that of its Middle Eastern neighbors for some time. That fact, coupled with the end of Soviet military aid to Syria following the Cold War, has further altered the economic correlation of forces. According to the International Institute for Strategic Studies, in 1985 the combined defense expenditures of Egypt, Syria, and Jordan amounted to $8.8 billion, compared to roughly $6.6 billion for Israel; nearly a decade later, the comparable sums were about $9 billion for Israel, but only $5.4 billion for its immediate neighbors.[34] Thus, despite a decline in Israeli defense expenditure over the last decade (measured as a percentage of GDP), the relative gap between it and its immediate Arab neighbors has if anything tended to grow. To be sure, the Israelis measure themselves not merely against these states but against more distant opponents (Iraq and, more recently, Iran), and not against any enemy singly but against potential coalitions. Nonetheless, at least when counting dollars—a quantitative index if ever there was one—it is difficult to maintain that the balance of defense expenditure has been shifting against Israel over the last decade or more. Israeli defense expenditure is triple that of Greece, and nearly double that of Turkey. This does take into account the IDF's low manpower costs for soldiers during their first three or four years of military service, which in this respect makes Israeli soldiers considerably cheaper than their U.S. or British counterparts. Compared to other Middle Eastern states, of course, the Israeli budget is dwarfed by the Saudi defense budget (much of it spent on infrastructure, however) but it is roughly three times that of Iran and two and a half times that of Egypt or Syria.

More important, by the 1980s the IDF was, in many key respects, no longer a small military in absolute terms. Its highly effective reserve system meant that its nearly one dozen armored divisions and ancillary brigades could be counted as frontline forces that, when called up, would number nearly 600,000 troops—a total armed force comparable in terms of end strength to that of Germany. When equipment is considered in the roughest way (see Table 3.1), the Israelis look very much comparable to a middle-sized European power, and certainly the equivalent of any of its immediate neighbors.

The Right Size, Lean Organization, and Social Egalitarianism

In a famous essay written in 1927 "On Being the Right Size," British biologist R. B. S. Haldane suggested that organisms can grow too large, and that, conversely, "just as there is a best size for every animal, so the same is true for every

---

[34] All in constant 1993 dollars. International Institute for Strategic Studies, *The Military Balance 1995–96* (London: Brassey's, 1995), p. 265.

institution," an observation endorsed by student of management Peter Drucker.[35] The same holds true for military organizations, and in that regard Israel's military, and the geographical space in which it operates, has surely been close to being "the right size" for innovation. This is certainly true at the technological level, where the distance between the laboratory and the field is often no more than an hour or two by car or fifteen minutes by helicopter. It is true at the human level as well, where the same scientist working on a new piece of technology is likely to have had his own experience of service in the ranks, to have close friends who will use the end item that he is developing, or to have children who themselves may come to depend upon it. Not only does this promote the highest level of seriousness in defense-related industrial work; it makes for a sense of what is practical and doable. Israeli scientists probably need fewer reminders than their counterparts elsewhere about the need for "soldier-proofing" all new types of equipment.

Table 3.1. Comparative Equipment Holdings[36]

Type of equipment	Israel	Germany	France	Egypt, Syria, and Jordan
main battle tanks	3,850	2,700	970	9,500
artillery	1,300	590	410	3,800
combat aircraft	450	540	680	1,150

This intensely practical sense, however, also predisposes Israeli technologists to look askance, for the most part, at great technological leaps ahead. They are conditioned by the general military culture of the IDF, which has always valued technology, but only in its place. The head of the Israeli Air Force (IAF) until just before the 1967 War, and IDF deputy chief of staff during the war, Maj. Gen. Ezer Weizman, now Israel's president, later told one American: "The military world has become a victim of its own sophistication in weaponry. . .It has forgotten that brains, nerve, heart, and imagination are all beyond the capacity of

---

[35] J. B. S. Haldane, "On Being the Right Size," reprinted in John Gross, ed., *The Oxford Book of Essays* (Oxford: Oxford University Press, 1991), p. 457; Peter F. Drucker, *Management: Tasks, Responsibilities, Practices* (New York: Harper & Row, 1974), p. 638ff. Drucker uses Haldane's metaphor as the point of departure for his discussion of the relationship between size, structure, and function.

[36] Ibid.; Gazit, *Middle East Military Balance, 1993–1994.*

the computer. No computer can go 'beyond the call of duty,' but that is what medals are given for."[37] Reuven Gal notes that

> The IDF's senior officers' approach to new technology is nonetheless somewhat ambivalent: on the one hand, they are always eager to acquire the latest equipment, always be one step ahead of other militaries, particularly those of their adversaries who historically have always received the latest technology. On the other hand, however, there is a certain amount of skepticism concerning overreliance on technology, seen as a possible threat to the importance of the essential human component. When these officers finally do decide to acquire a new weapon system, they will, almost always, modify it slightly so that it better suits the 'Israeli mind.'[38]

Maj. Gen. Benyamin Peled, commander of the Israeli Air Force during the 1973 War, is said to have remarked that "the best electronic warfare is a Mk.84 bomb on the target"—an attitude that got the IAF in considerable trouble in the early days of the 1973 war. One senior Israeli officer, commandant of the command and staff college, commented in a twenty-year retrospective on that technology "cannot be the decisive force" in war.[39] Even IDF officers in the research and development field, whom one would expect to be the most technologically disposed of all, show considerable caution.[40] Friction, the fog of war, and the dominance of the human element—all these are themes repeated by Israeli military scientists, not merely skeptical infantrymen.

When Israel *has* pursued dramatic technological leaps, it has generally done so with foreign resources: This has been true of the nuclear program (which depended on French aid), the ill-fated Lavi project of the 1980s, and the as yet uncertain Arrow anti-ballistic missile system. Even the Merkava tank required more than $100 million dollars of American funds in 1975 and more since.[41] The case of the Merkava makes another point: Although the overall design of the hull and the layout involved radical changes (particularly the placement of the engine

---

[37]   Tuchman, "Swift Sword," p. 181.

[38]   Reuven Gal, *A Portrait of the Israeli Soldier* (Westport, Conn.: Greenwood, 1986), p. 175.

[39]   Yitzhaki Chen, "Technology is not Everything," *Ma'arachot* (September–October 1993), pp. 2–7 (Hebrew).

[40]   See one of the most interesting of Israeli general officers writing on military matters, Yitzhak Ben-Israel, "Back to the Future," *Ma'arachot* (March–April 1993), pp. 2–5 (Hebrew); "Technological Lessons," *Ma'arachot* (September–October 1993), pp. 8–13 (Hebrew).

[41]   Hellman, "Israel's Chariot of Fire."

in front of the crew compartment, where it could absorb enemy fire), much of the system emerged from a fairly conservative technological base (the power plant, gun, and fire controls, for example were all "off the shelf" items).

The natural consequences of small size have been reinforced by the austerity and simplicity of the Israeli military bureaucracy. The IDF, which is perhaps one-third the size of the U.S. Army, has, effectively, two fewer ranks. Whereas the U.S. Army has eleven four-star generals, the Israelis have none, and they have only one three-star general: the chief of staff of the entire armed forces.

Lean organization reflects in part the demands of a conscript-based, reserve-oriented military system initially took in young men and women for only two years (rising to three years for men in 1968). This simplicity reflects itself even in combat organization, as noted above. Because of Israel's size, the relative simplicity of its military chain of command, and its social egalitarianism, ideas for new ways of tackling problems can flow remarkably quickly to the top. The case of the seizure of a new Russian P-12 radar in December 1969, alluded to earlier, is a case in point. IAF photo interpreters sifting through routine pictures noted the camouflaged station, and the same day, a sergeant prompted his superior, a lieutenant, to suggest to the head of IAF intelligence, a colonel, that the station could be snatched by commandos for evaluation, rather than bombed. The colonel went to the commander of the IAF, who agreed, and the next day in turn went to the Israeli chief of staff, who concurred and ordered a paratroop general to plan the seizure, which took place a day later in a complicated but successful military operation—a 48-hour turnaround on a land operation launched on the initiative of a junior air force sergeant, and involving only three levels of command.[42] Most militaries evolve such organizational shortcuts in wartime, to be sure, but few have made them standing operating procedure to the extent the Israelis have.[43] Military traditions of leadership from the front often bring the most senior military commanders to the point of decision, thereby cutting through the layers of bureaucracy that might otherwise stifle new ideas. Not surprisingly, the Israelis pay a price for this style. An Israeli major general was killed on the front lines in the October 1973 War, and another in the Lebanon war. Even in much lower level operations, senior Israeli leaders pay for being at the front. During fighting with Palestinian civilians and soldiers that cost

---

[42]   See the description in Louis Williams, *Israel Defense Forces: A People's Army* (Tel Aviv: Ministry of Defense Publishing House, 1989), pp. 168–174.

[43]   Compare, for example, U.S. targeting procedures for aircraft in the Gulf War. Thomas Keaney and Eliot Cohen, *A Revolution in Warfare? Air Power in the Gulf* (Annapolis, MD: Naval Institute Press, 1996), pp. 124–137.

the IDF eleven dead and fifty-five wounded in September 1996, the dead included four officers (one a colonel), and the wounded included two brigadier generals and five colonels and lieutenant-colonels. Furthermore, the IDF adheres to a tradition of having senior officers bear the burdens of failure when matters go poorly. Following the September 1996 fighting, for example, the chief of staff of the IDF personally relieved a brigade commander and censured a battalion commander for an episode in which half a dozen soldiers were killed.[44] A proclivity to hold higher officers accountable—"for the failure of a company commander, relieve the brigade commander" is a military maxim[45]—makes it easier, one suspects, for junior soldiers and officers to put ideas forward.

Israel's egalitarian culture, an artifact of Zionist ideology, is similarly conducive to ready communication, although as in the United States, military leaders sometimes feel that to overcome such informality they must resort to particularly rigorous forms of discipline. To be sure, the ready use of first names and what strikes American observers as a surprising laxness about matters of uniform and military courtesy belies a discipline that can be harsh and unforgiving (in the regular forces, in particular) on such matters as having dirty weapons, neglecting guard duty, or behaving poorly in the face of the enemy. But the culture of military informality is surely conducive to the broaching of new ideas. Moreover, many soldiers, most of the junior officers, and even some senior ones (reservists on extended tours of active duty) have no career ambitions in the military whatsoever. Having thus little to lose from the point of view of professional advancement, they will frequently make their feelings known to superior officers with a brashness stunning to those familiar with more formal militaries.[46] The egalitarianism of a culture molded by socialist pioneers has, in some respects, receded in the face of Israel's capitalist boom. But the military culture, molded as it was by those experiences, has attempted to retain an informality and openness that it prizes for its own reasons.

---

[44]   Arieh O'Sullivan, "Shahak Fires Colonel over Joseph's Tomb Rescue," *Jerusalem Post News: Internet Edition*, October 23, 1996.

[45]   Gal, "Current Model of the Israeli Officer," p. 21.

[46]   The author of this chapter witnessed such an interaction in Gaza in 1988, between a (reserve) lieutenant-colonel and the chief of staff of the IDF. The latter was berating local commanders for failing to pursue stone-throwing Arab teenagers with adequate vigor; the former got up and, in no uncertain terms, told his superior that he did not understand local circumstances. The discussion was conducted with a vigor that bordered on rudeness, but with complete attention on the part of the senior and complete candor on the part of the junior.

The Social Base

From the outset, Israeli strategic thinkers believed that Israel's ultimate strength resided not simply in the IDF *per se,* but in the social base on which it rested. Israel is a highly developed society and, like all such societies when mobilized for war, can produce an exceptionally sophisticated military machine. Conscripts and recruits in the IDF are well-educated, particularly by comparison with their neighbors. By the early 1980s, some 65 percent of Israelis aged 18–24 had some secondary education, and an additional 20 percent had some postsecondary schooling.

The IDF can, and does, draw on the cream of Israeli youth, who still compete to enter elite units and various specialized and technical branches, such as intelligence. Through a variety of innovative service programs (some of which allow young men and women to complete their bachelor's degree while in the ranks), the IDF can bring the country's finest minds to serve national defense. It would be like the U.S. military guaranteeing a minimum of three years of active duty, and more of reserve service, from the very best college undergraduates—the entering classes of Harvard, Yale, Stanford, Johns Hopkins, and several score of other top-notch institutions. One Israeli program, *talpiyot,* does just this by selecting a handful of outstanding high school students for university education in math or science at IDF expense, followed by rigorous military training and five years of active duty in positions demanding advanced technical skills.

The sophistication of the Israeli social base has other military benefits. Most Israeli conscripts are reasonably comfortable with all manner of electronic and mechanical devices, including the full panoply of information-age tools and toys. Farmers, mechanics, and factory workers are accustomed to caring for sophisticated machines and machine tools. Thus, within days, an army composed primarily of reservists could, in 1973, effectively learn to handle weapons like the U.S. Army's TOW antitank missile, which until then had not been in the IDF inventory. And in 1991, when Israel received Patriot air defense batteries, its soldiers soon began to tinker with a system that they had only just learned to operate. Although the prevalence of high-tech sometimes creates problems—the proliferation of cellular phones in the field, most notably, poses a serious threat to operational security—it provides the Israelis a notable high-tech edge.[47] As one Israeli officer noted, "It's very convenient for me to be able to call my soldiers if

---

[47]   On Israeli use of cellular phones, including their military significance, see Sheldon Teitelbaum, "Cellular Obsession," *Wired* (January 1997), pp. 144–149, 194–196.

they are taking a walk in the city and have them report to me in 15 minutes if I need them."[48]

In many ways, Israel remains in a state of war—with the total mobilization of all social and economic resources that the term implies. Behind the soldiers exists a well-developed economic and industrial base that can supply the Israeli military with many of its wants and develop new products to meet its needs. Although Israel's leaders have studiously attempted to maintain an air of normalcy in their embattled country, its citizens have nonetheless felt the kind of personal stake in national defense familiar to Western publics only during World War II. Israel has, until fairly recently, spent high percentages of its gross national product on defense (up to 25 percent after the October 1973 War)—comparable to, if less than, that of the United States during World War II, and even today, proportionate to the U.S. defense effort at the height of the Cold War. In all other respects it has engaged in the same psychological and organizational mobilization for war characteristic of nations engaged in the global conflicts of the first half of this century. If this mobilization has exacted a price in spirit, cash, and blood, it has nonetheless produced military excellence.

THE SOURCE AND NATURE OF ISRAELI MILITARY CONSERVATISM

The Power of the Old Paradigm

Even in the discussion above we have noted some forces that, despite the IDF's image of constant and daring innovation, induce a certain conservatism in Israeli military thinking and practice—the awareness of strategic stalemate, a sobering awareness of the high stakes involved in failure, and an acute sense of practicality that would not inhibit less immediately threatened states. The IDF mixes the persistent innovation noted above with a generally incremental and conservative approach that fits new techniques, inventions, or operational outlooks into a deeply rooted and relatively fixed military paradigm.

For two decades, Israel's national security doctrine succeeded—at least through the 1967 war, which represented its high point. Since then, its limitations have become increasingly apparent—but never to the point of forcing a high-level reconsideration of its merits, or a repudiation of any of its basic tenets. Many Israeli analysts in fact interpreted the calamity of 1973 as a kind of perverse vindication of this doctrine, which called for a preemptive attack on Egypt and Syria that Israeli leaders had refrained from launching. Had the IDF only acted on the warning it received, attacked, and thereby fought according its

---

[48]   Ibid., p. 196.

doctrine, they claimed, the *mechdal*—the "October earthquake"—would not have occurred.[49] The few military critics—most notably Col. Ya'akov Hasdai, a staff member to the Agranat Commission investigating the war—who saw 1973 as revealing deeper flaws in Israeli doctrine, were shunted aside.[50] The 1982 Lebanon war could be defined as revalidating that doctrine up to a point, in that Israel successfully drove the Palestine Liberation Organization out of Lebanon, only to err in immersing itself too deeply in Lebanese affairs. Even here, the problem seemed to be one of implementation rather than of doctrinal flaws: Ground operations attracted criticism from some Israelis who believed the IDF had moved at a lumbering pace and had thereby failed to reach one of its goals, the Damascus–Beirut highway.[51] Many Israelis felt that their country's passivity in 1991 in the face of Iraqi missile attacks represented another failure to implement the doctrine, but not a reflection on the doctrine itself.

Generations of Israeli officers have grown up with the old doctrine. Until recently—the last few years, in fact—most have found it hard to conceive of any alternative, even as it has of late been subject to a number of serious critiques.[52] The IDF, for all its receptivity to tactical and operational innovation, can be powerfully resistant to more thorough-going reconsideration of its first-order assumptions. Col. Emanuel Wald, an officer commissioned to do an internal study of the army in the mid-1980s, subsequently published an unclassified version of his report in 1987 fiercely criticizing the IDF. The official reaction included prohibition of his speaking at IDF units and his exclusion from reserve duty—punishments lifted only recently.[53] Even well after the Lebanon War, the

---

[49] This was the view of the former chief of staff, Lt. Gen. Chaim Bar Lev, who became the *de facto* southern front commander after the first few days of the war. Chaim Bar Lev, "The war and its objectives against the background of the IDF's wars," *Ma'arachot* (October–November 1978), pp. 2–8 (Hebrew).

[50] Ya'akov Hasdai, *Truth in the Shadow of War* (Tel Aviv: Zmora, Bitan, Modan, 1978) is a powerful collection of essays. On the IDF's response to criticism of this kind, see Gal, *A Portrait of the Israeli Soldier*, p. 182.

[51] See, *inter alia*, Ze'ev Schiff and Ehud Ya'ari, *Israel's Lebanon War*, Ina Friedman, trans. (New York: Simon & Schuster, 1984), especially Chapter 7, "The Lame Blitz."

[52] See most notably, Shimon Naveh, "The Cult of the Offensive Preemption and Future Challenges for Israeli Operational Thought," *Israel Affairs* (Autumn 1995), pp. 168–187; Reuven Pedatzur, "Israel—an Updated Military Doctrine," *Ma'arachot* (June–July 1990), pp. 20–29 (Hebrew); Ariel Levite, *Offense and Defense in Israeli Military Doctrine* (Tel Aviv: Jaffee Center for Strategic Studies, 1989).

[53] Emanuel Wald, *The Wald Report: The Decline of Israeli National Security Since 1967* (Boulder, Colo.: Westview, 1992). The Hebrew version was published in 1987.

belief of many senior officers was that Israel's basic doctrine remained sound.[54] Furthermore, Israel has not escaped the bureaucratic opposition to new systems that other countries have experienced: Even unmanned aerial vehicles were initially resisted by the IAF, and General Tal's conception of the Merkava tank ran into opposition within the army.[55]

It should be noted that the old paradigm assigns the highest priority to the ground forces. Because of Israel's small size and contiguity with potential opponents, the navy, although of high quality, has traditionally had a weak voice in shaping national strategy, and the air force, although much larger and more important, has nonetheless seen its chief role as paving the way for effective action on the ground. One source of change in the future may be the rise of these two services, both of which have steadily extended their reach with the acquisition of new, longer-ranged systems (from Sa'ar V missile boats to F-15Is). Yet, many Israeli officers, including some in the air force, doubt the effectiveness of air action alone to achieve strategic results. The views of ground force commanders dominate much of Israel's military culture—or at least have done so until the present. Where dissent from the central paradigm breaks into the open, it usually comes from journalists, civilian technologists, or reserve officers.

The final part of the old paradigm that retains its grip is the mass army system, that in itself creates a brake on innovation. In the nineteenth century, countries that could not exploit their national manhood thoroughly were at a disadvantage against those who could. Today's armies may find themselves in the reverse predicament—burdened by manpower systems that produce too many recruits serving for short periods of time. Some European states—France most notably—have, in fact, reluctantly discarded conscription to adapt their militaries to a new order of military affairs. For a nation in arms, any new military hardware or concept must be fitted into an army that is heavy with manpower and burdened with the need to equip and train the many conscripts it accepts. Moreover, to the extent that the IDF remains an institution with a social as well as a military mission, it finds it difficult to break away from the mass conscript

---

Upon petition, the chief of the general staff decided in 1992 that a ban on Wald lecturing at IDF events could be lifted. "Ban Off IDF Officer," *Jerusalem Post*, January 31, 1992. It should be noted that many more balanced critics of the IDF viewed Wald's critique as poorly done. For a reaction see Dov Tamari, "Military Intellectual Conservatism in the IDF—Is It Still There?" *Ma'arachot* (October–November 1989), pp. 23–35 (Hebrew).

[54] See, for example, an article by the major general commanding Israel's northern command, Yossi Peled, "The Operational Conception of Israel: Does it Need to Change?" *Ma'arachot* (January–February 1990), pp. 2–5 (Hebrew).

[55] Personal communication, senior Israeli defense scientist, February 1997.

and reserve system. Although not everyone would agree today with the officer who wrote fifteen years ago that "the IDF should be seen not just as an instrument of security but also as the school of the nation, the crucible for our youth, that contributes to the process of the ingathering of exiles," that view still resonates with many in the IDF.[56]

The obvious solution would be for Israel to reduce the length of active military service and trim reserve duty requirements. Such a move, however, would in some ways exacerbate its problem by increasing the churning of soldiers through units and, if anything, raising training costs. Israel's heavy reliance on a reserve-based system similarly has a conservative effect, making it more difficult to retrain the military on new pieces of equipment. As long as the idea of even a semiprofessional army remains out of bounds, there will be limits on the kinds of radical change the IDF can imagine. The institution of near-universal military service has been a powerful rite of passage for young Israelis (men more than women) and a means for acculturation of new immigrants. To step away from its basic principles, no matter how strong the pressure to do so, would mean a major and traumatic departure for army and society alike.

The Influence of *Batash*

The IDF has traditionally distinguished between two types of military operations: *bitachon shotef* ("current security") and *bitachon yisodi* ("fundamental security"). The former (usually abbreviated to the term *batash)* includes responses to terrorist attacks, retaliatory raids, and border skirmishes; the latter refers to big wars, real or potential. More than most armies, the IDF has found itself torn between these two demands, which create conflicting requirements in many areas, and which, during the Palestinian *intifada* that erupted in 1987, became an acute problem. Active duty units (composed primarily of conscripts rather than professionals) routinely find their training for conventional war disrupted by the need to man roadblocks or checkpoints, or simply to preserve order in turbulent streets. Although for some units (primarily infantry) *batash* may have training benefits (e.g., patrolling or small-scale raids), by and large it is a mission that detracts from overall readiness. The psychological frame of mind for many *batash* operations—which, as seen during the *intifada,* requires restraint in the use of deadly force—is often at odds with the aggressiveness that characterizes the IDF at war. And, perhaps most important of all, *batash* absorbs the energies and attention of the senior military leadership. Until fairly recently,

---

[56]   Col. Nissim Solomon, "Education in the IDF: Established Directions and Processes of Change," *Ma'arachot* (July 1982), pp. 32 (Hebrew). Significantly, this article barely discusses the question of professional education within the IDF.

the Israeli land forces had three major commands, North, Central, and South, and no central training and doctrine command. All three regional commands are involved in current security operations, and the burden posed by such operations have only grown over time. For the Israeli Air Force and Navy, of course, *batash* influences fewer of their routine activities, although the air force operates constantly over Lebanon, and the navy maintains constant patrols along Israel's coasts.

The magnitude of the *batash* problem is considerable. In one particularly bad year, 1991, there were more than 4,500 incidents involving Palestinians, including 561 incidents involving the use of weapons (a number that continued to climb in succeeding years). On the northern front, in Lebanon, the Israelis and their South Lebanese Army allies have experienced hundreds of attacks every year by Hizballah guerrillas, resulting in a steady trickle of IDF casualties—at least twenty dead and anywhere between eighty and one hundred twenty wounded every year since 1992.[57] It is only recently, however, that the IDF set up a special anti-guerrilla training school for operations in Lebanon. "This is one of the first times the IDF has acknowledged it is fighting a 'guerrilla' war and actually put that above preparing for a conventional war."[58]

For a number of reasons, the prominence of *batash* predisposes the IDF away from radical views of the future of warfare. For one thing, the combination of current security and the demands of rigorous training for a large-scale war that Israel, even today, must anticipate simply leave very little time for experimentation, rethinking of doctrine, or organizational forms. In making the case for increased use of war-gaming and simulation in the IDF, two senior officers write, "The accumulated experience in *batash*—at least in part—is not relevant to the IDF's preparation for war. More than this, the different commands are likely to draw from *batash* operational lessons whose application in war would lead to severe errors."[59] Both forms of security are simply too deadly serious to be slighted. This is as true (perhaps even more true) for colonels and generals as it is for privates and sergeants. The result is what one reporter terms

> the generation-old disease among Israeli troops. With their modern equipment,
> Israeli soldiers are schizophrenic. On one hand, they are trained to fight a

---

[57]   Statistics from IDF Spokesman's Unit, Information Branch, IDF Web Page http://www.israel-mfa.gov.il/idf/facts.html.

[58]   Arieh O'Sullivan, "IDF Sets Up Anti-Guerrilla Combat Training School," *Jerusalem Post: Internet Edition*, November 28, 1996.

[59]   Lt. Colonel Y and Colonel Y, "Computerized Wargames in the IDF," *Ma'arachot* (November 1995), p. 29 (Hebrew).

conventional war against a conventional enemy and battlefronts. On the other, they and their commanders—and even their commanders' commanders—have been engaged in police action and fighting terrorists for the past 15 years.[60]

Second, the Palestinian *intifada* and, at least until recently, progress in the Arab–Israeli peace process have disposed many senior Israeli officers to brush off conventional warfare as an issue of secondary importance.[61] After a period in which the Israelis could think that a combination of active and passive measures had either intercepted, deterred, or blocked cross-border infiltrators and home grown guerrillas, the *intifada* and succeeding troubles in the 1990s, to include the use of suicide bombing, suggested that the IDF could at best contain such attacks but not stop them. To the extent that such tactics not only persisted, but actually led to large political consequences (most notably a willingness to recognize and negotiate with the Palestine Liberation Organization and, arguably, the 1996 electoral defeat of Shimon Peres and his Labor-led coalition), the IDF had to concede their effectiveness. Almost as successful was the guerrilla war waged by Iranian-backed members of Hizballah in southern Lebanon, a struggle in which Israel has repeatedly suffered minor but painful and humiliating losses.

To some extent, this preoccupation by Israeli military leaders reflects an understandable focus on immediate problems. But it reflects as well a more considered assessment that the IDF, like the U.S. military, has demonstrated such a convincing superiority in conventional warfare that opponents will hesitate to tackle it head on. Rather, adversaries will attempt indirect or asymmetric responses, using forms of conflict that liberal democracies like Israel and the United States will find hard to handle. There is, of course, a substantial risk here: The IDF has not fought a conventional war for fifteen years, and some Israeli officers worry that it is losing the experience and attention to conventional tasks that it requires. Whatever their assessment of Israel's vulnerability to conventional attack, virtually all Israeli officers agree, however, that the problems of cross-border raiding and domestic insurrectionary violence pose problems utterly unlike those of conventional warfare.

---

[60] Arieh O'Sullivan, "Keeping a Watchful Eye," *Jerusalem Post: Internet Edition*, April 20, 1997.

[61] In repeated interviews, Israeli senior officers argued that the problems of *batash*, and in particular, coping with suicide bombers and Hizballah attacks, were likely to dominate the IDF's mission in coming years. To be sure, the IDF would need to maintain its conventional deterrent power, but many of them seemed to believe that the IDF would not need to use it. This perspective, however, may have changed during the past year, as the possibility of a war with Syria is taken more seriously now more than at any time in the past fifteen years.

Anti-Intellectualism

Radical change in the conduct of war, in many cases, is nurtured in bookish militaries—the Germans in this century and the last, most notably. It requires, at some level, groups of officers willing to think in a broad and disciplined way and capable of making imaginative leaps into the future. Substantial change certainly requires some kind of intellectual ferment.

The popular image of the IDF as an army of unusual cleverness is partly, but only partly, right. That there is abundant tactical and operational cleverness is beyond doubt, but this has not translated into intellectual rigor or indeed, a very high valuation of military thought in general. Here again, there are signs of change from the past, but a core anti-intellectualism persists. Unlike many militaries, the IDF has not made a university education a prerequisite for officership, although it has gradually moved to give officers opportunities for abbreviated bachelor's degrees if they decide to make a career of military service. Extraordinarily, by American and European standards, attendance at the command and staff course *(pikud umateh* or Pum—the equivalent of Fort Leavenworth for the U.S. Army or Camberley for the British Army) has usually preceded completion of an undergraduate degree. Pum is, for the majority of Israeli officers, the highest level of military education they will receive, the Israeli war college *(michlala l'bitachon leumi* or Mabal) being a small institution that focuses more on political matters and includes many nonmilitary governmental participants. (In a remarkable act of hubris Mabal was, in fact, disbanded after 1967 and re-established only after 1973.) Thus, at the stage in their careers in which Israeli officers should be ready to engage in systematic reflection about the higher levels of warfare, they do so without the benefit of the basic intellectual training offered by an undergraduate degree—a deficiency only partly offset by the high quality of some Israeli high schools. Pum itself has, traditionally, had a mixed reputation, and the question of its reform, including expansion to a longer and more academic course, is a perennial matter of debate.[62] As late as 1989, however, the commandant of Pum confessed to a tension between his students' desire to get a bachelor's degree and to complete their military studies.[63]

The IDF values higher education, to be sure, but primarily in the hard sciences, in which many officers do obtain advanced degrees. Knowledge of

---

[62] Lt. Colonel Muli, "The School of Command and Staff: a Military Academy," *Ma'arachot* (April 1996), pp. 47–48 (Hebrew) proposes the creation of a two year course.

[63] Uzi Lev-Tsur, "The Plan for Training the Commander at the Command and Staff College: a New Assessment," *Ma'arachot* (May–June 1989), pp. 30–31.

warfare is more often conveyed informally and orally than through a formal doctrinal system like that of the United States.[64] There is a strong defense publishing house and a high quality journal, *Ma'arachot* (loosely translated as "Campaigns"), but here too a certain reduction in intellectual power is noted relative to twenty or thirty years ago. On close inspection, many of the articles in *Ma'arachot* are either translations or (increasingly) produced by academics or relatively junior officers. Fewer senior officers write than in the past—a reflection, perhaps, of a generational change that has brought to the fore a more narrowly focused, professional general officer corps as compared to the more eclectic band of founding fathers of the IDF.

At a deeper level, Israeli officers are suspicious of "big ideas" in the art of war. Acutely sensitive to the predominance of what Karl von Clausewitz called "friction" and "the fog of war," they mistrust grand theories. In a military constantly at war, advancement comes not through educational achievements, eloquence, or intellectual reputation, but through demonstrated success as a field commander. This overwhelming preference for the practical doer *(bitsuist)* over the thoughtful speculator reflects as well the founding labor Zionist ideology of the early part of the century, which self-consciously rejected the caricature of the Jew as a bookish and timid victim for the equally caricatured muscular, fighting farmer and worker who would redeem the land and build a country.[65] Although the strength of such stereotypes has diminished over time, they remain potent. Avigdor Kahalani recalls that of three Israeli officers in his class at Fort Leavenworth after the October 1973 War, none had a college degree. But that struck him as no particular disability in a course that was entirely too academic and focused on higher-level national security issues.[66] Time off for academic work can hurt an officer's chances for promotion.[67] More important, particularly

---

[64] See the remarks by Avigdor Kahalani, a retired brigadier general (now Cabinet minister) who performed brilliantly as a battalion commander on the Golan Heights in 1973. *A Warrior's Way*, p. 147.

[65] See, in particular, Ya'akov Hasdai, "'Operator' *(bitsuist)* and 'Ideologue': Priest and Prophet of the IDF," *Ma'arachot* (May 1981), pp. 41–46 (Hebrew). Hasdai's essay uses a phrase from a famous essay by the early Zionist thinker Ahad Ha'am.

[66] Kahalani, *A Warrior's Way*, p. 263. Curiously, Kahalani does not mention the presence of Vietnam veterans in his class, yet they must have been there in 1978—many with more days under fire than he had.

[67] Gal, *A Portrait of the Israeli Soldier*, p. 169. Not always, however—a number of senior generals have picked up master's and even Ph.D. degrees. Much rests, however, on the personal decisions of the chief or deputy chief of staff, who exercise unusual control over appointments.

in the combat arms, the IDF continues to place the highest possible value on courage, persistence, and leadership: Military intellectual achievement trails far behind.

Resource Constraints and the Price of Technological Advances

The IDF is, by and large, a parsimonious army and hence unlikely to risk large sums of its own money on futuristic or highly uncertain technological systems. Like the U.S. Marine Corps, with which it has some affinities, it generally prefers to innovate in relatively inexpensive ways while waiting for richer forces to make the larger leaps, and then to follow quickly. Israel, as noted above, has not had the resources for great technological leaps in the military realm. When it has attempted such advances (the Lavi aircraft, the Arrow anti-missile system, or the Tactical High Energy Laser) it has usually done so with direct foreign assistance, or it has waited until the technology in question had matured and thus become affordable for a small country. On a small scale, however, Israeli soldiers believe in the merits of being willing to try out "half-baked technologies" in operational environments.[68] The IDF's incremental technological style reflects not only fiscal constraints but a belief that small technological advantages—marginal edges in range, accuracy, or maneuverability—can yield large differentials of combat power.

Typically, the IDF has pursued a pattern of extremely thorough exploitation of old or essentially civilian technologies, coupled with aggressive and continuous marginal improvements. For instance, the Super Sherman was a modified American M4 World War II–era tank, which, though long obsolete elsewhere, rendered useful service to Israel through the June War. Retaining the old hull of the thirty–five ton tank, the Israelis replaced the engine and main armament (swapping the inadequate 75 mm cannon for a 90 mm gun and later a French 105 mm gun) and made a number of improvements to the fire-control system.[69] Similarly, as a way of extending the life of older tanks that would have proven vulnerable to modern antitank missiles, the Israelis took an old idea, reactive armor on tanks (first conceived by the Germans at the end of World War II) and developed it.

Through the June 1967 War, the Israelis retained and cultivated the use of guns in their aircraft, even as the United States shifted to the use of heat-seeking or radar-guided missiles. The older gun technology proved perfectly adequate to Israeli needs, as long as it was in the hands of skilled pilots.

---

[68]   Interview, senior Israeli officer, June 1996.

[69]   Luttwak and Horowitz, *The Israeli Army*, p. 191 and *passim*.

In the early 1970s, the Israelis were similarly late in adopting advanced electronic countermeasures (ECM) for aircraft against radar-guided surface-to-air missiles, preferring instead to rely on simpler electronic countermeasures and evasive maneuvering and low-level attacks on enemy batteries: This led to a less happy outcome and to a swift turn to U.S.-supplied ECM in the early days of the 1973 war.[70]

Israel historically has extracted the maximum out of its air fleet, flying World War II vintage C-47's well after the United States had stopped using them, and using obsolete trainers as second-echelon fighter-bombers. Although Israel has acquired some of the best U.S. aircraft available, in the shape of F-16 C/D and F-15 C/D/E fighter-bombers, it has not merely modified them but has taken older platforms and extended their life considerably. Perhaps the best example of this is the venerable F-4 Phantom, which the Israelis have converted to the Phantom 2000—an overhauled aircraft with new avionics that has guaranteed that Israeli F-4s (and those that they modify for other countries) will continue to have combat roles into the first decades of the next century.[71]

Even where the Israelis appear to have been technological pioneers, a close look reveals the same pattern of aggressive but incremental development of relatively mature technology. In 1982, foreign military observers were much taken by the Israeli use of UAVs in Lebanon. The UAV was, again, an old concept, used by the United States in Vietnam a decade earlier. Where American UAV development, however, had bogged down in the 1970s in a quest for very long ranges, large reconnaissance payloads, and secure communications, the Israelis contented themselves with what were, in essence, model airplanes equipped with cameras.[72] From here, resting on work done in the 1960s, the Israelis gradually evolved more and more sophisticated versions of such platforms. In the end, the Israeli UAVs could not compete with the far more ambitious American programs such as the ill-fated Aquila and the more successful Darkstar—but they did not need to.

An Over-Taxed Senior Leadership

Contributing to the IDF's spirit of conservative innovation is the fact that its senior leadership is, by any standard, terribly overworked. Because of the small size of the country, and because of a tradition of leading from the front, Israeli

---

[70] Ibid., 351.

[71] Glenn E. Bugos, *Engineering the F-4 Phantom II: Parts into Systems* (Annapolis: Naval Institute Press, 1996), pp. 212–213.

[72] Azriel Lorber, "The Mini-RPV Comes of Age," *Miltech* (June 1983), pp. 46–50.

military leaders will appear on location whenever a crisis occurs. They probably spend more time in the field than their European or even their American counterparts. Again, to a greater extent even than their American counterparts, they are continuously engaged in planning and conducting operations—both for current security and the large-scale conventional threat.

Beyond these requirements, however, are two others that eat into the time of the senior military leadership. First, although Israel has a defense ministry, the security system remains dominated by the uniformed military.[73] Senior generals and staffs thus handle many of the issues that in the United States would be the province of civilian under secretaries, assistant secretaries, or a national security council staff. And, in fact, a recent effort to create a national security council apparatus was stymied by opposition from the Ministry of Defense and the IDF, which saw in such a body a threat to their dominance in security issues.

Second, after the 1973 war, senior Israeli officers participated in military disengagement talks with Egypt and Syria, and with the start of the Madrid Peace Process in 1991, senior Israeli officers have been intimately involved in negotiations with the Palestinians and Syrians. At the same time, the IDF's senior leadership, operating in a more critical and open domestic environment, finds itself preoccupied with responding to an ever more inquisitive press—again, at the expense of more traditional military concerns.

SIGNPOSTS OF CHANGE

Notwithstanding such conservatism, some Israeli military thinkers have begun to criticize the old paradigm and to suggest new and different ways of approaching Israeli security. Increasingly, these notions have found expression outside official circles as well, sometimes reflecting internal deliberations that have remained confidential. Academics like Ariel Levite (now in government service), retired military leaders like Shimon Naveh, Knesset members such as Dan Meridor, journalists like Reuven Pedatzur, and technologists like Ze'ev Bonen are examples of creative Israeli thinkers who, to varying degrees, called the old national security doctrine into question. Within the Israeli military educational establishment, some change is evident as well, including the creation of an advanced operational doctrine group at the Israeli war college.

Conditions for a thoroughgoing reassessment of Israeli doctrine are improved by a further fact: The IDF no longer considers itself, and is no longer treated by others, as invincible or infallible. In the wake of the calamity of the 1973 war,

---

[73] For a good survey, see Yehuda Ben Meir, *Civil–Military Relations in Israel* (New York: Columbia University Press, 1995).

Israeli attitudes toward the IDF began to shift and, perhaps more important, so too did the attitude of the Israeli press. From a generally reverential and certainly discreet attitude in military matters, Israeli journalists have gradually developed instead something closer to the critical and skeptical outlook of their U.S. counterparts. This may stem from the October 1973 War and the domestically divisive Lebanon war, which shook the country's faith in the IDF, but it may also reflect the exposure of Israeli journalists to an international press that inundated the country after 1967. Minor scandals and personal politics in the officer corps receive abundant attention in the Israeli press, and few journalists treat the IDF with the deference to which it was once accustomed. At the same time, new sources of defense expertise (primarily in the form of think tanks) have begun to emerge and to offer alternatives to official thinking. To be sure, the Israeli press remains, by American standards, remarkably cozy with and solicitous of government officials and military officers. Nonetheless, although Israeli officers retain a privileged status in Israeli society, neither they nor their doctrines are likely to remain free from the scrutiny of a well-informed press.[74]

In sum, the IDF has produced a culture of conservative innovation that has fostered incremental change, but, until recently, has resisted fundamental transformation. The givens of recruitment, professional military education, and organization, remain largely as they were twenty or thirty years ago, or even longer. According to one source, the IDF's capstone two-volume doctrinal manual dates back to before the June 1967 War.[75] Increasingly, however, the IDF faces a chorus of criticism from those who can knowledgeably make the case for thorough-going change, and has been softened up enough by bruising experience and continuous criticism to consider the need for it. Indeed, there is evidence that elements of its senior leadership believe the IDF requires drastic overhaul. The question remains whether objective circumstances require substantial change, and it is to that subject that this paper now turns.

---

[74] See, for example, the none too friendly treatment accorded revelations that the Israeli general officer corps has grown by more than a third in the last decade. Alex Fishman, "Too Many Generals," *Yediot Ahronot*, February 6, 1995, pp. 12–13; Gidon Alon, "MK Merom: the Number of Senior Officers in the IDF Has Grown by an Average of 33 Percent Since '86," *Ha'aretz*, February 7, 1996, p. 1 (Both Hebrew).

[75] Personal Communication, January 7, 1998.

Chapter 4

The Israeli Revolution in Security Affairs

This chapter will address three questions: (1) Do IDF thinkers discern a revolution in military affairs (RMA) on the horizon that resembles that discussed by U.S. thinkers? (2) To what extent have external and internal forces—acknowledged to a greater or lesser degree by the IDF—created circumstances that might transformation of the IDF? (3) And if there is an Israeli security transformation underway, what are its likely contours?

FROM MOBILE WARFARE TO 'THE SATURATED BATTLEFIELD'

From a structural point of view, today's IDF is still in many ways the army that was created in the late 1970s and early 1980s to fight a war with Syria. Following the 1973 war, and particularly after the 1977 Egypt–Israel Peace Treaty, the Israeli defense establishment developed a variety of technical and operational responses to the challenges of a war on the Golan Heights, and in particular to the emergence of what they termed "the saturated battlefield." Where previously Israel had sought to defeat its enemies by mobile operations and indirect attacks in the open field, it now faced on the Golan a front bristling with modern antitank defenses arrayed in depth, with limited and unpromising avenues for flank attacks.

Every war has left its mark on the Israeli defense establishment. If the 1956 and 1967 wars were models of how the IDF prefers to fight, the 1973 war remains, even today, of paramount importance in shaping the IDF's thinking about warfare. The 1973 war was Israel's conventional worst case scenario come true—a surprise attack on multiple fronts reinforced by expeditionary forces from second-line Arab states. Moreover, many of the operational problems the IDF faced in 1973 it expected to encounter again: a surprise attack; the air force compelled to participate in the land battle despite a lack of air superiority; and the necessity of breaking through dense defenses in the Golan. For all these reasons, a repeat of the 1973 war scenario provided the model for Israeli war planning throughout the 1970s. Planners assumed an Arab surprise attack on multiple fronts, but this time involving forces much larger and more sophisticated than those faced in 1973, because of the massive post-1973 influx of petrodollars. The

Israeli planners also included well-equipped expeditionary forces from the outer-circle Arab states in their wargame scenarios.

The 1973 October war forced a major reassessment of the IDF's ability to obtain early warning to enable the unhindered mobilization of its reserves. The war also drew attention to the role of the tank and airplane in the IDF's force structure in light of the heavy losses suffered by the armored corps and air force during the war. The IDF concluded that the tank and fighter were still essential but that their survivability on the modern battlefield could not be taken for granted. Moreover, because it could not take early warning for granted, and because it expected to face larger, more modern Arab forces than in 1973, the IDF dramatically expanded its force structure. Thus, between 1973 and 1977, the IDF increased its tank inventory by more than 50 percent, its inventory of armored personnel carriers by 80 percent, its artillery inventory by 100 percent, and its combat aircraft inventory by 30 percent, while at the same time doubling the size of its order of battle.[1] Moreover, as a hedge against future surprises, it increased the size of its standing forces relative to the reserves, a tacit acknowledgment that there is a point beyond which quality cannot offset quantity. Although the IDF gave some thought to a radical technological transformation at this time, immediate operational requirements led to a preference for quantity at the expense of a substantial qualitative leap forward.[2] Finally, because Israel expected to face large enemy expeditionary forces in future wars, the IDF began placing greater emphasis on the development of a long-range strike capability, to deter second-line states from participating in future wars or to interdict such forces en route the front.[3]

The Egypt–Israel peace treaty in 1979 and the outbreak of the Iran–Iraq war in 1980 transformed Israel's strategic environment without altering the IDF's primary operational problem. With Egypt no longer an Arab confrontation state, only Jordan and Syria could pose direct military threats to Israel. Jordan itself offered no major threat, although improving Jordanian relations with Iraq caused Israel some anxiety; the Iran–Iraq war left the latter country preoccupied and, for the moment, reduced the threat from that quarter. At the same time, with the

---

[1] Yehuda Wallach, Moshe Lissak, and Arieh Itzchaki, *Atlas of Israel* (Jerusalem: Carta, 1980) pp. 48, 119.

[2] Interview, senior Israeli officer, May 1996.

[3] During the 1973 War, although Israeli air and airmobile forces harassed Iraqi ground forces as they moved through Syria en route the front, they did not have a decisive impact on the deployment of these forces. Zvi Ofer and Avi Kober, eds., *The Iraqi Army in the Yom Kippur War* (Tel Aviv: Ministry of Defense, 1986) (Hebrew).

Soviet Union continuing to provide Syria with weapons, Syria's avowed intention of gaining military parity with Israel seemed within reach. Accordingly, throughout the 1980s and into the 1990s, Israeli military planners focused most of their attention on the possibility of a war with Syria—augmented, after Iran and Iraq stopped fighting, by a substantial Iraqi expeditionary force.[4] Israeli concerns focused in particular on the possibility of a Syrian "standing start" surprise attack intended to retake the Golan Heights—or at least part of it. Israel feared that Syria would exploit its advantage in standing forces (five to six Syrian divisions deployed near the Golan versus one reinforced Israeli division) to achieve gains on the ground before the IDF could mobilize, with a UN-imposed cease-fire then freezing these gains in place. In support of the ground effort, Israelis believed Syrian commandos, strike aircraft, and missiles would attack airfields, armories, and command-and-control facilities to neutralize Israel's air force, disrupt and delay the mobilization of its reserves, and degrade Israel's ability to interpret developments on the battlefield. Simultaneously, missile attacks against Israeli population centers might weaken the resolve of Israeli decision makers and demoralize frontline troops concerned for the welfare of their families. This combination of circumstances would, Israelis feared, let Syria achieve its battlefield objectives during the initial phase of a war.

If Syrian efforts to achieve a cease-fire failed, or if they chose to continue the war to exploit early gains, Israeli planners foresaw the expansion of the war. On the internal front, Syria could encourage Palestinians in the West Bank, Gaza, and perhaps even Israel, to undertake an uprising, thereby disrupting Israeli mobilization efforts and diverting Israeli forces to internal security duties. Likewise, the arrival of major expeditionary forces from Iraq (believed capable of providing eight to ten divisions) and possibly other Arab nations several days after the outbreak of fighting could slow or stop Israeli counterattacks.[5]

The main problem the IDF faced in planning to fight the Syrians was that conditions in the Golan were not conducive to implementing Israel's traditional operational concept, with its emphasis on early offensive action and the indirect approach. The narrow front, the density of Syrian forces there, and the depth of the Syrian fortifications built since the 1973 war limited opportunities for maneuver and raised the possibility that a breakthrough battle would be won only

---

[4]   Interview with Director of Military Intelligence Maj. Gen. Ehud Barak, *Bamahane,* May 30, 1984, p. 10 (Hebrew).

[5]   For an Israeli perspective dating to the late 1980s on the future characteristics of Arab–Israeli warfare, see Maj. Gen. Moshe Bar-Kochba, "Trends and Developments in the IDF's Force Structure," *Skirah Hodeshit,* nos. 3–4 (1988), pp. 30–32.

at the cost of unacceptably high losses. Facing this daunting prospect, Israeli military experts proclaimed a crisis created by the saturated battlefield.[6]

Israel devoted itself in the 1980s to developing equipment and methods to address the problems posed by the saturated battlefield. The particular operational problems of a war on the Golan, combined with the apparent potential of emerging military technologies, spurred a debate about the continued efficacy of Israel's traditional commitment to the offense versus the defense in war. The participants in the debate fell into two camps: traditionalists and reformers. According to the traditionalists, Israel's singular adherence to offensive action was dictated by its strategic circumstance and had stood the test of time. There was, accordingly, no need for change. In the words of one of the most prominent proponents of this line of thought:

> Israel's strategic position . . . demands placing the offensive at the forefront of our strategy. . . . In this category, preemptive war and the offensive are preferable (to) even the shortest possible defensive with a quick transition to the counteroffensive. . . . The answer to the question [which form of war is preferable for Israel] is unequivocal: the offensive in the air, on land, and at sea.[7]

On the other hand, the reformers questioned the efficacy of offensive action and maneuver warfare under conditions obtaining on the Golan—a narrow front with enemy defensive fortifications arrayed in great depth, with the enemy capital located immediately to its rear. Under such conditions, offensive operations focusing on a breakthrough battle could well result in enormous casualties for Israel, could prompt early superpower intervention (because of the proximity of Damascus to the front) while the IDF was still struggling to achieve its objectives. Combat of such character could also leave Israel weakened during the crucial postwar negotiations. The reformers thus offered an alternative to the breakthrough battle. They proposed that the IDF exploit new and emerging technologies—precision munitions, automated command-and-control systems, and day/night target acquisition capabilities—to create new war–fighting options for Israel. According to one proponent of this view, this would entail three elements:

---

[6] See Brig. Gen. Dov Tamari, "Thoughts on Tactics," *Ma'arachot* (May–June 1980), pp. 2–5; Lt. Azar Gat, "On the Crisis of Maneuver," *Ma'arachot* (October 1980), p. 43 (Hebrew); Colonel S., "Who Needs a Pyrrhic Victory? The Principle of Economy of Force—the Basis for a Change in Israeli Doctrine," *Ma'arachot* (February 1983), pp. 34–37 (Hebrew).

[7] Israel Tal, "The Offensive and the Defensive in Israel's Campaigns," *Jerusalem Quarterly* (Summer 1989), p. 47.

1. Deployment for defensive combat. Instead of plastering its forces against an almost impenetrable wall, the main force could be deployed for an economical defense for a period of time while using the air force, navy, and airmobile forces for long-range guerrilla operations against vital systems deep in the enemy's rear. Perhaps that kind of war will not bring about an impressive victory, but we will be able to assure the preservation of our strength for later stages or as a basis for negotiations without absolute dependence on our superpower patron;

2. Vertical envelopment;

3. The use of ground or aerial envelopment maneuvers to force the enemy to redirect his armored forces and anti-aircraft batteries from the front toward the threat, and implementation of the offensive on the front after acquiring air superiority over it and weakening the enemy's forces.[8]

Although the IDF could continue to emphasize preemption, implementation of the latter approach would entail a shift in emphasis from maneuver to fire, and from offensive action to an active defense on the ground—at least during the initial phase of a war.[9] While most Israeli ground forces would remain initially in defensive dispositions, the IDF would initiate massive air and artillery strikes against Syrian troop concentrations and air defenses and, in concert with airmobile operations and naval raids, against vulnerable Syrian rear areas. The purpose of these attacks would be to inflict heavy losses on Syrian front–line units, and to divert second- and third-echelon Syrian units for rear area protection. The air force would also launch long-range preemptive strikes to destroy Syrian ballistic missiles before launch (those that escaped would be dealt with by missile defenses), and to interdict any expeditionary forces en route the

---

[8] Colonel S., "Who Needs a Pyrrhic Victory?" p. 37.

[9] For other Israeli defense thinkers implicitly or explicitly calling into question the traditional offensive orientation of Israel's national security concept, see Saadia Amiel, "Deterrence by Conventional Means," *Survival* (March–April 1978), 58–62; Dr. Zvi Lanir, "The Qualitative Factor in the Arab–Israeli Arms Race of the 1980s," *Ma'arachot* (February 1983), pp. 26–33 (Hebrew); Shmuel Gordon, "Principles of Combat with Precision-Guided Munitions," *Ma'arachot* (April 1987), pp. 22–26 (Hebrew); Ariel Levite, *Offense and Defense in Israeli Military Doctrine* (Tel Aviv: Jaffee Center for Strategic Studies, 1989); Reuven Pedatzur, "Updating Israel's Military Doctrine," *IDF Journal* (Winter 1991), pp. 32–35; and Ze'ev Bonen, "The Impact of Technological Developments on the Strategic Balance in the Middle East," in Shlomo Gazit, ed., *The Middle East Military Balance: 1993–1994* (Boulder, Colo.: Westview, 1994), pp. 148–163.

front.[10] Only after thus preparing the battlefield would Israeli air and ground forces launch the initial phase of the breakthrough battle, shifting and massing fires from stand-off range to create gaps in Syrian deployments.[11] The maneuver phase of the breakthrough battle would begin only after Syrian first-echelon forces had been sufficiently weakened—at least at select breakthrough points— and second- and third-echelon forces reduced by deep-strike systems or diverted to protect vulnerable rear areas. Committed Israeli forces in the Golan or Bekaa could then breach Syrian defenses and defeat Syrian forces in detail through maneuver and close combat, with many fewer losses.

Although it is not clear which school of thought has prevailed in influencing Israeli planning for a war on the Golan, it *is* clear that many systems developed since the 1973 war, and many of the organizational changes in the IDF since then, respond to anticipated operational problems of conflict with Syria. For instance, the problem of breaching the dense Golan defenses spurred Israeli interest in combat engineer equipment and led to the development of armored bulldozers, the Puma engineer assault vehicle, remotely controlled tanks and various means for clearing minefields. Likewise, the imperative of suppressing Syrian air defenses encouraged the development of the Keres (a ground-launched version of the Standard antiradiation missile), Samson and Delilah deception drones, and the Harpy antiradiation attack drone.

The need to rapidly destroy large enemy formations before they could close with IDF ground forces spurred Israeli interest in stand-off precision munitions, sophisticated command-and-control systems, and airborne sensors. The Israelis developed a number of long-range precision weapons. The artillery corps acquired modern fire-control systems and large quantities of self-propelled tube and rocket artillery systems.[12] The Israelis also pursued an all-weather, day/night

---

[10]   The outlines of this approach can be found in statements by Israeli officers dating back to the late 1970s and early 1980s. See Benny Morris, "Changed Options," *Jerusalem Post Magazine,* June 8, 1979, pp. 7–8; Maj. Gen. Israel Tal interviewed in R. D. M. Furlong, "Israeli Lashes Out," *International Defence Review* (August 1982), pp. 1006; James Doyle, "In the Shadow of War: Israeli Generals See Future Clashes Fought on Changed Battlefields," *Army Times,* August 15, 1988, pp. 27, 31.

[11]   Chief Artillery Officer Brig. Gen. Oded Tira, "Artillery: Weapon of Destruction," *Ma'arachot* (September 1983), pp. 15–17 (Hebrew).

[12]   Ibid.; some Israeli officers, in fact, began describing the artillery as an arm of decision, that would destroy large numbers of enemy forces, thereby reducing the size of the maneuver force required to complete the victory.

target acquisition capability using ground sensors, manned and unmanned aircraft, and satellite reconnaissance systems.[13]

The Israeli interest in threatening the Syrian rear encouraged the development of airmobile, amphibious, and naval strike forces. The IDF initiated a modernization program for its CH-53 fleet in the mid-1980s to enable these aircraft to fly long-range low-altitude night penetration missions. Likewise, the IDF's resurrection of the *Givati* infantry brigade in 1983—in addition to addressing the perennial shortage of infantry in the IDF—was intended to bolster Israel's amphibious capabilities, because the *Givati* was initially envisaged to have such a role as a secondary mission. (This mission soon fell by the wayside as amphibious operations in wartime were deemed too risky.) The reequipping of the Israeli Navy has likewise given the IDF new capabilities for striking high-value targets along Syria's shoreline.

During the 1973 war, Israeli air and airmobile forces attacked a division-sized Iraqi expeditionary force en route the Golan heights. This effort succeeded in harassing and delaying the attacking force on its way to the Syrian front, but did not prevent its arrival. As a result of this experience, and the massive military buildup in the outer-ring states after the 1973 War, the IDF devoted significant resources to enhancing its long-range aerial, airmobile, and aerial strike capability to interdict Arab expeditionary forces. The IDF took a number of initiatives along these lines, including upgrading its CH-53s, acquiring aerial refueling capability by converting B-707s into tanker aircraft, and providing its combat aircraft with a long-range low-level night precision strike capability (represented by the acquisition of Lantirn and Litening navigation/targeting pods for its F-16s and F-15s).

By 1990, the IDF had assembled many of the pieces it thought it would need for a conventional war against Syria. It did not look forward to such a struggle, realizing how costly it could prove. Israel had no assurance that it could prevent Syria from disrupting the mobilization of its forces or foiling its counterattacks, or that it could successfully shield its civilian population from missile attack. On the other hand, although the end of the Iran–Iraq war in 1988 and Iraq's bellicose anti-Israeli rhetoric thereafter increased Israel's fears of a renewed Eastern front, the Gulf War of 1991 diminished the threat from that quarter, at least temporarily.

---

[13] One of the main findings of the 1982 war was that the IDF still had problems getting target intelligence to potential shooters. As a result, many opportunities for engaging targets were lost. Reuven Pedatzur, "The Integration of Field Intelligence," *Ha'aretz,* December 14, 1987, p. 9 (Hebrew).

ISRAELI VIEWS OF DESERT STORM AND THE FUTURE OF WARFARE

As previously noted, the Israeli military tradition includes a powerful strain of skepticism. Israeli soldiers tend to shun grand concepts of warfare. This mistrust of grand theories is especially apparent in Israeli views of the Gulf War, views that differ significantly from those of most U.S. military officers and defense specialists. American analysts take as a given the notion that studying Desert Storm can yield important insights into the future of warfare. Given the Gulf War's preeminence in the contemporary debate regarding military affairs (not just in the United States but throughout the developed world), the comparative indifference of Israeli officers toward that conflict is notable. For that reason alone, Israeli views of Operation Desert Storm deserve careful examination.

In the eyes of many Israelis, Desert Storm hardly qualified as real combat. Most tend to view the conduct of the air and ground campaigns against Iraq (as opposed to their outcome) as only marginally relevant to their own security concerns. In a speech delivered in June 1991, Prime Minister Yitzhak Rabin stated the point bluntly: "The Iraq–U.S. confrontation has little relevance for, or can teach us little about, the Arab–Israeli conflict."[14] Israelis tend to emphasize the extent to which the "extremely asymmetrical nature" of the war diminishes its significance. For them, American conclusions derived from the Gulf War are not so much erroneous as uncorroborated. They cite, moreover, the unique character of the adversary and President Saddam Hussein's adherence to a war strategy that rendered the Iraqi army "not only impotent offensively, but also otherwise largely defenseless."[15] They dismiss the ground war as an unnecessary afterthought, "more like a march to collect prisoners and booty, than a combat operation."[16]

No doubt, a measure of professional envy and resentment motivates this Israeli tendency to downplay the significance of Desert Storm. After all, the ease with which the Americans and their allies dispatched Saddam Hussein's massive army can only deflate the IDF's own reputation by calling into question its achievements. The Israeli critique of the Gulf War, however, does not entirely

---

[14]   Yitzhak Rabin, "After the Gulf War: Israeli Defense and Its Security Policy," reprinted in *Yitzhak Rabin and Israeli National Security* (Ramat Gan, Israel: Bar-Ilan University, The BESA Center, 1996), p. 8.

[15]   Ariel Levite, "The Gulf War: Tentative Military Lessons for Israel," *War in the Gulf: Implications for Israel* (Boulder, Colo.: Westview, 1992), p. 148. See also Aharon Levran, *Israeli Strategy After Desert Storm: Lessons of the Second Gulf War* (London: Frank Cass, 1997).

[16]   Aharon Yariv, "Conclusions," *War in the Gulf,* p. 391.

lack merit, and it provides a useful corrective to the common American tendency to overrate the military significance of Desert Storm.

Israelis do concede that Desert Storm represents a major advance in what some Israelis call "sophisticated conventional warfare," and that it offered a demonstration of superior technology and technique against a conventionally armed and conventionally minded opponent. But the operative term throughout is "conventional." In Israeli eyes, sophisticated conventional warfare responds only to a narrow range of threats. Moreover, attaining superiority in this specific form of warfare requires vast resources—precisely when the threats facing Israel are becoming more ambiguous and diverse, and when the country's shifting priorities have reduced the financial resources available to deal with those threats.

The Israelis note that the Iraqis obligingly arrayed their forces in terrain hospitable to precision weapons, remained passive while the United States mustered its military might, labored under the burden of inept strategic and operational leadership, eschewed unconventional methods such as terror or people's warfare, and did not use weapons of mass destruction.[17] They note as well that the United States had the luxury, which Israel lacks, of allowing the opponent not only to seize a large chunk of territory, but then to hold it for some months while a counterblow was prepared.

The Israelis do not, of course, disregard their own Gulf War experience, which served to alert them to the nature of emerging threats. For Israel, the key feature of that experience was that the rear became the front. The Scuds falling in and around Israeli population centers made it clear that the rear no longer stood immune from attack. This reality shook Israeli confidence in its ability to protect its civilian population and provoked a reevaluation of defense priorities, leading to the creation after the war of a Home Front Command.

Israeli analysts are by no means oblivious to the potential of high-technology systems employed in the Gulf War to enhance elements of traditional IDF conventional doctrine: deterrence, early warning, transferring the fight to the enemy's territory, and the pursuit of rapid battlefield decision. Generally, however they have tended to deprecate the military significance of Desert Storm. This tendency informs their reaction to speculation about an emerging RMA. As one analysis has noted, "The Israeli military is inclined to think less in terms of revolutions in military affairs than in terms of unceasing measure-

---

[17]   Ze'ev Bonen, "Sophisticated Conventional War," in *Advanced Technology and Future War,* BESA Security and Policy Studies No. 28 (Ramat Gan, Israel: Bar Ilan University, 1996), pp. 19–30.

countermeasure interactions within a relatively constant military framework."[18] Israelis put little stock in the recent U.S. theorizing about an RMA. The more ambitious technological formulations—Admiral Owens's system of systems, for example—many Israeli officers simply dismiss out of hand as either impractical or, at best, irrelevant to a state that operates under completely different geopolitical conditions than those of the United States. At the most, they say, it reflects not the harbinger of new forms of warfare, but the culmination of changes (e.g., the introduction of precision weapons) that had been under way for several decades.

If this negative reaction to the bolder U.S. visions of an RMA derives from a deep-seated aversion to grand concepts, it is also rooted in clear-headed analysis and judgment. It reflects both decades of battlefield experience and an appreciation of post–Cold War Middle Eastern realities. The great and painful lesson of Israel's recent military history is that conventional military dominance simply invites adversaries to develop alternative methods—popular resistance, terror, guerrilla warfare, and weapons of mass destruction—that may mitigate that advantage or even render it largely irrelevant. Given the diverse forms of politically motivated violence Israel faces, the prospects of achieving decision through adherence to a single overarching military paradigm has become a chimera in the eyes of many Israelis. The notion that a technology-driven revolution can solve Israel's security dilemmas is profoundly at odds with Israeli experience. From the Israeli perspective, therefore, one defect of most U.S. theorizing about the RMA fails the first test of Clausewitz: it describes a vision of warfare divorced from politics.

The Israelis speak here from bitter experience, acknowledging as they do the extent to which many of their own past military practices have been strategically and politically barren.[19] Brilliant military victories—in 1956, 1967, and, after a brush with disaster, 1973—did succeed in preventing the destruction of Israel and have persuaded some former enemies to give up their efforts to destroy the Jewish state. But none of these victories secured lasting peace or even an extended respite from violence. Recognition of the limitations of Israel's own

---

[18]   Patrick J. Garrity, "Why the Gulf War Still Matters: Foreign Perspectives on the War and the Future of International Security," Center for National Security Studies Report no. 16 (Los Alamos, N. Mex.: Los Alamos National Laboratory, Center for National Security Studies, July 1993), p. 61. See also pp. 62, 80–83. This analysis rests on papers and presentations by several senior Israeli officials and retired military personnel after the Gulf War.

[19]   See, for example, Naveh, "The Cult of Offensive Preemption and Future Challenges for Israeli Operational Thought," pp. 168–187.

efforts to translate military power into political purposefulness has made Israelis all the more sensitive to that very defect in current American thinking about the RMA.

Although Israelis challenge American interpretations of the Gulf War's significance and view with skepticism American theories of an RMA, it is not because they view the old military formulas as adequate. The reverse is true. Events are persuading increasing numbers of Israelis that traditional approaches to security have outlived their usefulness, making significant change an imperative. Where Israelis differ from American advocates of an RMA is in the character of that change.

This is reflected in their preference for the term "the future battlefield" *(sdeh hakrav ha'atidi)*. This concept reflects the Israeli view that in the operational realm, warfare will be characterized more by *continuities* than by dramatic or even revolutionary *discontinuities.*[20] In the words of Maj. Gen. Israel Tal, one of the founders of the Israeli tank corps:

> The transformation of an arsenal is a very lengthy and costly process. The revolutionary means enter the craft of war and conquer their place in a gradual way. When these new means have proved themselves in practice, they are already considered regular and "old," and on their doors even newer ideas and means are knocking and threatening their position. Thus the new and the old are continually swirling about one another and refashioning the art of war. This is, so to speak, the dialectic of war.[21]

Although cognizant of the need to innovate continually to maintain the IDF's qualitative edge over conventionally armed adversaries, proponents of the future battlefield emphasize the extent to which those technologies leave the basic geometry of combat unaffected. Weapons become more lethal, their range and precision increase, and command-and-control capabilities improve, but the dynamic by which the outcome of conflict is decided remains largely intact. Such a perspective on the future reflects and fosters a preference for incremental change and for integrating technological advances into existing organizations and routines—rather than experimenting with radically different organizations or methods designed to capitalize on the full potential of technology. In short,

---

[20]   For an example of such thoughtful skepticism, see Maj. Gen. Yitzhak Ben-Israel, "Back to the Future," *Ma'arachot* (March–April 1993), pp. 2–5 (Hebrew). Ben-Israel is in charge of research and development for Israel's Ministry of Defense and is considered one of its most creative thinkers.

[21]   Israel Tal, *National Security: The Few Against the Many* (Tel Aviv: Dvir, 1996), p. 226 (Hebrew).

implicit in the Israeli vision of the future battlefield is a bias in favor of renovating or rejuvenating orthodoxy to save it.

Yet if this preference for the future battlefield is consistent with the Israeli penchant for conservative innovation, in a broader sense Israelis reject the RMA not because it is too extreme but because it is too restrictive. In Israeli eyes, U.S. thinking about the RMA is flawed by the implicit assumption that the RMA is a phenomenon that a small elite can direct or tailor to the advantage of the United States. Israelis criticize the American tendency to characterize their military revolution as a top-down affair. Disagreement on this point is fundamental and relates to the very definition of revolution. In the view of many Israelis, a true revolution—by its very nature—will elude control by any single agency or organization or nation. As one senior Israeli analyst, exasperated with what he viewed as American hubris, has observed: When speculating about an RMA it is essential to remember, "It's not a coup—it's a revolution."[22]

However quick to take issue with U.S. formulations concerning a particular RMA, most Israeli defense experts agree at least on this point: Matters relating to defense and security in the Middle East are currently undergoing profound and far-reaching changes. As a description of these changes, the preferred U.S. characterization—the so-called RMA—is inadequate and misleading. Yet, despite these reservations, Israelis have begun to recognize that there is indeed a revolution in progress.

FORCES FOR CHANGE

A confluence of developments in four distinct areas persuades many Israelis that a fundamental transformation is underway.[23] The first is technological: advances in military technology that do, as many Americans argue, presage important changes in the conduct of "sophisticated conventional warfare." The second is strategic, reflecting the continuing flux in Middle East politics since the Egypt–Israel peace agreement of 1979 and more recently, the progress toward Arab–Israeli peace since 1991. The third is economic, the product of changes in basic Israeli economic policies and the recent, spectacular acceleration of Israeli economic growth. The fourth factor—and arguably the most influential—stems from profound shifts in the make-up and temper of Israeli society. These changes affect Israeli public attitudes toward defense issues and the military, and have

---

[22] Personal interview, Tel Aviv, May 29, 1996.

[23] See, for example, Tal, *National Security*, p. 218. His list includes three factors: (1) the advent of surface-to-surface missiles; (2) the peace process; (3) and the spread of weapons of mass destruction.

begun to redefine the hitherto sacrosanct relationship between the IDF and the Israeli people.

Technology

Technological advances that figure so prominently in discussions about a military revolution elicit from Israelis responses that vary between ambivalence and selective enthusiasm. Although certain technologies promise to reinforce key tenets of traditional Israeli military doctrine—advanced means of intelligence collection and analysis enhance early warning, and standoff delivery systems take the fight to the enemy's territory with minimum risk to Israeli soldiers—Israeli defense experts are decidedly cool to the notion that as a whole these technologies provide a comprehensive solution to the security threats facing Israel.

Nonetheless, there are a number of emerging technologies and systems that promise to offer dramatic payoffs for the IDF as it faces the future battlefield. The most obvious of these, of course, are long-range precision strike systems—the homegrown Spike family of fire-and-forget top-attack antitank weapons; the Nimrod laser-guided antitank missile (several of which can be launched simultaneously at different targets from the same launch vehicle); the Popeye air-to-surface missile; and the air-launched Modular Standoff Vehicle (MSOV) guided container weapon system that carries a cargo of advanced submunitions. These systems permit extended standoff—thus reducing the risk to Israeli soldiers, while potentially inflicting high attrition rates on enemy formations in very short periods of time. Collectively they help account for a noticeable shift in Israeli military thought that increasingly emphasizes fire over maneuver.

Unmanned aerial and ground vehicles have also attracted Israeli attention. Israel has established itself as a world leader in the production and employment of unmanned aerial vehicles (UAVs). It is likely to continue to expand its UAV capabilities for reconnaissance and strike missions. In addition to upgrading short- and medium-range UAVs already fielded, the IDF is likely to field a high-altitude long-endurance reconnaissance UAV to collect information concerning distant targets in Iraq and beyond. The IDF is also likely to expand its existing range of attack UAVs (such as the Harpy) to include systems capable of attacking ballistic missile launchers and missiles during their initial phase of flight. The IDF may also pursue the development of unmanned ground vehicles for employment in high-risk environments. The IDF is also pursuing automated command-and-control systems for sorting, analyzing and depicting data on friendly and enemy forces. This includes, for example, the Combat Vehicle

Integration System for Israeli combat vehicle crews, similar to the U.S. Army's "digitization of the battlefield" initiative.[24]

The IDF is also developing directed-energy weapons, such as the Tactical High Energy Laser (THEL) system currently being jointly developed by the United States and Israel. Each THEL unit will provide the ability to detect and destroy a variety of threats, including short-range rockets, UAVs, long-range cruise missiles, and attack helicopters.[25]

Finally, the IDF is probably devoting great efforts to enhance its electronic and information warfare capabilities. Although these efforts are—for good reason—shrouded in secrecy, electronic warfare played a key role in the IDF's highly successful naval operations during the 1973 war and in its rout of Syrian air and air defense forces in Lebanon during the 1982 war, and it is likely to play a key role in future wars. Furthermore, with a large number of world-class computer software designers and engineers, Israel is likely to exploit the potential for waging information warfare against its enemies wherever the opportunity may present itself. Together, these two capabilities may enable the IDF to defeat its adversaries by neutralizing sensors, jamming communications, or introducing viruses into weapons and comand and control systems.

In several respects, the Persian Gulf War affirmed Israel's qualitative edge over its most likely adversaries. Indeed, by revealing the limited capabilities of Arab armies participating in the war, it suggested that Israel's edge is even greater than previously appreciated. Desert Storm provided clear evidence of the inferiority of Arab tank armies and air forces that rely on dated Soviet equipment and doctrine; such armies have no future on the modern battlefield. This statement applies to Syria just as much as it did to Iraq. For its former clients, the fact that the Soviet Union no longer exists as a cheap source of arms complicates the problem of replacing weapons as they become obsolete. With the exception of the oil-rich states in the Gulf (themselves increasingly strapped for cash), few Arab states possess the economic wherewithal to purchase large quantities of modern arms.

On the other hand, the Gulf War raised disturbing questions for Israel about how to deal with the proliferation of advanced conventional arms in the region. American willingness to provide moderate Arab states with sophisticated arms (for instance, M-1A1 tanks, AH-64 Apache attack helicopters, and Harpoon

---

[24]   Rupert Pengelley, "Battle Management System for Israel," *International Defence Review* (August 1996), p. 10.

[25]   "Israel and U.S. Forces Warm to High-Energy Laser Weapons," *International Defence Review* (February 1997), p. 5.

antiship missiles to Egypt; and M-1A2 tanks, F-15S strike fighters, and multiple-launch rocket artillery to Saudi Arabia), along with Russia's willingness to offer its most advanced weapons at bargain prices (Kilo class submarines with wake-homing torpedoes to Iran; MiG-29 fighters with AA-11 Archer missiles to Syria, Iraq, and Iran), insures that Israel will not be able to take its security from conventional threats for granted.

Even more challenging conventional threats loom on the horizon. The introduction of a new generation of highly accurate, long-range standoff weapons currently under development in the West—such as the French Apache container weapon—could have a significant impact on Arab military capabilities. The Apache is a subsonic-guided cruise missile with a range of 150 km (although plans exist for a 600 km range variant). Carrying either conventional or brilliant submunitions and launched at extended stand-off ranges, Apache will enable Arab aircraft to deliver large volumes of accurate fires against high-value targets in Israeli rear areas—air bases, armories, and command centers—without having to penetrate Israeli airspace.[26] Likewise, the transfer of advanced air-to-air missiles such as the American AIM-120 AMRAAM or the Russian AA-12 Adder to Israel's adversaries could complicate the IAF's efforts to achieve air superiority. Both are highly capable long-range air-to-air missiles with a fire–and–forget capability that will enable Arab pilots to engage multiple Israeli aircraft simultaneously beyond visual range.[27]

The introduction into the region of highly capable rocket artillery systems such as the American MLRS and the Russian BM-30 Smerch could similarly complicate the land battle. (Egypt, Saudi Arabia, and Bahrain have acquired the MLRS; Kuwait has purchased the BM-30.) These systems are capable of rapidly delivering very large quantities of highly accurate and lethal artillery fire over great ranges and large areas, and brilliant submunitions have been developed for both systems. The basic MLRS round has a 32 km range, the BM-30 round has a 70 km range, and each launcher carries a dozen rounds that can be fired in rapid

---

[26] The Apache is very similar to the Modular Standoff Vehicle (MSOV) built by Israel Military Industries and in service with the IAF. "France Selects Apache for Long Range Strike," *International Defence Review* (February 1995), pp. 14–15; Erich H. Biass, "The Guided Dispenser: The Ultimate Attack Weapon?" *Armada International* (April 1991), pp. 6–14.

[27] Enzio Bonsignore and Ian Bustin, "Air-to-Air Missiles: The Battle Begins," *Military Technology* (May 1994), pp. 10–20.

ripples. Moreover, because of their ability to "shoot and scoot," these systems are themselves difficult to target and destroy.[28]

Arab acquisition of advanced attack helicopters could pose a new threat to Israel's armored forces. Egypt and Saudi Arabia now have American AH-64 Apaches, Syria and Egypt have French SA-342 Gazelles, and Syria and Iraq have Russian Mi-24/25 Hinds. Both Syria and Israel used attack helicopters during the 1982 War in Lebanon, as did Iran and Iraq during their 1980–1988 war. So great is the IDF's concern about the attack helicopter threat that it has equipped the Merkava III with a system to track and engage attack helicopters with its main gun.[29]

Finally, the acquisition of modern submarines by potential adversaries could complicate efforts to protect Israel's sea lines of communication and to defend its coastline. Modern diesel submarines can run almost silently, and the Mediterranean Sea—which is characterized by high ambient noise levels—is an ideal arena for undersea warfare. Submarines can interdict surface shipping to Israel or provide platforms for cruise missiles attacks against Israeli population centers. In this regard, the modification of Egypt's four operational Romeo class submarines to accommodate U.S.-produced Harpoon antiship missiles (which have a range in excess of 100 km) is a source of concern to the IDF.[30] Although none of these weapons will fundamentally alter the Arab–Israeli military balance, their acquisition by Israel's enemies means that future wars will be more costly for Israel, and will complicate the challenge of defense for an already overburdened military.

---

[28] N. A. Makarovets, "A Tradition in MLRS," *Military Technology* (December 1993), pp. 74–75.

[29] During the 1982 War, the IDF demonstrated the potential of the modern attack helicopter. Although still experimenting with tactics and concepts of employment, Israel's twelve AH-1 Cobras and thirty MD-500 Defenders destroyed twenty-nine enemy tanks, twenty-six armored vehicles of various types, and thirty other vehicles. Yet, four helicopters were lost (two to friendly fire) in the process—an attrition rate that was considered unacceptably high. Interview with anonymous senior IAF officer, "Bekaa Valley Combat," *Flight International* (October 16, 1982), p. 1111; Karl Schnell, "Experiences of the Lebanon War," *Military Technology* (July 1984), p. 30.

[30] Responding to a growing submarine threat, Israel converted many of its first generation Sa'ar class missile boats to ASW platforms during the 1970s. R. D. M. Furlong, "Israel Lashes Out," *International Defence Review* (August 1982), p. 1006. The development of the Barak point defense missile may likewise have been partly motivated by a desire to protect Israel's coast from sea-launched land-attack cruise missiles.

The Gulf War also exposed troubling Israeli vulnerabilities to nonconventional threats. Relatively crude surface-to-surface missiles, armed with conventional warheads and employed in modest numbers, disrupted Israeli society and the functioning of the Israeli economy on a massive scale. Postwar revelations about Iraq's nuclear effort, the influx of newer missile technologies into the Middle East from China and North Korea, the emergence of a black market in fissile material following the collapse of the Soviet Union, and evidence that regional rogue states continue their efforts to develop weapons of mass destruction all point to a deadly serious threat. The prospect that such systems might be employed again as weapons of terror and intimidation against civilian populations has forced the Israeli government to give heightened attention to civil defense against chemical and biological attack.

In the future, missiles will be more accurate, lethal, and capable of hitting targets over greater ranges. Moreover, the use of solid-fuel motors will increase mobility, shorten launch preparation times, and boost rates of fire, making it even more difficult to locate and destroy enemy missiles. Thus, today's liquid-fueled Scud-B and -C missiles will be replaced by more capable successors, as well as first-generation land-attack cruise missiles possibly derived from long-range antiship missiles such as the HY-2 Silkworm.

Similarly, the nature and scope of nonconventional weapons proliferation in the Middle East will become increasingly difficult to ascertain. Proliferators have improved their skills at concealing their activities by dispersing and hiding production and storage sites. This will make it more difficult to discover new programs, identify relevant facilities, and assess the scope and maturity of programs once they are underway. This will make preventive and preemptive strikes against a country's nonconventional weapons infrastructure more difficult to undertake than in the past and will thereby increase the relative importance of deterrence and defense in dealing with the threat.

Moreover, just as Desert Storm demonstrated the obsolescence of mass armies based on the old Soviet model, so too did it serve to expose certain shortcomings in the IDF. The problems faced by the infantry on the modern battlefield illustrate this point. Israeli infantrymen continue to trundle about the battlefield in M-113 personnel carriers, a vehicle that, however upgraded, nonetheless remains in its essentials a product of the 1950s. The survivability of infantry on a battlefield saturated with modern anti-tank guided missiles (ATGMs), advanced artillery munitions, and air-launched precision-guided munitions is highly problematic—even when the infantrymen are ensconced in the most up-to-date infantry fighting vehicles (IFVs) such as the American M2

Bradley or the British Warrior. The problem of assuring the survival of infantry on the highly lethal modern battlefield thus remains unresolved.

On the other hand, if Desert Storm highlighted the vulnerability of certain elements in the Israeli force structure, it also affirmed the wisdom of the IDF's past insistence on quality elsewhere: in reconnaissance, main battle tanks, precision-guided munitions, tube and rocket artillery, helicopters, strike aircraft, and, above all, sophisticated command-and-control systems. Even where employed in relatively small numbers, such systems made a huge contribution to determining the outcome of Desert Storm. According to the old saw, in war, quantity has its own quality. The Gulf War may have turned that axiom on its head. As exemplified by the massive but ineffective Iraqi army, quantity without quality was all but meaningless.

Yet even if levels of U.S. financial support for Israel remain constant, steep increases in the cost of advanced systems and the acceptable limits of the Israeli defense budget are such that Israel will be hard-pressed to procure large numbers of systems critical to success on the modern Middle Eastern battlefield, most notably attack helicopters, high-performance combat aircraft, and precision-guided munitions. Even funding the upgrades needed to sustain the utility of existing high-tech systems will tax Israeli resources. To be sure, some Israelis believe that in the long run, modern high-tech armies are no more expensive than their low-tech predecessors—although *initial* costs might be higher—because fewer platforms, munitions, and sorties are required to destroy a given target or achieve a given outcome now than were needed in the past.[31] For the moment, this remains a minority view, particularly given the pressing need to modernize a whole host of basic systems, from machine guns to night vision devices.[32] Gaining an adequate return on the investment made in training a high-tech warrior means retaining him (or her) in uniform for an extended period. Given the increasingly attractive opportunities available in the private sector for well-educated and talented young Israelis, that means providing compensation sufficiently generous to persuade military specialists to forgo those opportunities and to remain in the service. This makes a high-tech force even more expensive.

---

[31] Ze'ev Bonen, "The Impact of Technological Developments on the Strategic Balance in the Middle East," in Shlomo Gazit, ed., *The Middle East Military Balance: 1993–1994* (Boulder, Colo.: Westview, 1994), p. 152.

[32] Alon Pinkas, "Army Too Concerned with High-Tech Systems," *Jerusalem Post*, May 24, 1995, p. 2, quoting a senior IDF officer in the Ground Forces Command, who, interestingly, goes on to say, "we have been drawing too many conclusions from the American experience in the Gulf War . . ."

Moreover, high-tech weapons divert scarce national resources from other needs that have a more direct and palpable social benefit. With an economy that has since 1991 enjoyed robust economic growth, it may appear that Israel is in a position to support a policy of both guns and butter. Yet, for reasons to be discussed below, the Israeli polity has become increasingly reluctant to sustain the nation's traditionally high levels of defense spending. Impatient with the traditional practice of pouring the national coffers into defense, Israelis want their tax revenues to address other societal needs as well. Israeli defense analysts and senior officers tacitly accept this new and probably irreversible political reality. The IDF must learn to live with less. Thus, for example, as early as April 1988, Maj. Gen. Ehud Barak, then serving as IDF deputy chief of staff, acknowledged publicly that when it came to defense, "We have almost exhausted the resources of our economy and our society."[33] Nothing has occurred since to persuade IDF leaders to alter that judgment.

By exploiting its strategic partnership with the United States and by tapping Israel's own sophisticated defense industries, the IDF will continue to field a force qualitatively superior to any likely opponent; of that there is no doubt. What is increasingly subject to question, however, is whether Israel can afford to maintain its technological advantage while also clinging to its model of a mass army in which the ground forces field more than 3,500 tanks, 6,000 APCs, and 1,000 artillery pieces. Economic, social, and technological considerations may well bring about a major restructuring in which the IDF shrinks in numbers and in which firepower is of paramount importance. This will result in a shift from an army built on masses of armored fighting vehicles to a smaller force in which attack helicopters and sophisticated artillery systems share center stage with reduced numbers of modern tanks.

Traditionally, the IDF has adhered to the model of the "nation in arms": a short-service conscript force that relies on large, readily mobilized reserves. That such a force is well-suited to exploit the most advanced types of military technology is by no means apparent. To judge from recent U.S. experience, the military establishment best suited to exploit the full potential of military technology is small, elite, and professional. Indeed, absent an unlimited defense budget, advanced-technology and mass are two mutually exclusive alternatives. This reflects both the price-tag of the most advanced weapons systems and the expense of training soldiers to operate those systems. For a generously endowed military, a mass army built around a large number of tanks that cost $2 million to $3 million each may appear to be within the realm of possibility. But not even the

---

[33]   *Davar*, April 21, 1988, pp. 16–17, in FBIS-NES, April 22, 1988, p. 32.

wealthiest nation can afford a mass army built around attack helicopters that cost five or six times as much as tanks.[34] The investment required to produce a tank crewman compared to that required to train a combat-ready helicopter pilot—the difference between months and years of training—only reinforces this gap. Given a force structure consisting largely of tankers, artillerymen, and infantry soldiers who can be trained in three to four months, short-term conscription might be viable. Given a force that relies on aerial systems as its main killing arm—and considering that it takes much more than a year of training simply to qualify a pilot—long-service enlistments become all but mandatory.

Such considerations may help explain the oft-quoted call of Lt. Gen. Dan Shomron, IDF chief of staff in 1987–1991, for a "slimmer and smarter" force, evidence that at least some senior IDF commanders are already signaling their preference for an all-volunteer professional army.[35] Yet for Israelis, such a change would be fraught with difficulties that have little apparent connection to military effectiveness as such. To adopt such a professional model would be to discard what is widely recognized as one of the organizing principles of Israeli society. As a result, the Israeli political establishment has at least until now shied away from addressing the issue directly, maintaining a "people's army" that in a structural sense is increasingly detrimental to Israel's efforts to exploit advanced military technology.

Strategy

Israel in 1998 enjoys a higher level of national security against conventional attack than it has at any other point in the past fifty years. Yet at the personal level, the Israeli people feel *less* secure. And Israeli government officials and senior military officers confront a range of security problems far more complex and confounding than those faced by their predecessors.[36] The result of the peace process is not peace, but new forms of conflict and competition that in some cases transcend military affairs.

---

[34]   By way of illustration, the M-1A1 Abrams tank costs approximately $2.5 million dollars. The cost of an AH-64 Apache attack helicopter is approximately $14 million.

[35]   For a discussion, see Stuart A. Cohen, "The Peace Process and Its Impact on the Development of a 'Slimmer and Smarter' Israel Defense Force," *Israel Affairs* 1 (Summer 1995), pp. 1–21. A few academic economists have already begun to make this case. See Allison Kaplan Sommer, "Reserved Anger," *Jerusalem Post*, August 20, 1993. See also, Shmuel Gordon, "In Favor of Selective Conscription," *Ma'arachot* (1993), pp. 32–37 (Hebrew).

[36]   See Stuart A. Cohen, "Israel's Changing Military Commitments, 1981–1991," *Journal of Strategic Studies* (1992), pp. 330–350.

Why this apparent paradox of increased anxiety and confusion at a time of temporarily reduced threat? If the old Israeli security environment was unforgiving and dangerous, it offered the compensatory advantages of clarity and predictability. At least Israelis knew who and what they were up against. In this regard, the peace process has proved to be a mixed blessing. It has spawned new, sometimes deadly threats while at the same time fostering higher expectations among Israeli citizens of what peace and security should signify. In the new environment, danger remains, but clarity and predictability have given way to ambiguity, uncertainty, and a disconcerting sense that the geopolitical setting in which Israeli military planners must operate remains highly unstable. By virtually any measure, Israel remains the dominant conventional military force in the Middle East. It is not conventional threats, however, that principally worry Israelis, but ones coming from one end or the other of the spectrum of conflict.

At one end of that spectrum lies an emerging class of over-the-horizon threats. These are adversaries that do not share a border with Israel, but that appear bent on acquiring a capability to strike Israel directly. Cruise or ballistic missiles tipped with nuclear, biological, or chemical warheads are the likely weapons of choice. Once the exclusive preserve of the richest or most advanced military powers, missiles today are becoming increasingly available to nations of lesser means. Whether purchased or developed indigenously, such systems offer an apparent shortcut to redressing a conventional military imbalance that might not be overcome even with massive resource outlays. In this category of over-the-horizon threats, Iraq and Iran top the list of suspects.[37]

At the opposite end of the spectrum of conflict lurk "low-end" threats. Recent or ongoing examples of such threats include the Palestinian *intifada*, Hamas's campaign of urban terror, and the protracted struggle with Hizballah in the "security zone" in southern Lebanon. In Israeli military parlance, these are "current security" problems. Yet that bland label is inapt, concealing a costly and debilitating reality. In truth, traditional military practice and doctrine have availed the IDF little in its efforts to devise an effective response to Israel's current security problems. Israeli military excellence has traditionally manifested itself at the tactical and, to a lesser but still significant extent, at the operational level of wars. But such an outcome presumes that the conflict has shape or structure. By comparison, the "current security" challenges that the IDF has

---

[37]   On the threat posed by Iran and Iraq, see Michael Eisenstadt, *Iranian Military Power: Capabilities and Intentions* (Washington, D.C.: The Washington Institute for Near East Policy, 1996) and Michael Eisenstadt, *Like a Phoenix from the Ashes? The Future of Iraqi Military Power* (Washington, D.C.: The Washington Institute for Near East Policy, 1993).

found so daunting in recent years have lacked such crisp definition. In the view of one retired senior Israeli officer, such conflicts represent war not as an extension of politics, but "war as a social phenomenon."[38] In such a conflict, the military outcome of engagements has little intrinsic significance; success does not translate into eventual political advantage. As a result, the IDF's excellence in conventional warfare goes unrewarded.

Rather than preempting current security threats, the IDF has found itself repeatedly surprised by opponents thought to be inferior in strength and skill. Rather than achieving a quick decision, it has found itself bogged down in seemingly interminable conflict. Sometimes it has given in to the temptation to rely excessively on firepower, with results that have been politically embarrassing and militarily counterproductive. Operation Grapes of Wrath, launched by the IDF in the spring of 1996 to eliminate the threat of Katyusha and mortar attacks from southern Lebanon, exemplified both the appeal and the dangers of this approach.

Relying on attack helicopters and self-propelled artillery supported by counterbattery radar, and using UAVs for reconnaissance, Israeli units pummeled villages in southern Lebanon suspected of harboring Hizballah terrorists. They did so with what they claimed was pinpoint precision, thereby deflecting international criticism and propping up the effort's apparent political legitimacy. Best of all from the Israeli perspective, this new method for dealing with a nagging current security problem entailed virtually no risk to Israeli soldiers. The apparent benefits of this approach evaporated on April 18, however, when shells from an Israeli 155 mm battery smashed into a United Nations compound at Qana filled with approximately 800 refugees who had fled their homes to escape Israeli shelling. More than 100 of those refugees were killed, including women and children, with dozens more wounded. The debacle at Qana transformed Grapes of Wrath from an apparent success into a military and political disaster.[39] Perhaps hardest of all for Israeli soldiers, the incident at Qana tarnished the IDF's reputation in the eyes of many Israelis and of the world at large.[40]

---

[38] Personal interview, Tel Aviv, May 29, 1996.

[39] See, Mary Dejevsky, "Error is Ruled Out by Military Expert: Massacre at Qana," *Independent*, May 9, 1996, p. 9, for an edited version of the official report on the shelling, submitted to the United Nations. The Israeli version is summarized in Joris Janssen Lok, "Israel Defends Record on 'Grapes of Wrath,'" *Jane's Defence Weekly*, June 5, 1996, p. 20.

[40] Hillel Halkin, "Claude Lanzmann and the IDF," *Commentary* (June 1995), p. 50, which predates Qana, makes some of these points.

Moreover, the dilemmas of current security are not likely to diminish in the future—a point driven home with acute clarity in September 1996 when Palestinians reacted violently to the Israeli opening of an archaeological tunnel in Jerusalem. Palestinian police fought side by side with civilians in rioting that left eleven Israelis and more Palestinians dead. Indeed, Israel's unquestioned dominance in the conduct of sophisticated conventional warfare will provide a continuing incentive for adversaries to exploit alternative modes of warfare that are cheaper and more accessible.

In a larger sense, the awkwardness of being suspended indefinitely between war and peace has become emblematic of Israel's present-day security situation. It is central to the management of current security problems, like dealing with challenges posed by Hamas or Hizballah. But it also figures in a large way in defining Israel's relations with several of its neighbors, to include those ostensibly removed from the list of Israel's enemies.

Thus, rather than eliminating altogether the potential for such a conflict, the peace process—in the eyes of many Israelis—at most modifies the terms of competition with Israel. Whether or not Syria—thus far the most obstinate of Israel's neighbors—will ever sign on to that process remains an open question. Beyond such doubts about Syria, experience with nations that have already made peace with Israel is not especially reassuring. Israel's partners in peace are not stable democracies. They suffer from overpopulation and poor economic performance. And with some former adversaries, indicators of genuine reconciliation are sparse. Hence, Israelis are wary of viewing existing agreements as permanent.

Egypt is a prime example. Twenty years after Anwar Sadat's dramatic trip to Jerusalem, Israeli–Egyptian relations have not progressed beyond an atmosphere of cool correctness. Given the perceived potential for political instability there, Egypt could one day reassert its claim as leader of the anti-Israel camp. Thus, "war after peace"—the possible revival of open antagonism after peace has been nominally secured—is a scenario that Israel can ill afford to ignore and a contingency that further complicates the problem IDF military planners face.

The full array of security challenges Israel faces today entails a complex mix of contingencies: protracted current security problems that defy easy resolution through military means; the danger, albeit reduced, of conventional attack by traditional adversaries; outer-circle states wielding weapons of mass destruction; and the fear of "war after peace" instigated by former adversaries whose embrace of peace appears less than ardent. Dealing with each of these four major security problems requires Israel to maintain different kinds of forces:

- To deal with current security concerns, the IDF needs high-quality special operations forces and well-trained and -equipped infantry, preferably regulars rather than conscripts, for border security duties and preventive, preemptive, and retaliatory purposes.
- To deal with traditional conventional threats—at the moment apparently limited to Syria—the IDF's current force structure is generally adequate: a conscript-based army centered on large combined arms tank formations, supported by a high-quality tactical air force for a war in a confined theater.
- To deal with the threat posed by outer-ring states, the IDF needs to invest heavily in capabilities that provide for strategic early warning, protection against missile and air attack, and long-range strike aircraft, ballistic and cruise missiles to hit targets well outside the Levant.
- Finally, to deal with the revival of hostilities with current partners in peace— Egypt, for example—the IDF will wish to conduct a conventional defense far from Israel's borders. Ensuring that such a battle will occur deep in the Sinai will put a premium on having airmobile antitank units, and armored formations supported by tank-killing helicopters and aircraft for a war characterized by far more maneuver than a war with Syria.

To be sure, substantial overlap would exist between each of these forces. For example, high-quality special operations units and precision-guided munitions could play a role in all four cases. The point, however, is to suggest that the wide range of contingencies that Israeli planners must consider creates a demand for new capabilities or capabilities that previously figured only marginally.[41]

If the Israeli people were prepared to subordinate all other considerations to security, with all that would imply in terms of sacrifices and social priorities, perhaps Israel could muster the wherewithal to create an army capable of responding to all four notional categories of threat described above. As we shall see, however, that is not the case in today's Israel. That disparity—between a strategic environment that is becoming more complex and a society that is assigning a higher priority to non-security interests—lies at the core of Israel's security dilemma.

---

[41]   For a senior IDF officer's concise summary of the multi-faceted security challenge facing Israel, see the comments of Maj. Gen. Matan Vilna'i, former deputy chief of defense staff, published in "Country Briefing: Israel," *Jane's Defence Weekly,* June 19, 1996, pp. 53–54.

The Economy

The third factor transforming Israeli views regarding security is economics. Impelled by a surge of economic growth, Israel is changing in ways both exhilarating and, for some, highly disconcerting. For the moment, Israel remains an odd and yet attractive blend of a society in which the exotic (to an American) sights, sounds, and smells of a developing country jostle with an emerging identity that is sophisticated, affluent, and thoroughly Westernized in its tastes and aspirations. Yet long-term co-existence between the two is likely to prove difficult.

Thanks to the unprecedented economic boom of recent years, Israel is a society in rapid flux. For today's visitor to Tel Aviv or one of its many bustling suburbs, the dominant impression is of sprawling apartment blocks under construction, of streets clogged with late-model automobiles, of battalions of shoppers charging in and out of stores that feature glitzy Western-style goods, of young Israelis crowded into "milk bars" and fast-food restaurants, and of the ubiquitous cellular telephone, no longer a convenience but something like an essential feature of life in modern Israel. Israel is booming.

The data describing recent Israeli economic performance support such impressionistic evidence. Since 1990, the Israeli economy (gross domestic product, or GDP) has grown at an average of more than 6 percent per year, a performance all the more impressive considering the large influx of immigrants from the former Soviet Union during that period. That influx of relatively young and well-educated new citizens imposed short-term resettlement costs but within a few years added energy to the Israeli economy. Some 1,800 high-tech firms have sprung up in well-planned industrial parks around Haifa and Tel Aviv, achieving exports by 1995 of $9 billion per year, double what they were only five years earlier.[42] By 1996, Israeli per capita GDP exceeded $15,000, putting Israel just slightly behind the United Kingdom, Italy, and France.[43]

In short, Israel is well on its way to becoming a consumer-oriented market economy, a society in which there is not only a good deal of money to be made, but in which the making of money is acquiring a new respectability. According to Uzia Galil, founder of Elron, a holding company that does $1 billion in business annually, 90 percent of that in exports, "Many, many years ago in Israel the

---

[42]   John Rossant, "Out of the Desert, Into the Future," *Business Week*, August 21, 1995, p. 78.

[43]   Central Intelligence Agency, *The World Factbook 1996*, at www.odci.gov/cia/publications/nsolo/wfb-all.htm. It should be noted, however, that since mid-1996, the rate of economic growth has slowed.

connotation of making money was negative. That has changed. The fact is that money as a measure of entrepreneurial success is getting more deeply rooted into society."[44]

Rapid economic development with the concomitant spread of consumer-oriented values has implications for security in three different respects. First, it reduces popular willingness to sustain the high levels of defense spending that have been standard throughout most of Israel's history. Israeli spending on defense as a percentage of GDP has fallen sharply since the mid-1970s for a number of reasons, including a diminished sense of threat, redirected national priorities, and rapid economic growth. More important, Israeli defense spending has stagnated in real terms throughout this period.

Figure 1.
Israeli Defense Consumption as a Percentage of Gross Domestic Product[45]

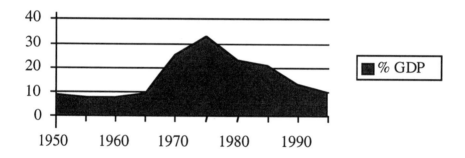

The election of Binyamin Netanyahu as prime minister and the Likud Party's return to power in 1996 have not reversed that trend. Netanyahu's first budget imposed a further 3 percent cut in real defense spending, reducing direct defense expenditures to only 10 percent of GDP, the lowest level in decades (though some of this was reinstated in early 1997 in response to concerns about a possible

---

[44]   Gwen Ackerman, "Israel Growing into Role of High-Tech Player," *Austin American-Statesman,* February 5, 1996, p. C3.

[45]   State of Israel, Central Bureau of Statistics, "Defence Expenditure in Israel 1950–1995" (Jerusalem: Central Bureau of Statistics, 1996), p. 37. These figures should be used with some caution, since they do reflect certain choices about what to measure; they are, however, indicative.

war with Syria). Netanyahu's second budget continued this trend, trimming an additional one percent from the defense budget.[46]

The second implication for security is that economic development is redefining the aspirations and motivations of younger Israelis. Traditionally, among Israeli occupations, military service has ranked first in prestige and has been viewed as providing the essential path to achieving prominence in other fields such as politics and business. Increasingly, however, opportunity, influence, and excitement lie in the private sector. Business is where the action is—and increasing numbers of Israelis in recent years have become wealthy. For many, the ideal of Israel as a historic Zionist enterprise has become passé. "Each person wants his own big villa and car," remarks Israeli historian Benny Morris. "What's important is what's good for the individual, not for the collective."[47] As a result, young Israelis today, not unlike their contemporaries throughout the West, are less interested in self-sacrifice than in self-realization.[48]

Finally, the private sector also offers an alternative outlet for nationalist aspirations: This is the third way that economic growth affects security considerations. As one Israeli sociologist puts it, "You can fulfill yourself not by serving in the army, but by serving your nation on the export front or the computer front."[49] For growing numbers of Israelis, the global economy has become the chief arena in which the competition between nations plays itself out. From this point of view, that Israel manufactures its own main battle tank or maintains a powerful air force matters less than the fact that it now ranks second globally in the number of companies traded on the New York Stock Exchange. The real issue is no longer what Israel must do to survive but what it must do to

---

[46]   James Bruce, "Arms Buys Safe as Israel Cuts Defense by \$260m," *Jane's Defence Weekly,* July 17, 1996, p. 17; Ed Blanche, "Netanyahu Deals Blow to IDF with \$57m Cut," *Jane's Defence Weekly*, July 30, 1997, p. 5.

[47]   Quoted in Glenn Frankel, "Israeli Army, Society Slip Out of Step," *Washington Post*, August 5, 1996, p. 1.

[48]   The shift from a culture of self-sacrifice to a culture of self-realization may also be eroding the toughness that has figured prominently in the national character of Israel. The panicky reaction to Gulf War missile attacks suggests that Israeli civilians are less willing to "pay the price." More recently, in response to a handful of suicide bombing incidents, the Israeli government temporarily caved in to public demands that soldiers be provided to guard each and every public bus in the country—a highly dubious use of military manpower. The threat of civilian casualties on even a modest scale may well be emerging as Israel's Achilles' heel.

[49]   Dr. Oz Almog, quoted in Arieh O'Sullivan, "The Waning Image of the IDF," *Jerusalem Post*, August 9, 1996.

flourish economically in a highly competitive world. Given this perspective, the traditional Israeli willingness to support high levels of military spending has dwindled and competes with an insistence on government policies that will enhance the nation's ability to hold its own in the global marketplace.

Society

Whatever the impact of the new military technology, of the shifting strategic context in the Middle East, or of economic growth, one of the most far-reaching challenges to traditional Israeli security practices and institutions is emerging as a by-product of changes in Israeli society. This concern led Chief of Staff Lt. Gen. Amnon Shahak, in his eulogy to the slain Prime Minister Yitzhak Rabin, to undertake an anxious review of the relationship between the IDF and Israeli society. "How far have we gone, my commander, from the days when the IDF uniform was a source of pride, a source of honor."[50]

To a greater or lesser extent, all military doctrine serves political and social as well as strictly military purposes. This has been notably true in the case of IDF. Now various changes in Israeli society—demographic, cultural, and religious—are making elements of traditional doctrine either irrelevant or counterproductive. The old model of a militia-based people's army may well have outlived its usefulness and may soon be obsolete, both in terms of its military suitability and in terms of its long-standing role as cornerstone of national unity.

Long viewed as above politics and beyond criticism, the army today is well on its way to becoming just another institution. Viewed in retrospect, that tendency had its origins in the aftermath of the October 1973 War, the conflict that first exposed chinks in the armor of the IDF that a mere six years earlier had seemed invincible. Certainly, it became evident by the time of the Israeli invasion of Lebanon in 1982 and the ensuing unhappy occupation of southern Lebanon. Having said that, it is only with the events of recent years—notably the Palestinian uprising of 1987–1993 and the Persian Gulf War of 1991—that the essential relationship between the IDF and Israeli society has undergone significant change. This is most immediately evident in the changing relationship between the IDF and the media.

As elsewhere in the developed world, the Israeli news media have become increasingly aggressive and intrusive. Defense and security issues are no longer accorded special treatment and the IDF is no longer permitted to evade critical scrutiny. Young Israeli reporters and editors refuse to practice the self-censorship

---

[50] "The words of the Chief of Staff Amnon Shahak at the memorial service for Yitzhak Rabin," *Ha'aretz,* October 31, 1996 (Hebrew).

common among their predecessors. For journalists whose exposure to combat extends only to "dirty wars" like the 1982 incursion into Lebanon or the *intifada*, security is more a beat to cover than an epic of national survival. As a result, a younger generation of editors and reporters delight in skewering the IDF, exposing instances of waste, incompetence, and malfeasance, and even revealing military secrets.[51] Israeli officers, long accustomed to gentle treatment, have not adjusted easily to the media's changing attitude. And yet, this is only one manifestation of change in the hitherto sacrosanct relationship between the Israeli military and Israeli society. Others, although less obvious, are even more important.

The fabric of Israeli society is changing in ways that are fundamental. Israel is no longer a grand socialist experiment, having moved since the late 1960s in the direction of a market economy, a trend accelerated in the 1980s and 1990s. Israelis who, in the past, would have expected to work for the state in one way or another, now work for privately owned firms. The Israeli ideal—never Israeli reality, to be sure—is no longer defined by the *kibbutz*. Increasingly, Israelis live in suburbia and commute to office blocks in congested cities where their days do not differ substantially from those of their counterparts in Western Europe or the United States. Where young Israelis once affected (if they did not entirely feel) a disdain for the softness and materialism of American culture, they now embrace everything from McDonald's to Madonna with uncritical enthusiasm. These broad developments have enormous implications for the way that Israelis view military service and the army itself. Israel's new preoccupation with the achievements of those engaged in private enterprise has the ancillary effect of puncturing the aura of prestige surrounding the IDF and in particular the officer corps. The authority of the high command, hitherto unquestioned on matters touching however remotely on national security, has been diminished. The assumption that the IDF must have first call on the human and material resources of the nation no longer carries the weight that it once did. For individual Israelis, military service is no longer a prerequisite for gaining entry into the upper echelons of social and political life.

These changes in social attitudes have a direct effect on the willingness of young Israelis to serve in the army. Although there has been no large-scale resistance to conscription as such, there is evidence of a growing tendency among draft-eligible Israelis to contrive physical or psychological excuses to

---

[51]   See, for example, a very American-style story: Arieh O'Sullivan, "IDF Using Soldiers as Guinea Pigs in Nerve Gas Tests," *Jerusalem Post: Internet Edition*, January 9, 1997.

avoid military service.[52] Although more than adequate numbers of high-quality volunteers are still available to fill elite units, conscripts overall manifest a growing inclination to avoid service in the less glamorous combat branches (armor and artillery), not to mention combat support and combat service support units. *Sayeret o nayeret* ("commando or paper pusher") is said to be the motto of some Israeli youngsters, who want either the challenge of the elite units or a comfortable office job in Tel Aviv, but not the grinding, often boring work of IDF units engaged in routine field duties. The deputy chief of staff has acknowledged a "lack of motivation to serve in combat field units," and when Defense Minister Yitzhak Mordechai recently asked a group of recruits where they wanted to serve, one (anonymous) draftee shouted, "the rear!"[53]

Even crack units have seen their share of troubles. In January 1998 a company of soldiers in the *Golani* brigade, a tough unit with a glorious and grim record, mutinied against their commander, who had deprived older recruits of customary privileges. Not surprisingly, the mutineers were arrested and expelled from the unit. In the new Israel, however, the episode did not end there: Parents of conscripts protested loudly, eliciting from the general in charge of Israel's Northern Comand a promise to reexamine the sentences and possibly readmit to the brigade those mutineers who apologized for their actions. The episode echoed an even more troubling case a year earlier, when a company of reserve paratroopers abandoned an outpost in southern Lebanon in protest against a similarly martinet-like officer.[54]

Indications of a drop in soldier motivation have provoked concern—publicly expressed—that the IDF may be losing its vaunted fighting edge.[55] The IDF's regular surveys of young people on the verge of conscription seem to bear out

---

[52]   See, for instance, Ya'akov Erez "'A 21 Profile' is No Longer an Embarrassment," *Ma'ariv Weekly Supplement*, August 23, 1996, p. 1ff. The reference is to a "profile" that gives its holder an early discharge on grounds of unfitness for service.

[53]   Steve Rodan, "Vilna'i: IDF Prepared for Syrian Attack," *Jerusalem Post: Internet Edition*, December 27, 1996; O'Sullivan, "Waning Image," p. 9. The head of the IDF's Planning Branch, Maj. Gen. Shaul Mofaz, recently confirmed this trend. Arieh O'Sullivan, "IDF's Planning Branch: The 'What If' People," *Jerusalem Post,* September 13, 1996, p. 11. "The drop in motivation is not a product of the army," he insisted. "It is a product of processes in Israeli society."

[54]   See Arieh O'Sullivan, "IDF Meets Formidable Foe: the Jewish Mother," *Jerusalem Post*, January 4, 1998; Amos Harel, "Apologetic Golani Rebels Get Shorter Sentences," *Ha'aretz English Edition*, January 7, 1998.

[55]   Leslie Susser, "Going Soft?" *Jerusalem Report*, September 5, 1996, pp. 18–20.

leaders' anxieties: One survey found 93 percent of secular Israeli youth in 1986 planned on being drafted, compared with 75 percent, less than a decade later.[56]

This decline in zeal affects the reserves above all. For major contingencies, Israel has always placed heavy reliance on the instant availability of large combat-ready reserve formations. Toward that end, reserve duty in Israel has always been demanding, with an obligation for all physically fit males to serve until age 54 and with active training typically amounting to a month each year— not counting mobilization for emergencies. Yet, if arduous by the standards of most other nations, reserve duty in Israel has also been viewed as integral to citizenship, a moral obligation to be neither dodged nor shirked.

That may now be changing. Unlike the 1950s and 1960s, when reserves were mobilized for conflicts lasting only days or weeks, the "emergencies" for which reservists have been activated in recent decades have been protracted and at times morally problematic. The IDF high command has learned that reserve formations organized and trained for conventional operations are not necessarily well-suited for missions that involve pacification or low-intensity combat in a densely populated urban setting. For their part, reservists have come to resent the fact that the burden of duty necessitated by current security contingencies has fallen unevenly. Although certain units, such as infantry battalions, have drawn repeated assignments to the West Bank and Gaza or along the security zone with Lebanon, other units go scot free.[57] In addition, in a society increasingly responsive to the attractions and imperatives of a market economy, many Israelis see the price exacted by Israel's system of reserve service—and its disruptive impact on other career pursuits—as unacceptable. According to a report released in mid-1996 by Israel's state comptroller, for example, absenteeism among reservists has reached 20 per cent in some combat units and 40 per cent in some non-combat units.[58] According to a classified report cited by an Israeli newspaper in September 1996, "tens of thousands" of reservists "are evading service for what officers consider illegitimate reasons."[59] As one indicator of waning

---

[56]   Arieh O'Sullivan, "Youth Less Willing to Serve in IDF," *Jerusalem Post,* May 7, 1996, p. 2.

[57]   As an indication of the growing inequity of reserve service, according to one scholar, at present in the IDF "as much as 60 percent of the burden of all current reserve service is borne by just nine percent of the available complement." Stuart A. Cohen, "The Peace Process and its Impact on the Development of a 'Slimmer and Smarter' Israel Defense Force," *Israel Affairs* (Summer 1995), p. 3.

[58]   *Jane's Defence Weekly* (May 8, 1996), p. 19.

[59]   Arieh O'Sullivan, "Reserve Commanders Declare War on Service Evaders," *Jerusalem Post,* September 11, 1996.

motivation, a recent IDF survey indicated, "Half of Israeli men say they would not do reserve duty if they were not forced to do so."[60]

In short, Israel finds itself entering a new security environment that imposes new requirements on citizen-soldiers, requirements for which part-time soldiers may not be especially well-suited. At the same time, citizen-soldiers are less willing to fulfill even the level of commitment that their fathers and grandfathers had supported. The army's response has been to de-emphasize the reserve system, lowering the maximum age ceiling for reserve service for combat units from 54 to 42 and reducing the frequency with which reserve units are activated.[61]

Nor are effects of social change limited exclusively to conscripts and reservists. Regular officers are not immune to the changes in national priorities and collective motivation within Israeli society. In a booming economy, business executives and lawyers may displace the officer corps from its position atop the ladder of social prestige. With Israel's survival (apparently) no longer in jeopardy, the nation's best and brightest no longer feel the same obligation to commit themselves to a life of military service. As a result, the civilian sector is now drawing quality away from the officer corps—precisely when it is becoming increasingly important for the IDF to develop a generation of officers who are not only brave and resourceful warriors but also flexible, imaginative, forward thinkers.[62]

But if Israelis are distancing themselves from the principle that every citizen has an obligation to participate in the nation's defense, the IDF itself is contributing to that change. The metamyth undergirding the Israeli way of war is that the IDF is a true "people's army." According to the central premise of that myth, apart from a small number of the truly unfit and of those excused for religious reasons, every Israeli youth, male or female, serves in the army. Actual practice, however, diverged from this ideal. In the early 1980s, only 88 percent of 18-year-old males and 62 percent of all 18-year-old females were actually conscripted.[63]

---

[60]   Arieh O'Sullivan, "Poll: 50 Percent of Reservists Would Opt Out if They Could," *Jerusalem Post,* September 11, 1996.

[61]   Stuart A. Cohen, "Small States and Their Armies: Restructuring the Militia Framework of the Israel Defense Force," *Journal of Strategic Studies* (December 1995), p. 82.

[62]   This is not a new complaint, however: Maj. Gen. Meir Pa'il made such arguments as long ago as the early 1970s.

[63]   Moshe Nativ, "IDF Manpower and Israeli Society," *Jerusalem Quarterly* (Summer 1984), p. 140.

Recently, however, exemptions from conscription and early discharge of conscripts have increased even further, so much so that the ideal of universal service is itself becoming unsustainable. Without fanfare—indeed without acknowledging that it is departing from past practice—the army has adopted a system of de facto selective service. According to Israeli press reports, approximately 83 percent of eligible males currently serve, though another 15 percent of these receive early discharges for various reasons.[64] This drop stems from three factors. First, the huge influx of immigrants from Russia since 1990—which helped swell Israel's population by more than 20 percent in a half dozen years—has expanded the pool of draft-eligible youths well beyond the army's requirements. Second, the army has raised its standards—the mental and physical prerequisites to entering active duty—in effect eliminating from consideration substantial numbers of young Israelis who in earlier years would have been inducted.[65] Third, the army has become more generous in issuing exemptions to those wishing for whatever reason to avoid service. The Israeli military, which still depends on a draft system predicated on the need to put every able-bodied male under arms, has more men than it knows what to do with, partly because of demographic changes over the years. In 1950, Israel had fewer than a quarter of a million men of military age; in 1975, perhaps half a million; and today, close to 900,000—a better than tripling of the manpower base.[66] As all armies know, and as Israeli leaders acknowledge, underemployed soldiers breed trouble.[67]

The fact that Israeli women too are subject to conscription has been an essential component of the IDF's image of as a true "people's army." Yet when it comes to actual practice, here too the drift away from the ideal of universal service is apparent. In recent years, the term of service for female conscripts was reduced from twenty-four to twenty-one months. Even so, only an estimated 50 percent of women actually serve.[68]

Yet there is another sense in which the military contribution of Israeli women is in flux, a change that further suggests of the way shifting attitudes in Israeli

---

[64]   Clyde Haberman, "Israelis Deglamourize the Military," *New York Times*, May 31, 1995, p. A10.

[65]   Cohen, "Small States and Their Armies," pp. 82–83.

[66]   State of Israel, Central Bureau of Statistics, *Statistical Abstract of Israel*, years indicated.

[67]   Yitzhak Rabin made this point to the Knesset foreign affairs and defense committee in 1993. Dan Izenberg, "Army Considers National Service for Men, Women," *Jerusalem Post*, November 30, 1993, p. 12.

[68]   Frankel, "Israeli Army, Society Slip Out of Step," p. 1.

society at large are calling into question practices that were previously accepted as inviolable. Much as it has in the United States and elsewhere in the developed world, the politics of gender has begun intruding into Israeli military affairs. And as has been the case with the U.S. military establishment, the IDF has found itself obliged to accommodate the desires of women intent on pursuing careers— including military careers—regardless of traditional gender-defined boundaries. Confined in the past to administrative and clerical roles to "free up" men for combat, female Israeli conscripts are increasingly resistant to being consigned to what many regard as mere busy work. Simultaneously, other women, led by a cadre of career officers, are demanding the removal of bars that prevent women from serving in combat specialties.[69] The IDF is currently in the process of implementing a ruling of the Israeli Supreme Court issued in November 1995 ordering that women have the opportunity to qualify as pilots in the air force.[70] The politics of gender has other dimensions as well. Israeli courts recently compelled the IDF to grant survivor's rights to the companion of a prominent homosexual officer.[71] Quite aside from the challenge (entirely familiar to the U.S. military) to traditional attitudes about gender and sexuality, these episodes reveal yet another trend: the increased intrusion of courts into the IDF's daily affairs.

From the point of view of an army high command that does not need and cannot afford the entire annual cohort of Israeli 18-year-olds, the shift away from true universal service makes eminent sense. Yet, from another perspective, adjustments to the practice of conscription also mirror and may serve to endorse a decline in the general willingness of Israeli youth to serve. In political circles and the media, this decline in motivation among would-be conscripts is acknowledged and openly discussed.[72] But in tampering with a practice that has until recently been viewed as sacrosanct, senior IDF leaders are further complicating an already complex national security picture. Suddenly, the lack of

---

[69]   Louise Lief, "Second Class in the Israeli Military," *U.S. News and World Report* (May 22, 1995), p. 47.

[70]   James Burke, "Israeli Military Moves towards Equality," *Jane's Military Exercise and Training Monitor* (April–June 1996), p. 5.

[71]   Esther Hecht, "Ruling against IDF Sets Gay Rights Precedent," *Jerusalem Post: Internet Edition,* January 13, 1997.

[72]   On a report concerning declining motivation rendered to members of the Knesset's Foreign Affairs and Defense Committee by the IDF chief of staff, see Alon Pinkas, "17 Percent of Eligible Males are Exempted from Military Service," *Jerusalem Post*, March 30, 1995, p. 3. In addition, see James Bruce, "Poor Discipline Blamed for Surveillance Exercise Fatalities," *Jane's Military Exercise and Training Monitor* (April–June 1996), p. 15.

military service no longer carries with it the stigma that it once did in Israeli society. As more and more role models—notably, rock stars and athletes—rise to prominence without ever having worn a uniform, the imperative of serving in the IDF erodes further.[73] Talented young Israelis no longer see the absence of military service as an impediment to their own prospects of future success. Thus, for example, in the current Knesset, 30 of 120 seats are filled by members who lack any military experience. Indeed, in some quarters, the lack of such experience is perceived as an emblem of daring and of independence from traditional norms.

Few officers are willing to entertain publicly the prospect that the IDF may one day abandon conscription altogether (though privately, some acknowledge the advantages of such a step). But the general trend points toward a largely volunteer system that sustains a professional army. In effect, the army is drifting away from the concept of a people's army, despite the profound implications, military and otherwise, of such a change and without entertaining any national debate that an issue embodying the essence of Israeli citizenship surely deserves.

Paralleling the decline in motivation among conscripts and reservists is evidence of a shift in the motivation within the officer corps. Thus, the IDF has felt compelled of late to devote increasing attention to issues of officer pay and benefits such as housing and education. The hope, apparently, is that assurances of generous compensation can stop the talent drain.[74] But such blandishments are likely to be self-defeating. Their real effect is to undermine further the traditional military ideal, displacing the concept of service to the state in favor of a new ethos that is occupational in character. Furthermore, when it comes to material compensation, the army is unlikely to win a competition with the private sector. The attempt to do so is producing unanticipated but worrisome results. The requirement to spend more on personnel has exacerbated the impact of recent cuts in defense spending as a percentage of GDP. In 1984, personnel costs absorbed 19 percent of the defense budget; by 1991, they absorbed 39 percent of the defense budget; and today, the IDF spends 48 percent of a shrinking budget on salaries.[75]

---

[73]   One sign of the times is the career of Aviv Geffen, Israel's most popular rock star, who boasts on stage about his avoidance of military service. Frankel, "Israeli Army, Society Slip Out of Step," p. A16.

[74]   Cohen, "Small States and Their Armies," p. 84.

[75]   R. A. Kaminer, "Israel Reveals Unprecedented Level of Defense-Budget Details," *International Defence Review*, January 1994, p. 20; Leslie Susser, "Going Soft?" *The Jerusalem Report*, September 5, 1996, p. 20.

In a sense, all of these developments—the intrusive media, the growing preoccupation with private concerns, the diminishing motivation for military service, even the evidence of bureaucratization of the officer corps—stand as a tribute to the progress that Israel, fifty years into its existence, is finally making toward becoming a normal state. Yet if there is truth in that analysis, it does not by any means tell the whole story. Israel today is a variant of what Samuel P. Huntington has termed a "torn country."[76] The nation's Jewish population is divided into a number sharply antagonistic camps. In addition to the traditional divisions between Jews of European and those of Middle Eastern origin, and between recent immigrants and the native-born, there has arisen greater tension between secular and religious Israelis. This gap goes beyond the tension between ultra-Orthodox Jews (who, because of quirks in the Israeli political system, receive exceptional financial support and wield disproportionate power over certain aspects of daily life) and all others. Many Israelis aspire to continue the process of making Israel into a prosperous, modern, secular society anchored culturally and economically if not geopolitically in the West—a kind of Hebrew-speaking California. Other groups, traditional though hardly fundamentalist, seek a more religious and more nationalistic society. Defense policy and the role of the IDF figure prominently as battlegrounds in this internal conflict.[77]

From the point of view of the militant religious right, the IDF's record of service as an obedient and responsive instrument of state policy in the last few years has been anything but commendable. Leaders of this nationalist camp have not hesitated to use the most inflammatory language to denounce the army for its role in carrying out government policies opposed by the religious parties. Thus, for example, when the government tasked the army to prevent the establishment of new illegal Jewish settlements in the West Bank and Gaza following the September 1993 signing of the Oslo Accords, critics in the religious parties sharply criticized the IDF high command. The effect of such criticism, until very recently completely unknown in Israel, has been to further the process of dislodging the IDF from its position as the focal point of national consensus.

---

[76] Samuel P. Huntington, "The Clash of Civilizations?" *Foreign Affairs* (Summer 1993), p. 42.

[77] A good summary of their diverging views may be found in Gad Barzilai and Efraim Inbar, "The Use of Force: Israeli Public Opinion on Military Options," *Armed Forces and Society* (Fall 1996), pp. 49–80. For a profound look at this issue, see Stuart A. Cohen, *The Scroll or the Sword? Dilemmas of Religion and Military Service in Israel* (Amsterdam: Harwood Academic Publishers, 1997). This conflict has been fought out even in the rewriting of the IDF's code of ethics. See Tzvi Hauser, "The Spirit of the IDF," *Azure* (Spring 1997), pp. 47–72.

The religious right's interest in questioning the role of the IDF also translates into politicization of a more direct sort. When it comes to the broader trend of reduced enthusiasm for military service, the modern religious right (as opposed to the ultra-Orthodox Jews, who generally shun the uniform) constitutes an exception to the rule. Indeed, according to a poll conducted by researchers at Bar-Ilan University, young Israelis from religious families display "a greater motivation to volunteer for elite combat units than do young men from secular families."[78] Thus, according to one Israeli analyst, in today's IDF, 30 percent to 40 percent of conscripts in elite units come from religious families.[79] When the former chief rabbi of the armed forces and of Israel publicly urged soldiers to disobey government orders to remove settlers from the West Bank—if and when such an order would come—more than one commentator and some former military officers began to question the reliability of religious soldiers.[80] Events have yet to bear out their fears and may never do so. But it is certain that the noticeable growth in the number of religious officers will change the flavor of an IDF dominated in its early years by a considerably more leftist and secular leadership. Modern Orthodox youth, who generally take a harder line on foreign and defense policy than their peers, stream into preparatory one year programs designed to steel their souls and harden their bodies for military service. Fifty percent of the graduates of one such academy completed officer training, and more than two-thirds ended up in elite units of one kind or another.[81] Although some secular IDF officers applaud the advent of these well-motivated and disciplined youths into the service, others deplore it. One former chief of military

---

[78] Arieh O'Sullivan, "Poll: Decline in Army Motivation Starts at Home," *Jerusalem Post*, September 10, 1996, p. 1.

[79] Personal interview, Tel Aviv, May 27, 1996.

[80] In December 1993, Rabbi Shlomo Goren declared that for soldiers a directive to assist in evacuating the West Bank "would be an order against the commandments of the Torah." Such an order would be "a rebellion against Moses, against the Torah, against Judaism, and against the Almighty, and it must, absolutely must, be rejected and refused." Michael Parks, "Israeli Rabbi Urges Troops to Disobey Army," *Los Angeles Times*, December 20, 1993, p. A1. It should be noted, however, that several prominent religious figures and religious Knesset members publicly dissented from this position, as did the religious commander of the IDF Officers School, Col. Elazer Stern, on grounds that such rulings threatened the cohesion of the army, and thus ultimately the existence of the state. Alon Pinkas and Sarah Honig, "Rabin Slams Rabbis' Call to Soldiers," *Jerusalem Post*, April 19, 1994, pp. 1, 4; Herb Kernon, "Rabbis: Halacha Forbids Moving Army Bases from Judea, Samaria," *Jerusalem Post*, July 22, 1995, pp. 1, 2.

[81] Arieh O'Sullivan, "Guns and a Prayer," *Jerusalem Post*, January 31, 1997, p. 12.

intelligence growls, "The kippa [the skullcap worn by religious Jews] is a visible symbol which is not just an expression of observance, but an open political statement which says they have undergone political indoctrination. And that is dangerous."[82]

THE ISRAELI SECURITY REVOLUTION

There is within Israel a debate, or rather several distinct debates, about the various forces for change that we have identified. Regarding the military–technical sphere, most Israeli officers do not believe the debates portend an RMA—at least not in the way the term is understood by Americans. Nonetheless, some important Israeli military thinkers and officers have begun to talk of an impending revolution of some kind. For instance, nearly ten years ago Maj. Gen. Ehud Barak, then the deputy chief of staff talked about implementing in the IDF "a revolution begot through evolutionary means," though he provided few details about the precise nature or content of this revolution.[83] Within the IDF and the Israeli defense establishment, there have appeared in the past decade and a half several schools of thought on this matter.

According to one school, the main changes that need be made are conceptual—that is, doctrinal. According to one proponent of this view, the IDF, "which is still based on armor, mechanized infantry, and air power," could meet the challenges of the future battlefield with "the war materiel at its disposal" and without changing "the structure of its forces," provided it were to "bring about revolutionary change in existing doctrine." The author advocates a change in the IDF's war-fighting doctrine, from one emphasizing costly breakthrough battles, the destruction of enemy forces, and the seizure of territory, to one emphasizing defensive combat—with offensive operations following only after the enemy has been weakened. One result would be the conservation of force to enable Israel to undertake postwar negotiations from a position of strength.[84]

A second school emphasizes the need for both doctrinal *and* structural change. One proponent has criticized the IDF's "cult of the offensive" with its emphasis on heavy armored formations—at the expense of a more balanced force structure—employed to achieve the physical destruction of enemy forces in

---

[82]   Ibid., p. 14.

[83]   According to Barak, this revolution would yield "partial results" in "3–5 years" and would "ripen" when the IDF "produce(d) the weapons and prepare(d) the battle doctrine for the future battlefield" in "8–10 years." *Davar*, April 21, 1988, pp. 16–17, in FBIS-NES, April 22, 1988, p. 32

[84]   Colonel S., "Who Needs a Pyrrhic Victory?," p. 37.

wartime. Rather, the IDF should formulate "universal operational doctrine" embodying both offensive and active-defensive approaches. Such a doctrine would emphasize not the "mechanistic . . . destruction of the opposing forces," but rather "a systematic approach to disrupt [the enemy's] ability to accomplish its ends," and would result in a more balanced force structure involving a mix of both "armored" and "air mechanized" forces combining mobility and striking power.[85]

A third school—which more closely approximates Admiral Owens's system of systems—sees future warfare dominated by "the tactics of [target] destruction" made possible by combining precision-guided munitions with sophisticated command-and-control systems. Future battles will be won by the side that "most rapidly locates enemy targets and allocates them to its own units." Crucial to this effort is the integration of command-and-control elements into a "single super-system" that will have a "real chance of piercing the [fog of war]" because of its ability to identify enemy and friendly forces rapidly and precisely. The challenge facing the IDF, then, is to create such a "super-system."[86]

Finally, a fourth school holds that the main thrust of contemporary military developments involves "inserting sophisticated equipment and ordnance into existing platforms within present force structures" and the creation of command-and-control architectures "suitable for fast data fusion from various sources" and "rapid sensor-to-shooter connection." This will enable a more efficient waging of "sophisticated conventional warfare," but *not* a true revolution, which will occur only after the "massive transition to radically new major platforms." In the meantime, the future battlefield will be characterized by a greater role for attack helicopters and "platforms capable of fighting mainly by indirect fire."[87]

Each of these approaches, however, is primarily a military–technical response to military–technical challenges or opportunities. The challenges that Israel currently faces, however, have deeper roots and broader implications, that—in their totality—herald a full-fledged *revolution in security affairs*. This Israeli revolution in security affairs will proceed in a context in which conflict is ill-defined, possibly protracted, and occurs in a far more complex political environment than in the past; in which the population as a whole becomes

---

[85]   Naveh, "The Cult of the Offensive Preemption," pp. 168–187.

[86]   Zvi Lanir, "The Qualitative Factor in the Israeli–Arab Arms Race of the Late 1980s," *Ma'arachot* (February 1983), pp. 26–33 (Hebrew).

[87]   Ze'ev Bonen, "Sophisticated Conventional War," in *Advanced Technology and Future Warfare,* BESA Security and Policy Studies No. 28 (Ramat Gan, Israel: Bar Ilan University, 1996), pp. 19–30.

increasingly impatient and intrusive in military affairs; in which the incompatibility of maintaining a high-tech force and a people's army become increasingly difficult to reconcile; and in which highly unpredictable adversaries brandishing weapons of mass destruction lurk ominously over the horizon. The impact of this revolution in security affairs is likely to make itself felt in a number of ways. It will transform the basis of Israeli civil–military relations. It will serve as midwife to a new operational concept that will be at once more realistic and more modest in its expectations. Finally, it will reintegrate politics and military policy in new and somewhat unsettling ways.

The change in civil–military relations may well be the most controversial and difficult result of such a transformation. The concern, voiced privately by a handful of active and retired IDF officers, that there is a growing sense of "alienation" that divides the army and society in Israel, is overstated. Israeli society and the IDF are not headed toward estrangement or outright antagonism. Having said that, the unusually intimate relationship that has prevailed since Israel achieved independence, along with the extraordinary deference accorded the army, is fast becoming a thing of the past. As the autonomy previously enjoyed by the IDF is curtailed, civil–military relations in Israel are becoming "normalized." As a result, future Israeli civil–military relations are likely to resemble those of other advanced democracies: complex, contentious, and inextricably linked to the overall domestic and international political context. Yet at the same time, the adjustments that occur will make the civil–military relationship once again congruent with the new social and political realities of Israel.

By confronting Israel with an expanded range of threats—including some that conventional military means cannot solve—the new security environment robs the traditional Israeli way of war of much of its former salience. For the IDF, the imperative of deterring over-the-horizon attack, while also engaging in protracted low-intensity conflict, diverts attention from contingencies in which it would fight in its traditional style. The means and the doctrine employed with such great effect to win lightning victories in 1956 and 1967, and to recover from near catastrophe in 1973, may not be obsolete in all cases, but they do not cover the full range of contingencies to which the IDF must be prepared to respond.

Among other distinguishing features, the force that supersedes people's army will place less emphasis on the operational level of war that has been an abiding fixation of the IDF. No longer will operational requirements override strategic considerations, as occurred in 1967 and 1982. The IDF already finds itself locked in conflicts in which the slightest error or miscalculation at the tactical level—the misdirected artillery shell or the individual soldier provoked into violating rules of engagement—can have explosive strategic and political ramifications. Yet if Israel is entering an era in which force in its own terms will no longer be used to decisive effect, it may also acquire new opportunities in which force married to coherent strategy may achieve greater political benefits than have the IDF's many battlefield victories.

After decades of animosity, sacrifice, and bloodshed, the Israeli people are increasingly "beleaguered, war-weary, and impatient" to have an end to conflict.[88] At the same time, the opportunities and rewards of affluence have begun to redefine success and status in Israeli society—and to provoke a backlash among those who believe that Israel should be something more than just another prosperous, highly secularized nation-state. Israeli military history has turned a corner, embarking upon a new post-heroic age in which Israeli warriors are likely to find moral clarity and epic undertakings to be in equally scarce supply. As a result, the IDF finds itself today obliged to perform tasks that possess neither the martial glory, say, of a June 1967 War, nor the heroic resonance of an Entebbe rescue. Internal security, counterterrorism, counterinsurgency operations: Such is the dirty work that increasingly defines the lot of the Israeli soldier. For Israel as a whole, the military's changing role forms an integral part of a larger effort to adapt to a radically changed world, but the blessings that derive from that effort will be mixed at best.

To what kind of armed forces will the Israeli revolution in security affairs give birth? One can imagine several possibilities that are likely to combine some or all of the following elements.

The Abandonment of Universal Military Service

It is unlikely that Israel will ever find it possible to shift to an all-volunteer force. During the Cold War, the United States and Great Britain could neither afford, nor recruit to sufficiently high standards, professional forces numbering more than one percent of the population. This would, in the Israeli case, yield an unacceptably small force of perhaps 50,000 men and women. But historical experience suggests that a selective service–type draft, in which only a portion of the draft-age cohort of men serve, begins to lose popular support once something like half of the eligible population are no longer required to serve.[89] The IDF may try to postpone the day of reckoning by gradually reducing the term of military service, but it has, thus far, stubbornly fought cutting service time from three to

---

[88]   Efraim Inbar, "Israel: the Emergence of New Strategic Thinking," *International Defence Review (Defense '95)*, p. 95.

[89]   Eliot A. Cohen, *Citizens and Soldiers: The Dilemmas of Military Service* (Ithaca, N.Y.: Cornell University Press, 1985).

two years, and for good reason. Lowering service time while sustaining a high inflow of recruits will merely increase the turbulence in units and do nothing to abate training costs.

More promising will be a reduction in reliance on reservists, something that has already begun. Here too, however, a price will be paid, as the IDF loses the services of experienced citizen-soldiers. More likely, a hybrid system will emerge in which the principle of near-universal service is retained, but with very different tracks—a period of basic training followed by Swiss-style reserve duty for the average soldier, a longer three-year term of service for volunteers (who might receive various financial incentives to enlist) and longer contracts still for professional soldiers, whose numbers have already risen and can be expected to continue rising in the years to come. Such an overhaul of the system of military service, however, will have radical consequences for the place of the military in Israeli society, for the composition of the IDF, and for the self-image of its officer corps.

A Reduction in Force Structure

As noted above, the IDF, more than most militaries, has had to confront the tension between quality and quantity. On the whole, however, Israel will probably shift over time to emphasizing quality at the expense of quantity, particularly in its ground forces, which are, in relative terms, the least technologically advanced branch of the IDF. It will do this for financial reasons (the cost of tanks, modern artillery, and attack helicopters will make mass difficult to achieve), but it will move slowly—in part because Israel's reliance on a large reserve component (which trains for only several weeks per year) makes change difficult, and in part because its uncertain security situation makes radical change dangerous.[90] Moreover, as the Israeli security perimeter shifts outwards, toward Iran and beyond, the country is likely to require increasingly costly systems that can reach and do effective damage to enemies at considerable distances from the Levant. But the systems involved—long-range strike aircraft such as the F-15I, for example—will be costly and hence few in number.

A Rebalanced Force

Although its long romance with the tank and the fighter-bomber is hardly over, the IDF has evolved into a more complex military, deploying a sophisticated artillery arm, a large helicopter fleet, attack and reconnaissance UAVs, and an air force and navy capable of striking far afield. In the IDF of the future, therefore, it

---

[90] See Tal, *National Security*, p. 225, for a critique of the notion of a "small and clever army" advanced by Chiefs of Staff Daniel Shomron and Ehud Barak.

seems likely that the role of the tank and the fighter-bomber will change somewhat. Attack and transport helicopters will take on much of the maneuver role once played exclusively by the tank, and the IDF will create airmobile forces equipped with large numbers of antitank weapons, capable of attacking the Syrian army's rear, wearing down advancing units of the Egyptian army in the western Sinai, or opposing the Iraqi army in eastern Jordan, far from Israel's borders.[91] Likewise, attack and reconnaissance UAVs will assume some of the missions formerly fulfilled by manned aircraft. Although the IAF will still support the ground forces, it will play an increasingly independent role, hunting surface-to-surface missiles or striking nonconventional weapons-related facilities in neighboring states and beyond. The navy will retain much of its independence, though it will assume a more prominent role as a strategic strike force.

A different kind of rebalancing may occur if Israel gradually shifts responsibility for current security operations to more professional units. During the *intifada*, the IDF made a self-conscious decision to fight the Palestinian insurrection with regular active duty and reserve units, rather than by relying primarily on specialized counterinsurgency forces. The IDF was not certain that it could afford to create what would, in effect, be a separate armed force for counterinsurgency operations, and it questioned the wisdom of doing so. It paid for this decision in a variety of ways, including declining morale and disrupted training. In the end, increased reliance was put on specialized units (particularly undercover and Border Guard units) for some of this work.

At the same time, it should be noted that a transformation of the IDF may occur unevenly, with some branches (the smaller, more technologically intensive air force and navy, and perhaps some segments of the ground forces) pressing further into the realm of high-technology weaponry, leaving large parts of the armed forces behind. This high-tech core may take on the more difficult tasks of *batash* (current security) and carry the burdens of the more sophisticated kinds of conventional warfare (e.g., attacks on enemy missile batteries), although leaving routine current security and mobilization for all-out war to the mass of the IDF. Such an "uneven revolution" would pose new challenges for the IDF in the areas of training and morale.

---

[91] Naveh, "The Cult of the Offensive Preemption," pp. 180–183; Shimon Naveh, "Defending Israel in the 21st Century: Operational Implications of the Emerging Strategic Reality and the Revolution in Military Affairs," unpublished paper, June 1996, pp. 9–21.

An 'Americanized' Officer Corps

The IDF has begun to recognize that its officer corps will require an overhaul in the coming years—to include the provision of academic training earlier in the careers of its officers and a more generous compensation package to compete with the civilian sector. Accordingly, it has begun to imitate some features of the American approach to officer education and compensation. The IDF's officer selection and training programs guarantee it a supply of proven and talented leaders—such is the result of selecting officers only after they have completed a year or two of service in the enlisted ranks.[92] But it is clear to many Israeli observers that the current educational system is inadequate. Proposals have been put forward to convert the command and staff school to an advanced two-year course, and perhaps eventually to a military academy, complete with academic degrees.[93] Experimental programs along these lines have been attempted, including *ofek* ("horizon"), a program that puts officers on a fast track to battalion command, with expanded opportunities for academic study. Today some 40 percent of Israeli lieutenants have some post-secondary academic education—twice the ratio of a decade ago, but still far from the nearly 100 percent figure of other militaries.[94] The consequences for civil–military relations from the increasing professionalization of the Israeli officer corps, including its array of special perquisites, are as yet unknown but may well prove to be significant.[95]

New Operational Concepts

The IDF's operational concepts are swathed in secrecy. This is because Israeli military thought is highly concrete. Israel's doctrine for breaching defenses,

---

[92]   For a description of Israeli officer selection and training, see Reuven Gal, *A Portrait of the Israeli Soldier* (Westport, Conn.: Greenwood, 1986), pp. 90–110.

[93]   See Reuven Gal, "For a Review of the Current Model of the Israeli Officer," *Ma'arachot* (February 1996), pp. 24–25 (Hebrew); Lt. Colonel Muli, "The School of Command and Staff: A Military Academy," *Ma'arachot* (April 1996), pp. 47–48 (Hebrew).

[94]   Stuart Cohen and Ilan Suleiman, "The IDF: From People's to Professional Army," *Ma'arachot* (May–June 1995), p. 6ff, reprinted in *Armed Forces and Society* (1995), pp. 237–251.

[95]   They have already attracted more than a little unfavorable attention. See, for example, Nadav Zeevi, "The Guarded Secrets of the IDF," *Ha'aretz Supplement*, November 8, 1996, p. 18ff., which is a detailed and none-too-friendly description of how the IDF compensates senior officers.

suppressing air defenses, or attacking mobile missile launchers is tailored to deal with very specific operational problems and enemies. Israeli operational concepts resemble keys carefully crafted to fit particular locks, rather than a general approach to the problem of opening doors. It is highly unlikely that there could be an Israeli equivalent of the U.S. Army's Field Manual 100-5 (Operations)—a generic operations manual prescribing common principles and basic methods. There are, however, a number of areas where Israel will exploit new and emerging technologies to develop new operational concepts.

- *Enhancements to Israel's border security arrangements in Lebanon.* The IDF has long grappled with the problem of securing its northern border against terrorism and protecting its forces in southern Lebanon from guerrilla attacks. Part of the solution has been the creation of an integrated border security system employing sophisticated remote sensors, ground and aerial surveillance systems, and human intelligence networks to provide special forces, infantry units, and attack helicopter crews with real-time early warnings of hostile activity. Likewise, the IDF has developed sophisticated countermeasures to deal with command-detonated car bombs. Of primary interest here are how the Israelis integrate the various sensors, some of which in the American system would be "national," others "theater," and yet others "tactical" assets; and how the IDF coordinates different types of forces, employed in accordance with a uniqely Israeli integrated operational style.

- *The IDF's concept for ballistic missile defense.* The IDF approach to missile defense will be similar to the way that it approached air defense suppression after the 1973 War: a comprehensive approach that integrates air, ground, and naval forces to create attack capabilities to supplement active and passive defensive measures. Heavy emphasis is likely to be placed on using special forces, attack helicopters, strike aircraft, and attack UAVs to destroy launchers on the ground and to hit missiles during the boost phase of flight, thus reducing the burden of anti-ballistic missiles and civil defenses. Likewise, the navy—which possesses the Barak point defense missile—is likely to have a role in defending the coast against cruise missile attacks coming by way of the sea.

In press interviews, Israeli officers indicate that had the IDF acted against mobile Iraqi missile launchers in 1991, their approach would have involved a combination of special and conventional forces on the ground, cued by unmanned reconnaissance aircraft, working in conjunction with rotary- and fixed-wing combat aircraft overhead. By way of comparison, the U.S. coalition's campaign against Iraqi missiles consisted primarily of disparate special operations and air forces operations—coordinated in most cases, but not integrated into a harmonious whole.

• *Aggressive exploitation of unmanned aerial vehicles.* If there is one common technological thread in evolving Israeli operational concepts, it is the use of UAVs for a variety of purposes. Israel pioneered the use of UAVs in the late 1970s and early 1980s and will build on its comparative advantages by investing heavily in UAVs. The IDF has likely developed both short-range and long-endurance UAVs for intelligence and strike missions. Moreover, it has probably developed novel and unique concepts for employing UAVs to support not only naval strike, long-range airmobile, and air defense suppression operations, but also offensive counterair operations and Scud-hunting operations. Although the air force may resist the use of UAVs to displace manned platforms, this opposition is far less evident than in other countries, including the United States.

• *Extensive employment of electronic and information warfare.* The IDF is likely to use electronic warfare means on an extensive basis, exploiting its relative advantage in high-tech electronics to cripple its enemies' ability to fight. It is also likely to engage in information warfare whenever possible. Press reports that Mossad hackers have tried to intrude into Hizballah's web site, and that the Palestinian terrorist group Hamas has used the Internet to transmit encrypted orders and instructions to its operatives, indicate that information warfare may already be a reality. Israel's heavy reliance on high-tech weaponry, advanced electronics, and computers, however, may make it more vulnerable to information warfare than are its enemies. As a result, as much effort may have to be devoted to protecting Israeli forces against enemy information warriors as to exploiting enemy weaknesses in this domain.

A Revised Strategic Doctrine?

Israel's strategic doctrine has changed, albeit gradually, over the years. Nonetheless, Ze'ev Schiff, the dean of Israeli defense experts, recently wrote that the "divergence between this [Israel's national security] doctrine and the exigencies of the world in which we now live began after the Six Day War and has grown wider ever since. The doctrine is now obsolete, unsuited to present realities."[96] Although Israel will continue to rely on "red lines," conventional deterrence, and early warning because of its lack of depth, Israeli strategic doctrine is likely to change in important ways in the future. In this regard, at least five elements stand out:

---

[96] Ze'ev Schiff, "Facing Up to Reality," *Ha'aretz English Edition*, January 9, 1998.

• *Reduced military freedom of action.* In the past, because Israel believed that it faced implacable and—in the short-term—immutable Arab hostility, military considerations dominated its policy toward its neighbors. Rarely did Israeli decision makers consider the political impact of military actions on relations with its neighbors save in terms of deterrence. Yet Arab–Israeli negotiations since 1991 have placed new constraints on Israel's use of force. Israel must now consider the impact of its actions on its peace treaties with Egypt and Jordan, and on ongoing negotiations with the Palestinians and others, and it must develop more precise, discriminate retaliatory techniques to avoid undesirable political consequences.[97] Moreover, all future wars will be "wars after peace." Israel will conduct those wars mindful of how fighting will affect the durability of existing peace agreements. Moreover, the emergence of opponents armed with chemical, biological, and nuclear weapons will oblige Israel to find ways to fight wars without provoking the use of these horrendous weapons.

• *A mix of defensive and counteroffensive operational methods in the place of exclusively offensive ones.* Although not disavowing the preventive or preemptive option, Israel will face greater political obstacles to its use, particularly as the country contemplates wars in which it may hope for the tacit or even the overt cooperation of regional partners such as Jordan and Turkey. Aside from the threatened use of weapons of mass destruction by an opponent, which would surely evoke a preventive or preemptive Israeli response, Israel will in most cases be constrained from launching large-scale operations without some precipitating use of force against it.[98] Moreover, the IDF is likely to wage war differently that in the past. In the Golan, the IDF is likely to eschew offensive action for an active defense during the initial phases of the war, shifting to the offense only after Syrian forces had been sufficiently attrited through artillery and air strikes and airmobile raids. Conversely, in the event of a war with Egypt or Iraq, large Israeli airmobile forces might be inserted deep into western Sinai or eastern

---

[97] Israel's bungled attempt in September 1997 to assassinate a senior Hamas figure in Amman, Jordan, by using a poison that would leave no trace in the body of the victim, seems to have been motivated by just such a consideration. Ironically, the effort was poorly executed, and by prompting a crisis in relations between Israel and Jordan had precisely the opposite effect.

[98] For a more traditional view by Major General Tal, see Steve Rodan, "Leading Strategist Urges Secrecy for War Preparations," *Jerusalem Post: Internet Edition,* December 5, 1996.

Jordan to wear down advancing Egyptian or Iraqi units before they can close in on Israel's borders.

• *A quest for regional military partners.* In the past, Israel preferred to wage war with the support of a great power patron, and this will remain a core element of Israeli strategy. To the extent that Israeli strategy is governed by a vision of Israel as a member of the region, its leaders will seek to avoid the kind of isolation their country knew for the first four decades of its existence. Thus, in the case of confrontation with states beyond its immediate borders (Iraq or Iran, for example) Israel will strive for at least the tacit concurrence, if not the overt cooperation, of neighbors such as Jordan, Turkey, and perhaps some of the Arab Gulf states.[99] At the same time, the open acceptance of Israel as a legitimate player in the region may lead other countries to see new opportunities in an alliance with the most advanced military power in the region. Turkey's recent open military dealings with Israel provide the most prominent manifestation of this trend.

• *In the event of war, operations directed at destroying enemy forces rather than seizing terrain.* In past wars, territorial gains provided depth, a bargaining chip in peace negotiations, and a way to achieve secure borders. Destruction of enemy forces, although a normal aim of battle, had little long-term payoff, as Egypt's and Syria's Soviet patron replaced lost hardware with even better equipment. Conditions have changed dramatically. The seizure of terrain is now a much less appealing option for Israeli decision makers. The 1967 and 1982 wars suggest that ground, once taken, can be difficult to give up and yet difficult to control. It is often populated with hostile civilians who will greet their occupiers with Molotov cocktails and roadside bombs. Furthermore, to the extent that Israel desires normal relations with its neighbors, it has little interest in reinforcing Arab suspicions that it harbors expansionist designs. On the other hand, the collapse of the Soviet Union means that enemy forces, once destroyed, will no longer be reconstituted within a few years with the help of an unlimited air- and sea-lift directed by Moscow.

• *A less ambiguous nuclear posture.* Israel has long maintained a policy of ambiguity regarding its nuclear capabilities—neither acknowledging the

---

[99] Zalmay Khalilzad, David Shlapak, and Daniel Byman, *The Implications of the Possible End of the Arab–Israeli Conflict for Gulf Security* (Washington, D.C.: Rand, 1997); Dore Gold, *New Security Frameworks for the Middle East* (Washington, D.C.: The Washington Institute for Near East Policy, 1996).

existence of its nuclear arsenal, nor doing much to discourage the belief that it exists. Over time, the dissemination of Western intelligence about Israel's nuclear program, and in the mid-1980s, the revelations of a disgruntled Israeli nuclear technician, Mordechai Vanunu, disspelled all doubt about its existence. As Israel struggles to cope with longer range perils it will rely more and more on its own retaliatory capability. Deterrence, not pre-emption (as in 1981 against Iraq), nor even defense in the form of missiles like the Arrow, will have to protect the Jewish state from potential attack by nonconventional weapons. Israel's nuclear capabilities will figure increasingly in Israeli security policy, although official acknowledgement of those capabilities may still be some time off.

The speed with which the IDF will undertake a transition to new organizations, doctrine, strategy, and patterns of civil–military relationships will depend on personalities, politics, and the evolving strategic environment. Who leads the IDF and the government, and their willingness to take risks of various sorts, will matter a great deal; so too will Middle Eastern politics and the regional threat environment. Should war threaten or break out (be it with Syria or the Palestinians of the West Bank and Gaza), attention will be diverted from the effort to transform the IDF. But sooner or later, something like the changes sketched out above seem inevitable.

The IDF's revolution in security affairs will confront it with more complex strategic and operational problems than in the past. It will also make the IDF look, at first glance, rather more like the U.S. armed forces—high-tech, combined arms, more professional, perhaps developing an ethos that will place it at some remove from much of Israeli society. Yet this process of "Americanization" will have distinct limits. Indeed, the forces pushing the IDF to incorporate aspects of the U.S. military model will themselves generate resistance aimed explicitly at preserving the IDF's distinctive identity. Thus, the tactical and technological responses that Israel devises to its security problems will, in the final analysis, retain a unique Israeli flavor. In the meantime, controversy and contentiousness will mark the transformation of the IDF engendered by Israel's revolution in security affairs. That transformation will provide ample opportunity for Israeli officers to demonstrate the imagination and creativity for which the IDF is rightly well-known. But it will also require the abandonment of traditions once thought to be an indelible part of the national character. Finally—and inevitably—Israel's revolution in security affairs will give rise to new problems that are at present perceived only dimly, if at all.

Chapter 5

Implications

The Israeli military establishment faces a broad transformation that will result in an Israeli Defense Force that is smaller, more professional, less deeply rooted in Israeli society, and more reliant on a mix of operational methods for defeating its enemies on the battlefield. How is this transformation—which we have called Israel's revolution in security affairs—likely to affect Israel's national security interests? What problems is it likely to resolve, to create, and to leave unresolved? And what might American policymakers and experts learn from the Israeli case?

PROBLEMS RESOLVED

The specific character of the IDF's change will depend on three factors. First, Israel will need effective political and military leadership to make the transition, which will transform one of the central institutions of Israeli society. Second, the change may be an uneven one with Israel's naval and air forces—which are smaller, more professional (i.e., less dependent on reservists), and more technologically oriented—moving more quickly than the ground forces. Third, the pace of change in the IDF will respond to external events. The IDF's senior leadership contemplated a dramatic qualitative leap after the October 1973 War but, as a result of the pressures of that conflict and its aftermath, chose expansion instead. Similarly, the prospect or reality of a conventional war with Syria, for example, could for a time lead the IDF to concentrate on improving and updating its current structure rather than moving to a new one. Although the IDF has been investing in its future, it will, in a crunch, look to near-term readiness first.

That said, Israel's revolution in security affairs is likely to have several positive effects. First, assuming that a new IDF emerges, it will undoubtedly maintain and even increase the gap in conventional military capabilities that currently exist between it and potential Arab opponents. Drawing on a more literate and technically sophisticated population and equipped with military hardware comparable, at its best, to that fielded by the United States, the IDF will dominate the armies and air forces of its neighbors. Even when facing armies that can draw on U.S. or European hardware and training, there is little doubt that the Israeli edge in both skill and technology will remain. Furthermore—and this is a crucial point—with the Cold War over, Israel's Arab neighbors can no longer count on a superpower patron that will restore lost stocks of military hardware on lenient terms. To the extent that Israel's Arab neighbors have themselves become dependent on the United States for arms, they are now at the mercy of U.S. embargoes. By comparison, Israel's ability to manufacture and maintain advanced arms is much more solid than that of its potential opponents who lack sophisticated defense industries, and whose economies lag well behind that of the Jewish state.

Israel's sensitivity to casualties will, to some extent, mitigate these advantages.[1] In "wars of no choice" (such as the conflicts of 1948, 1967, or 1973), the Israeli public will remain willing to "pay the price" of hundreds or even thousands killed—but only so long as they are persuaded that their leaders truly had "no choice." Apart from such wars of survival, however, casualty sensitivity will constrain Israel's ability to exploit its military superiority. The traumas of the 1973 and 1982 wars and general societal changes will lead the IDF to shun high-risk military operations in peacetime and brinkmanship during crises; to search for technological solutions to operational problems, thus minimizing casualties to the IDF by means such as the use of artillery and the air force rather than ground units to strike at guerrilla bases in Lebanon. This may result in such a low tolerance for casualties in "wars of choice" (such as the 1982 invasion of Lebanon) that the price of battlefield success in such wars may be politically unacceptable. Furthermore, the proliferation of weapons of mass destruction increases the likelihood that future wars could feature terrorism or missile attacks on civilian population centers with such weapons, resulting in mass casualties. Under these circumstances, Israel will find it difficult to use force for purposes other than self-defense or survival, and Israelis will find themselves psychologically vulnerable to Arab strategies that exploit their casualty sensitivity.

A second problem the Israeli revolution in security affairs will resolve, albeit slowly, is the three-way tension between its manpower system, its military requirements, and its society. The "nation-in-arms" concept, devised for a struggling state of fewer than a million inhabitants at the end of the age of mass

---

[1] The sources of Israeli casualty sensitivity are complex and include traditional Jewish attitudes regarding the value of human life, the legacy of the Holocaust, and the increasingly cosmopolitan feel of the country, including European levels of comfort expected by the population, some of whose members choose to emigrate rather than endure excessive risk. Sensitivity to losses is particularly noticeable in public ceremonies and places: soldiers weeping at funerals of bombing victims in the mid-1990s attracted unfavorable comment from a more stoic older generation.

warfare, has outlived its usefulness. Already, the reserve component of the system, in particular, shows signs of strain, as the weight of military duty becomes increasingly burdensome and the tasks increasingly disagreeable. Even in the standing army, the IDF quietly admits that it suffers from having too large a draft cohort for its requirements. A new model IDF, which will have a much larger professional component and rest more on draftees and less on reservists, will adapt to demographic and cultural changes in Israeli society that make the old militia system increasingly problematic.

The third problem that the Israeli revolution in security affairs will resolve are those deriving from its past diplomatic isolation, and the constraints this isolation placed on Israel's military options. Israeli strategists have long dreamed of being *bündnisfähig*—an attractive potential coalition partner for a regional or great power. Their hopes—whether to serve as a *place d'armes* for British or U.S. forces in the Middle East, or to construct a grand coalition of minorities in the Middle East, or to build a grander coalition yet of marginal states on its periphery—have never borne fruit. As late as the Gulf War, Israelis had the mortifying experience of realizing that they were a potential strategic liability to the United States as it acted militarily in the Persian Gulf. Now, the combination of Israel's military sophistication and a more relaxed political atmosphere (because of the Madrid peace process and the end of the Cold War) makes Israel an increasingly plausible military ally. Its recent $650 million deal to refurbish Turkish air force aircraft and an agreement to gain access to Turkish training areas is an important breakthrough for Israel. On a much smaller scale, Israel's participation in United Nations peacekeeping operations in Haiti and humanitarian rescue operations in Africa bespeak the further normalization of Israel's external security relations. Although it is difficult to imagine the day when Israel overtly aligns with one Arab state against another, the peace process may have created new opportunities for cooperation with states that formerly shunned it.

UNRESOLVED PROBLEMS

In a recent interview, then–deputy chief of staff Maj. Gen. Matan Vilna'i summarized the dilemma Israeli force planners face:

> We have to prepare for three very different and often incompatible scenarios. First there's the day-to-day fight against terrorism. . . . Terrorist attacks such as the recent suicide bombings and the assassination of Prime Minister Rabin are a reality. . . . Secondly, we must be ready to fight the next major conventional war. There is no peace agreement with Syria. For this contingency we need to maintain and modernize our armored formations, our jets, and our navy. Thirdly,

we have to look beyond the horizon, because in our time Iran and also Libya
have developed into potential threats, being in possession of weapons of mass
destruction. We have to be able to counter those as well. That requires new,
over-the-horizon capabilities. The big difficulty with having to plan for these
three operational environments is that quite often a decision which is very good
for the fight against terrorism will be bad for the other requirements. . . . The
trouble is that a half-solution is not good, you must have the full answer for each
environment.[2]

The Israeli revolution in security affairs will neither remove nor even greatly
reduce the vulnerability of Israel to attack either by unconventional means (i.e.,
terrorism, popular insurrection, or guerrilla warfare) or nonconventional weapons
(i.e., surface-to-surface missiles or other delivery means for chemical, biological,
or nuclear weapons). Indeed, to the extent that Israel's conventional dominance
of its potential opponents grows, they will turn to these instruments of conflict
that Israel finds more difficult to counter. The Palestinians, one can argue, have
succeeded in achieving key political objectives—recognition for the PLO and
control over Palestinian population centers in the West Bank and Gaza—
precisely through such means.

The means of unconventional warfare have become more sophisticated over
time. Lebanese Hizballah guerrillas have proven themselves capable of punishing
Israeli forces in South Lebanon, and the spread of cheap video cameras and the
growth of the news media constrain Israel's ability to deal, for example, with
riots by Palestinian teenagers. Technology as such is not likely to give Israel a
substantial edge in waging low-intensity conflict operations because the objective
of these struggles is political, not military: to win "hearts and minds" and to
mobilize a civilian population on behalf of a cause. Paradoxically, military defeat
can actually aid in accomplishing this goal: Israel's 1967 victory was a boon to
Palestinian guerrilla recruiting. At the same time, democracies pay an
exceedingly high and debilitating price for winning dirty wars of this kind, to
include suspension of various civil liberties and even the use of torture.

Defending against certain types of nonconventional weapons is inherently
problematic; for instance, no country in the world currently has equipment
capable of providing reliable real-time warning of a biological attack. Strategies
of deterrence, and to a lesser extent of defense, will certainly be Israel's main
recourse. Preventive attacks will become more difficult as Israel's opponents
have learned the lesson of the raid on Iraq's lone Osirak reactor in 1981. Most
nonconventional weapons programs of interest to the Israelis will be located in

---

[2]   *Jane's Defence Weekly,* June 19, 1996, p. 53.

dispersed and hidden facilities. During the 1991 Gulf War, the United States—despite far greater resources—proved unable to root out the Iraqi nuclear program with air attack alone: Only a painstaking scheme of postwar inspections uncovered its full scope.

PROBLEMS CREATED

Security transformations of the kind discussed here create not only new opportunities or solutions to old problems—they breed their own. We may identify at least four in Israel's case. First, whereas world opinion, relations with great power patrons such as the United States, and the domestic stability of neighboring Arab states such as Jordan have constrained Israeli military operations in the past, Israel will face even greater limits on its military freedom of action in the future. These new constraints will stem from Israel's new diplomatic standing in the region, the existence of peace treaties with some of its neighbors (and continuing negotiations with others), and its own changing attitudes toward war. Thus, it will have to find ways to fight terrorism and perhaps engage in limited military operations or even wars against its remaining enemies without harming ongoing negotiations or endangering existing peace treaties. It is not clear that it will be possible in all cases to reconcile these potentially contradictory objectives. Furthermore, during the Cold War, Israel often chafed under United Nations or U.S. pressure or the threat of Soviet military intervention—any of which, the Israelis feared, would prevent them from achieving decisive battlefield victories.[3] To a large extent, these forces have abated, but others will replace them. In the future, the possibility that Israel's adversaries will respond with nonconventional weapons strikes against Israeli population centers will make decisive military outcomes by the IDF even less likely than in the past.

A second new problem has to do with Israel's reliance on the United States. Israel's strategic dependence on the United States will probably grow in coming years, while Washington's commitment to Israel will, at least, come under increasing scrutiny. Historically, the U.S.–Israel strategic relationship has rested on several factors: common values, the political influence of the American Jewish community, overlapping interests in the Middle East, Washington's perception of Israel as a strategic asset, and shared perceptions concerning the Soviet threat. The termination of the Cold War ended one common bond, and the waning electoral influence of American Jews, growing strains between American

---

[3]   Avi Kober, "A Paradigm in Crisis? Israel's Doctrine of Military Decision," *Israel Affairs* (Autumn 1995), pp. 188–211.

Jewry and the Israeli establishment over "who is a Jew," and the growth in size and organization of Arab American and Muslim communities in the United States pose another set of challenges. Moreover, Israel's security ties with other countries—such as sales of military technology to China—may pose another problem for the relationship. Maintaining strong strategic ties between the countries will require that the government of Israel not pursue policies perceived to be sharply at variance with U.S. interests. The common values remain intact, while the threats posed to both U.S. and Israeli interests by political and religious extremism; terrorism; rogue states such as Libya, Iraq, and Iran; and the proliferation of nonconventional weapons can provide a strong basis for the post–Cold War strategic relationship.[4]

Even under the most optimistic but plausible scenario, peace between Israel and its neighbors is unlikely to yield a significant "peace dividend" in the form of a further reduction in defense spending, though it may alter spending priorities (more money for counterterror forces, long-range strike and missile defense systems, and less for conventional ground forces).[5] To meet these threats, Israel will have to maintain, if not increase, its defense budget. Accordingly, Washington will be asked to continue current levels of technology transfer and security assistance to Israel. Yet, strains in relations between Washington and Jerusalem caused by differences over the peace process could cause the United States to curb cooperation in the security sphere (as it has several times in the past) and freeze efforts to further broaden and deepen strategic cooperation between the two countries, as a way of pressuring the Israeli government and placating Arab opinion.

Israeli defense companies will continue to seek joint ventures with U.S. firms as a way to gain access to the large U.S. market, enabling Israel to preserve its military industrial base. Developing an effective response to the threat posed by missiles and nonconventional weapons will likewise require a high level of cooperation. Few countries can deal with these kinds of challenges on their own (as Israel realized even before the 1991 Gulf War).[6] Israel will continue to depend on the United States for missile-launch warning data and technology

---

[4]   Shai Feldman, *The Future of U.S.–Israel Strategic Cooperation* (Washington, D.C.: The Washington Institute for Near East Policy, 1996).

[5]   Eliyahu Kanovsky, *Assessing the Mideast Peace Economic Dividend*, BESA Security and Policy Studies No. 15 (Ramat Gan, Israel: Bar-Ilan University, BESA Center for Strategic Studies, April 1994).

[6]   Even the United States had to rely on Czech chemical defense teams and German Fox chemical reconnaissance vehicles to fill gaps in its own nuclear, biological, and chemical defense capabilities during the 1991 Gulf War.

transfers while it develops its own missile defense capabilities. Likewise, the fact that some of the new threats facing Israel come from more distant countries—making them a more difficult collection target for Israel—will increase the importance of intelligence cooperation with the United States, which is better able to follow military developments in those countries because of its sophisticated global reconnaissance capabilities.

Finally, in the event of a new Arab–Israeli war, Israel will remain dependent on the United States for critical information and materiel. In a conventional scenario (such as a war with Syria), this might include target intelligence for counter-Scud operations and strikes on nonconventional weapon-related facilities, information to aid the interdiction of enemy expeditionary forces arriving from second-line states, specialized munitions to deal with hardened facilities, antimissile missiles to supplement Israel's own capabilities in this area, and of course a resupply of tanks and aircraft if combat losses are substantial. In the event of a nonconventional attack on Israel, aid might include the provision of medical supplies and personnel, to help treat and care for mass civilian casualties, and personnel and equipment, to aid in the decontamination of populated areas struck by chemical, biological, or nuclear weapons.[7] Thus, while theoretical adherence to the ethos of self-reliance will remain intact, Israel is likely to depend on direct U.S. assistance in future wars—expanding on the precedent established during the 1991 Gulf War when the United States dispatched Patriot missile crews to Israel.

A third problem Israel will face has to do with the gradual abandonment of its thoroughgoing "nation in arms" concept. The IDF has already begun to back away from its missions of "school of the nation," so critical in its early period. When, as occurred recently, the *Nahal (noar halutzi lohem* or "fighting pioneer youth") units of the army began experimenting with training young soldiers to become entrepreneurs in development towns rather than, as before, hardy farmers on the border, a milestone had been reached. Although conscription in some form looks likely to remain a feature of the IDF for years to come, it has already begun to lose its status as an indispensable rite of passage, without which a young Israeli man was doomed to dismal job opportunities and permanently wounded self-esteem. The IDF has always served as a unifying and assimilating force in a country built on immigration; that role will diminish. At a time when Israel faces growing fissures among groups—particularly secular and religious, but also

---

[7]   Michael Eisenstadt, "Arab–Israeli Conflict," in Patrick Clawson, ed., *1997 Strategic Assessment* (Washington, D.C.: Institute for National Strategic Studies, 1997), pp. 107–116.

various ethnic communities and opposing political persuasions—the loss of influence by such a powerful institution will have implications that reverberate across society.

Already the leadership of the IDF has changed from that of its formative period, when it was dominated by a largely self-taught group of commanders who had to build a military system from scratch. Today's leadership is older and more professional, if perhaps intellectually more narrow than that of the early decades of the IDF. Having grown up in an army that was completely identified with society, however, it finds itself shaken at the first signs—faint to an outsider perhaps, but alarming to those within the IDF—that Israel has taken the path toward the creation of a normal—that is, detached—officer corps. Israel's pattern of civil–military relations has allowed for an extraordinary degree of interpenetration of the society and the military, including a very high level of participation in politics by general officers upon their retirement from active duty. That practice, and certain institutional arrangements (for example, the weakness of the civilian Ministry of Defense bureaucracy vis-à-vis the military, and the absence of a national security council–type staff in the central government) may serve Israel poorly in the new security environment now emerging.

LESSONS FOR THE UNITED STATES

Despite the discrepancies in size, wealth, and strategic circumstances, Israel's revolution in security affairs is relevant to the United States. In the 1970s and 1980s, many American officers looked to the Israelis as an example to emulate; today, however, they are more likely to shrug off the IDF as a highly competent force whose experience is not very relevant to the U.S. in a post–Cold War world.[8] Having fought their own war against an Arab army, many officers have mentally downgraded their previously high estimate of Israel's military achievements. At the same time, they note the Israelis' apparent inability to prevail in a protracted, low-intensity conflict with irregular opponents, most notably Hizballah and Palestinian extremists.

This devaluing of Israeli achievement has probably gone too far. The war in the Gulf was fought under circumstances far more favorable to the United States,

---

[8] There were signs of increasing disdain already in the 1980s. See Edwin L. Kennedy, "Close-up View of IDF Models Offers Sharper, Truer Image," *Army* (March 1984), pp. 14–15. This article, like some of the Israeli discussions of the American military referred to above, indicates the difficulties proud and competent military organizations have in understanding one another.

at least in narrow military terms, than any of Israel's wars. Wealthy, overwhelmingly dominant in all spheres of military technology, fighting with an extensive array of allies against an opponent whose entire gross national product was not even one-third the size of the U.S. defense budget, given the advantage of a sustained air campaign to prepare the way for a ground offensive, the United States fought the Gulf War with advantages the Israelis could not dream of in their wars with their Arab enemies.

What do the Israelis have to offer students of contemporary military affairs? Israeli skepticism, grounded on near continuous military action against a variety of conventional and unconventional opponents over half a century, should serve to warn us about an overenthusiastic embrace of high technology. At the very least, something can be said for the Israeli system of continuous improvement and modification of basic weapons systems. Particularly at a time when the U.S. acquisition budget has fallen considerably behind what is needed for item-by-item replacement of major pieces of equipment, the Israeli approach of wringing the last iota of usefulness out of a basically sound platform will be one worth emulating. In some cases, this incremental approach has meant that the Israelis have fielded military capabilities in advance even of the United States, even though such a lead has almost always proven temporary (e.g., the introduction of UAVs and reactive and appliqué armors for armored fighting vehicles). The Israelis have indeed mastered the art of getting "half-baked" technologies quickly into the field.

More fundamentally, fifty years or more of combat experience has given the Israelis a deeply ingrained sense of the persistence of friction and the fog of war, even in modern combat, and a profound belief in the importance of military basics. Whether in their obsessive attention to topography and land navigation or in their relentless effort to simplify military organizations and procedures, they have focused on the essentials, and it has paid off.[9] The IDF can offer the U.S. military a kind of sanity check about large-scale conventional operations, an alternative view devised by a sophisticated organization. This said, the United States will continue to develop and deploy capabilities that dwarf those of the IDF. For instance, Israeli operations against Syrian air defenses in Lebanon in 1982 were properly regarded as a model action of the kind. It must be recalled, however, that the entire attack on those missile defenses took place in an area about half the size of one of the 30 "kill boxes" superimposed by U.S. air campaign planners over Kuwait and southern Iraq during the Gulf War, and that

---

[9]   This is one of the dominant impressions one takes away from memoir literature such as Ariel Sharon, *Warrior* (New York: Simon & Schuster, 1989).

the coalition air defense suppression campaign covered much of the entire, very large, country of Iraq.

The Israeli experience is of importance to the United States for other reasons, however, which go to the heart of the revolution in military affairs (RMA). The RMA as currently discussed in the United States is indeed an American revolution—one based on U.S. assumptions about geography, strategy, and space. The Israeli revolution in security affairs is also *sui generis*. Indeed, the Israeli case suggests that many countries will, under the pressure of information age technologies and broader changes (to include the end of the Cold War, rapid economic growth, and regional shifts in the balance of power) undergo their own revolutions in security affairs. They will not reconstruct their militaries in accordance with a single template for military power devised by the United States, although they will surely feel the influence of the U.S. example. Rather, these countries will devise unique solutions to unique problems. A further example of this phenomenon is Australia, whose revolution in security affairs began more than a decade ago with a formal departure from Cold War planning assumptions.[10] On the other hand, the United States and Israel face the same military dilemma in the post–Cold War world: Conventional superiority over their adversaries is likely to prod the latter to adopt "asymmetric" strategies involving the use of unconventional warfare and nonconventional weapons. The United States is thus likely to profit by studying how the IDF deals with these threats.

There will be, and in some measure already are, Chinese, French, and Japanese (and in the future, perhaps Russian, German, and other) transformations no less extensive. In evaluating these various "revolutions," Americans will look chiefly to technological indicators of change: Who is putting satellites in orbit, or how many late-model aircraft has a country acquired? We would be better advised to assess less technical measures, to include large changes in manpower systems, force size, operational concept, and deployments. Moreover, in locating

---

[10]   Over time, the Australian Defense Forces have undertaken a combination of measures to fit a new and rather different security concept than that of mere junior partner in a broader, United States–led alliance. These actions include redeployment of forces away from their traditional bases in the southern and more densely populated part of the country to the north; de-emphasis of heavy ground forces to the benefit of long-range air and naval power, augmented by light highly mobile infantry; and development of selected technologies uniquely suited to the Australian environment (most notably over-the-horizon radars that give the Australians a thousand-mile look over land and sea to their north). See Eliot A. Cohen, "Defending the Lucky Country," *National Interest* (Fall 1994), pp. 57–62.

the origins of such changes, U.S. students of revolutionary shifts in warfare should pay as much attention to changes in a country's political situation and socioeconomic indicators as to changes in military inventories or tables of organization and equipment. As we have seen, the vast ripples from the Cold War have had profound consequences for Israeli military policy and are likely to have no less significant consequences elsewhere.

A more sobering lesson the Israeli experience has to teach concerns the limits of revolutionary change in the conduct of war. Israel's military has, over the past twenty years, steadily widened the conventional gap over that of neighboring states. The Syrian quest for military parity with Israel in the 1980s failed, despite lavish Soviet funding and a single-minded focus on that task. The military–technological gap between Israel and the Arab states—nonexistent in the 1950s and barely visible in the 1960s—has widened noticeably; so too has the ability of the respective populations to exploit those technologies. But such a gap has not brought Israel security in important respects. Indeed, in some ways the Israeli revolution in security affairs seems to bring with it new constraints and problems almost as much as new opportunities.

Even at a conventional level, mass and the operational initiative still count for a great deal. A Syrian attack to recover the Golan Heights would end in Syrian defeat, but at a price that makes Israelis shudder. The technologically backward forces of Syria, much like those of North Korea halfway around the world, would succumb to superior firepower and military skill, but in the short run massed artillery fire, the size of the armored and mechanized formations they could bring to bear, and their high tolerance for casualties could make victory for their more sophisticated opponents a costly proposition. Like the United States in Korea, the Israelis could well find that such a victory would come at a cost in human life that is unacceptable to a modern liberal state.

The Israeli revolution in security affairs will not be a panacea for the Jewish state. Once complete—a process that might take a decade or more—Israeli conventional military power will appear more potent than ever before. The IDF will dominate neighboring armies and acquire the capability to deliver damaging blows to distant countries. For a nation that was born in war and that has lived ever since in its shadow, the prospect of surmounting such threats is no small accomplishment. Hard experience has taught the Israelis, however, the limits as well as the utility of military power, and the ways in which superiority in one form of conflict can merely goad an opponent to develop others. Israel's security will continue, as in the past, to require large sums of money and a spirit of dedication from soldier and civilian alike. But more than ever it will require a willingness on the part of Israeli politicians and the leaders of the IDF to change.

David Ben Gurion, Israel's founding Prime Minister and the father of its strategic doctrine, once warned that "The most dangerous enemy to Israel's security is the intellectual inertia of those who are responsible for security." Nearly a half century later, thoughtful Israeli leaders recognize the enduring relevance of Ben Gurion's counsel. The security challenges facing Israel today will require that Israel's soldiers henceforth demonstrate in the realm of intellect excellence to match their extraordinary achievements with the sword.

Appendix A

Five Scenarios for War

Despite occasional, even bloody setbacks to the peace process in the Middle East, it has been out of fashion for some time now to speculate about the contours of future warfare in that region. Yet general staffs must plan, and it behooves a student of the IDF to think about some of the contingencies that Israeli planners must consider. What follows are five possible scenarios for war in the Middle East, each of which illustrates the variety of demands on the Israeli military.[1]

INSURRECTION IN PALESTINE

Although Israeli forces have withdrawn from nearly all major Palestinian population centers in the West Bank and Gaza, the Palestinians still chafe at Israeli control over their movements outside of these areas, the presence of Israeli settlers—some in the heart of densely inhabited areas—and restrictions on commerce and trade. At the same time, horrifying terrorist attacks in Tel Aviv and Jerusalem and a brief but costly outburst of violence in September 1996 in which Palestinian police opened fire on Israeli soldiers have disillusioned and angered many erstwhile Israeli supporters of genuine peace and reconciliation.

Against this background, simmering Palestinian antipathy could erupt into violence, in the form of a spontaneous popular uprising, sustained guerrilla warfare sponsored by the Palestinian Authority, or independent terrorist action by groups such as Hamas and Islamic Jihad, or a combination of all three. Something harsher and far more violent than the *intifada* of 1987–1993 could occur, fueled by shattered hopes on both sides, and an ample supply of weapons within small but autonomous Palestinian enclaves. Israel could react in a variety of ways, including covert operations, reprisal raids, large-scale cordon and search operations, or a major operation to retake some Palestinian-controlled areas. Such

---

[1]   For alternative conflict scenarios, see Michael Eisenstadt, "Arab–Israeli Conflict," in Patrick Clawson, ed., *1997 Strategic Assessment* (Washington, D.C.: Institute for National Strategic Studies), pp. 107–116; Edward B. Atkeson, *The Powder Keg: An Intelligence Officer's Guide to Military Forces in the Middle East, 1996–2000* (Falls Church, Va.: Nova, 1996), pp. 138–154; and Anthony H. Cordesman, *Perilous Prospects: The Peace Process and the Arab–Israeli Military Balance* (Boulder, Colo.: Westview, 1996).

a conflict might spread to the Arabs of Israel and could exacerbate tensions between Israel and its Arab neighbors, who are liable to provide political and economic support to the Palestinians.

ISRAELI INTERVENTION IN JORDAN

The *intifada,* the 1991 Gulf War, and the growth of radical Islamic movements have helped radicalize segments of the Palestinian population of Jordan. The Hashemite monarchy has, thus far, managed to control such sentiments through a judicious mixture of indulgence, inducement, and repression. Yet the king is ill, his brother—the heir apparent—does not enjoy the king's popularity among the people of Jordan, and the legitimacy of the monarchy is not accepted by all the kingdom's subjects. Should domestic opponents to the monarchy make common causewith external enemies of the regime, Israel might feel obliged to act— particularly in the event of a move to bring Palestinians in the West Bank and Gaza and on the East Bank under unified Palestinian rule. The creation of a Palestinian mini-state in the West Bank and Gaza may pose manageable problems if Israel hems it in on one side and Hashemite Jordan contains it on the other. It becomes a very different proposition for Israel if that mini-state were to gain control of Jordan. During the Jordanian civil war in 1970, Israel stood ready to intervene to protect the kingdom against a Syrian invasion; it would surely have reason to threaten intervention again if an externally supported insurrection threatened the stability of the kindom, or if a third party once again threatened Jordan.

VIOLATION OR ABROGATION OF THE PEACE TREATY WITH EGYPT

Despite its chronic poverty, overpopulation, and problems with Islamic fundamentalism, Egypt will probably remain stable and supportive of efforts to peacefully resolve the Arab–Israeli conflict. Yet change is conceivable. Egypt has toed an increasingly critical line against Israel, manifested in hostile diplomatic moves and attacks in the government-supervised press. One president has already fallen to assassins' bullets, and his successor has only narrowly avoided the same fate. A more hawkish Egyptian government arising as a result of a change of regime, a coup, or a revolution, and influenced or controlled by radical nationalists or religious extremists, might decide to violate the peace agreement with Israel (for example, by exceeding permitted force levels in the Sinai). Already, the Egyptian army has conducted military maneuvers directed toward Israel. In the past, Israel has viewed large-scale Egyptian military deployments to the Sinai as a *casus belli,* and the forced withdrawal of the present-day multinational observer force there would evoke memories of 1967. Such a sequence of events could lead to an escalatory spiral that neither side might be able to control, leading ultimately to war.

WAR WITH SYRIA

During the fall of 1996, both Israel and Syria seemed, for a time, to believe that the chances of a war were greater than at any time in the recent past. Although Israel seems unlikely to attack Syria, save on explicit warning of a Syrian military move, Syria might launch a war to achieve limited gains. A quick grab of territory on the Golan Heights, coupled with a diplomatic offensive, might be one way to regain at least a part of the Golan, much as the Egyptian attack in 1973 led, over several years, to Egypt's recovery of the Sinai. Such an attack might include missile strikes on Israeli amories and air bases, and perhaps even the use of chemical weapons. War between Syria and Israel might also result from a deteriorating situation in South Lebanon, where Iranian-supported Hizballah guerrillas have inflicted a steady trickle of casualties on Israel. A major Israeli sweep into southern Lebanon to deal with Hizballah guerrillas, or a more direct attempt to punish Syria for allowing this organization to operate against Israeli forces, could lead to a broader war.

WEAPONS OF MASS DESTRUCTION FROM THE 'OUTER RING'

Finally, war in the Middle East might come from terrorist groups, or states such as Iraq, Iran, or Libya, that are acquiring nonconventional weapons and the means to deliver them. A nonconventional attack would most probably occur against the backdrop of a protracted and bloody guerrilla war with the Palestinians in the West Bank and Gaza, or a regional conflict in which Israel is targeted to deter U.S. intervention. Given the danger posed by the proliferation of nonconventional weapons in the Middle East and the potentially horrific consequences of their use, Israel might well be tempted to take preventive steps against nonconventional weapons-related facilities, and sites associated with possible delivery systems, such as air and missile bases. The Israeli attack on the Iraqi Osiraq reactor in June 1981 provided a model for operations of this kind. The IAF has a proven long-range strike capability, and its acquisition of 25 F-15I strike fighters further enhances this capability.

On the other hand, proliferators have learned the lessons of Osiraq, and can be expected to disperse and hide such facilities, making it difficult to repeat the success of the Osiraq raid. Under these circumstances, Israel's ability to deter the use of nonconventional weapons through the threat of retaliation in kind will be critical. This prospect of retaliation for overt attacks will create incentives for groups or states hostile to Israel to develop methods of delivering nonconventional weapons undetected, using covert means. This capability will, in turn, increase the difficulty of deterring nonconventional attack.

Appendix B

The IDF from War to War:
A Statistical Portrait[1]

The Wages of War: Israeli Losses in its Wars with the Arabs
1948–1996[2]

| | KILLED | | WOUNDED | |
	Soldiers	Civilians	Soldiers	Civilians
1948–49 war	4,500	1,700	12,500	unknown
1949–1956	222	264	580	477
1956 war	190	unknown	890	unknown
1957–1967	64	71	234	196
1967 war	777	unknown	2,811	unknown
1967–1973	650	188	2,243	955
1973 war	2,527	unknown	5,596	unknown
1973–1982	1,591	unknown	unknown	unknown
1982 war	214	0	1,114	0
1982–1985 (Lebanon)	306	0	1,756	0
1985–1996 (Lebanon)	179	6	704	131
Total	12,000+		30,000+	

[1] Note: Totals may not always be consistent across tables, owing to reliance on incomplete or multiple sources of information.

[2] Sources: Yaakov Erez and Ilan Kfir, eds., *IDF Encyclopedia* 1 (Tel Aviv: Revivim, 1982), pp. 53, 98, 117, 181; Yaakov Erez and Ilan Kfir, eds., *IDF Encyclopedia* 2 (Tel Aviv: Revivim, 1984), p. 61; Ze'ev Klein, *The War on Terror and Israel's Defense Policy 1979–1988* (Tel Aviv: Revivim, n.d.), pp. 111, 161; IDF web site, www.israel-mfa.gov.il/idf/wounded.html.

Comparative Strength: Israel and the Arabs
May 1948–October 1948[3]

| | ISRAEL | | ARABS | |
	May '48	Oct '48	May '48	Oct '48
Manpower	29,677	99,300	30,000	70,000+
Tanks	0	13	40	45
Armored cars w/guns	2	20	200	180
Armored cars/half tracks	120	280	300	440
Field guns	5	126	140	240
AT/AA guns	24	109	220	280
Fighters	0	13	60	86
Bombers	0	3	0	9
Misc. aircraft	28	49	57	56
Armed boats	3	5	12	16

Losses, 1948–1949[4]

	Killed	Wounded
Israel	4,500	12,500
Arabs	15,000	25,000

---

[3]   Sources: Yehuda Wallach, Moshe Lissak, and Arieh Itzchaki, *Atlas of Israel* (Jerusalem: Carta, 1980), pp. 13, 36, 47, 54; Edward Luttwak and Dan Horowitz, *The Israeli Army* (New York: Harper & Row, 1975), pp. 34, 36, 53; Erez and Kfir, eds., *IDF Encyclopedia* 1, p. 33.

[4]   Sources: Trevor N. Dupuy, *Elusive Victory: The Arab–Israeli Wars, 1947–1974* (New York: Harper & Row, 1978), p. 124. Note: Israeli figures do not include civilians killed and wounded.

Comparative Strength: Israel and Egypt, Mid- to Late 1955[5]

	Israel	Egypt	Czech–Egyptian arms deal, 1955
Manpower	100,000	150,000	n/a
Tanks (med/hvy)	200	200	230
Lt tanks, tank destroyers	50	173	100
APCs/half tracks	400	400	200
Artillery	230	375	500
Fighters	48	80	125
Bombers	2	0	40
Destroyers	0	0	2
Frigates	3	6	0
Torpedo boats	9	18	12

1956 War Losses[6]

	Israel	Egypt
Killed	190	1,000
Wounded	890	4,000
PoW	4	6,000
Aircraft	15	215

[5] Sources: Wallach, Lissak, and Itzchaki, *Carta's Atlas of Israel 1948–1961*, p. 124; Erez and Kfir, *IDF Encyclopedia* 1, pp. 120, 129; Luttwak and Horowitz, *The Israeli Army*, pp. 125, 129, 141; Dupuy, *Elusive Victory*, p. 212. Arms included in Czech deal arrived by October 1956. By the eve of the 1956 War, Israel had 350 tanks (250 M4 Shermans and 100 AMX-13s); 136 aircraft (16 Mysteres, 22 Ouragans, 15 Meteors, 29 Mustangs, 17 Harvards, 16 Mosquitos, 16 Dakotas, 3 Nords, 2 B-17s); and 11 Warships (2 destroyers, 9 torpedo boats). Conversely, Egypt had about 530 tanks and tank destroyers (230 T-34s and Stalins, 200 Shermans, 100 Su-100s); 129 aircraft (45 MiG-15s [30 operational], 30 Vampires [15 operational], 32 Meteors [12 operational], 49 Il-28s [12 operational], and 60 transport aircraft); and 38 warships (2 destroyers, 6 frigates, 30 torpedo boats).

[6] Sources: Dupuy, *Elusive Victory*, p. 212; Erez and Kfir, *IDF Encyclopedia* 1, p. 117.

Comparative Strength of Israel and the Arabs, June 1967[7]

	Israel	Total Arab	Egypt	Jordan	Syria	Iraq
Manpower	275,000	456,000	250,000	56,000	70,000	80,000
Tanks	1,093	2,750	1,300	270	550	630
APCs	1,500	1,845	1,050	210	585	unknown
Artillery	681	2,084	840	184	460	600
Combat aircraft	247	568	299	24	94	151
Warships	15	118	92	0	26	0

1967 War Losses[8]

	Israel	Total Arab	Egypt	Jordan	Syria	Iraq
Killed	777	16,000	15,000	200	450	unknown
Wounded	2,811	61,000	50,000	800	2,000	unknown
PoW	15	6,957	5,380	986	591	0
Tanks	394	898	600	180	118	0
Artillery	unknown	1,820	750	600	470	0
Combat aircraft	46	452	327	30	65	28

---

[7]   Sources: Wallach, Lissak, and Itzchaki, *Carta's Atlas of Israel 1961–1971*, p. 52; Dupuy, *Elusive Victory*, p. 337. Totals include non-operational equipment.

[8]   Sources: Erez and Kfir, *IDF Encyclopedia* 1, p. 205; Luttwak and Horowitz, *The Israeli Army*, p. 229; Dupuy, *Elusive Victory*, p. 333.

Comparative Strength: Israel and the Arabs, October 1973[9]
(forces committed)

	Israel	Arab Total	Egypt	Jordan	Syria	Iraq
Manpower	350,000	500,000	315,000	5,000	150,000	20,000
Tanks	2,100	4,841	2,200	170	1,650	500
APCs	4,000	4,320	2,400	100	1,300	700
Artillery	570	2,055	2,200	36	1,250	160
Combat aircraft	358	987	400	0	282	0
Missile boats	14	26	17	0	9	0
SAM batteries	10	185	146	0	34	0

---

[9]   Sources: Wallach, Lissak, and Itzchaki, *Carta's Atlas of Israel 1971–1981*, pp. 48, 94; Dupuy, *Elusive Victory*, pp. 606, 608. Total Arab expeditionary forces sent to fight in Syria included 2 armored divisions, 3 brigades, 500 tanks, 700 armored personnel carriers (APCs), and 160 artillery pieces from Iraq; 1 mechanized division, 170 tanks, 100 APCs, and 36 artillery pieces from Jordan; 1 paratrooper battalion, 1 armored carrier battalion from Saudi Arabia; 1 infantry brigade, 40 tanks, 40–50 APCs, 5 Hawker Hunter fighters from Kuwait; and 1 infantry brigade, 30 tanks, and 12 APCs from Morocco. Arab expeditionary forces sent to fight in Egypt included 1 infantry brigade and 12 tanks from Morocco; 1 armored brigade, 1 infantry brigade, 130 tanks, 30 APCs, 18 artillery pieces, and 59 combat aircraft from Algeria; 1 armored brigade, 100 tanks, 18 artillery pieces, 28 Mirage V fighters, and 3 helicopters from Libya; 1 infantry brigade, 1 commando battalion, 30 tanks, 30 APCs, and 12–14 artillery pieces from Sudan; and 73 combat aircraft from Iran. Arab expeditionary forces sent to fight in Jordan included 2 infantry brigades, 1 tank battalion, 54 artillery pieces, and 9 helicopters from Saudi Arabia. Most of these forces did not arrive in time to fight during the war. For instance, only elements of the Jordanian and Iraqi expeditionary forces sent to Syria saw combat.

1973 War Losses[10]

	Israel	Arab Total	Egypt (including expeditionary forces)	Syria (including expeditionary forces)
Killed	2,527	8,528	5,000	3,100
Wounded	5,596	19,549	12,000	6,000
PoW	294	8,551	8,031	411
Tanks	800	2,554	1,100	1,150
APCs	400	850	450	400
Artillery	25	550	300	250
Combat aircraft	102	392	223	118
Helicopters	5	55	42	13
SAM Bats	1	47	44	3
Missile boats	0	12	7	5
MTBs/patrol boats	0	5	4	1
Minelayers	0	1	0	1

---

[10]   Sources: Wallach, Lissak, and Itzchaki, *Carta's Atlas of Israel 1971–1981*, p. 98; Erez and Kfir, *IDF Encyclopedia* 2, p. 101; Dupuy, *Elusive Victory*, p. 609.

Comparative Strength: Israel, Syria, and the PLO: 1982[11]

	Israel	Syria	PLO (in Lebanon)
Manpower	450,000	250,000	15,000
Tanks	3,600	3,600	100
APCs	8,000	2,700	150
Artillery	1,000	2,300	300
Combat aircraft	600	450	0
SAM batteries	unknown	80	0
Missile boats	23	18	0
Submarines	3	0	0

1982 War Losses[12]

	Israel	Syria	PLO
Killed	214	1,500	2,000
Wounded	1,114	2,500	unknown
PoW	11	296	unknown
Tanks	140	400	100
APCs	135	90	unknown
Aircraft	2	99	0
Helicopters	4	6	0
SAM Batteries	0	19	unknown

[11]   Sources: *The Military Balance: 1982–83* (London: International Institute for Strategic Studies, 1983), pp. 56–57; Klein, *The War on Terror*, p. 97.

[12]   Sources: Trevor Dupuy and Paul Martel, *Flawed Victory: The Arab–Israeli Conflict and the 1982 War in Lebanon* (Fairfax, Va.: HERO Books, 1986), p. 225; Klein, *The War on Terror*, p. 110.

Comparative Strength of Israel and the Arab States, 1996[13]

	Israel	Egypt	Jordan	Syria	Iraq	Saudi Arabia
Manpower	175,000 (600,000 mobilized)	440,000	100,000	400,000	400,000	160,000
Tanks	3,850	3,650	1,050	4,800	2,200	900
APCs	8,000	3,850	1,100	4,200	2,500	2,800
Artillery	1,300	950	450	2,400	1,650	350
Combat aircraft	450	550	100	500	300	365
Missile boats	20	31	0	16	0	17
Submarines	3	8	0	3	0	0

---

[13]   Sources: Shlomo Gazit, ed., *The Middle East Military Balance 1993–1994* (Boulder, Colo.: Westview, 1994); International Institute for Strategic Studies, *The Military Balance 1996–97* (London: Oxford University Press, 1996), and other sources.